Will Wyatt.

A SEAMLESS ROBE

Broadcasting—
Philosophy and Practice

TO MY WIFE
FOR HER PATIENCE

A SEAMLESS ROBE

Broadcasting—
Philosophy and Practice

CHARLES CURRAN

COLLINS
St James's Place, London
1979

William Collins Sons & Co Ltd
London · Glasgow · Sydney · Auckland
Toronto · Johannesburg

First published in 1979
© Charles Curran 1979
ISBN 0 00 211864 5
Made and printed in Great Britain
by W & J Mackay Limited, Chatham

CONTENTS

PREFACE

WHEN IT BECAME KNOWN that I was to retire from the post of Director-General of the BBC I received many approaches from publishers about a possible book of memoirs. I was determined not to write a book of 'secrets', since I followed Lord Norman-brook's line that such private information as I had about BBC matters was not my property to disclose. Insofar as it should be available for publication it is available in the BBC's archives, for release at the appropriate time – which is for the BBC to decide – and I have taken particular care to ensure that the record is reasonably complete.

I was strongly pressed by Sir Michael Swann, and subsequently by Lady Collins, to write a different book – one which set down some of my thoughts about the philosophy and practice of broadcasting as I had known it. They suggested that what I had said in some of my speeches should be brought into some kind of synthesis and amplified, as a contribution to the information background which is often so sadly lacking in the public discussion of broadcasting policy. In the end, with some reluctance, I agreed. This book is the result.

I found, when I started on it, that a mere compilation of speeches would be inadequate. Some account of the formal constitutional background was necessary. Hence Part I. The philosophical statements about policy set out in Part II, which followed, needed to be amplified by the account of the major practical problems in Part III. And since broadcasting, both as an institutional phenomenon and as a programme service, is a matter of personal relationships, I have added an account of what I brought to the job of Director-General (Prologue), and a retrospective view of some of the personal issues which arose while I was doing it (Epilogue). The latter is self-explanatory by its contents. The former seems to me necessary for those who will rightly wish to assess the kind of man who is suggesting these philosophies. Writing this book has demonstrated to me how difficult it is to consider any single aspect of broadcasting without being drawn into considering a whole series of related aspects of the topic. One problem is inseparable from another. Hence my title – *A Seamless Robe*.

I do not claim that the range of subjects with which I deal is complete – simply that the philosophical, practical, and personal matters which I describe are those which most significantly occupied my time and thoughts during my eight and a half years. I am conscious of a large gap where there should be a chapter on relations with Trade Unions. I concluded that the individual problems I had experienced were too specific to be susceptible of extensive treatment in terms of general principle. Nor have I dealt with the arguments about the respective merits of Licence revenue and advertising revenue or direct grant for the BBC. The subject seemed to me to have been conclusively discussed by the Annan Committee, in its unanimous report, convincing even the doubters. I have tried, in dealing with personal matters, to reduce personal comment on people to the minimum which is necessary to convey an understanding of issues of principle.

My thanks are due to Sir Michael Swann and Lady Collins for their encouragement; to George Campey for a critical reading of the manuscript; and to Mrs Rosemary Haynes for producing the text from the unclarities of my dictation and manuscript amendments.

Finally, I should acknowledge the work of all those who helped me in the original preparation of the many speeches whose substance appears at various points in this book – among others, James Norris and his colleagues of the Secretariat; Geoffrey Buck and Michael Checkland of BBC Finance; and again, George Campey, whose advice as BBC Head of Publicity during most of my period of office was quite invaluable, and who pointed out to me, in almost every text I prepared, the pitfalls, both of argument and style, which I was digging for myself.

CHARLES CURRAN

PROLOGUE

DURING THE WATERGATE TRIAL we were frequently reminded of the classic American constitutional dictum that Government should be 'of laws and not of men'. It is easy to understand the fear of the arbitrary individual in command which lies behind those words, and the desire to regulate human activity by openly stated principles which are accessible to all and understandable by all. But in running institutions the innermost problems are always those of the relationships between men, and the safeguard for the public is that those men should have a respect for the laws within which they are formally required to operate. This principle holds in broadcasting, as in every other public activity. It holds especially in a public institution like the BBC, where a deliberate attempt has been made to set apart from detailed governmental scrutiny the activities of an institution which can have a profound influence on the opinions and actions of the society within which it operates.

In attempting to set down a description of the philosophy which ought to permeate the practice of the BBC, and in describing the precepts which that practice ought to follow, there is no escape from the problem of personality, and the central personalities are those of the Chairman and of the Director-General. They operate, it is true, within the formal constitutional framework provided by the various documents which establish the BBC and prescribe its activities and they have to remember constantly the expectations which have been set up by a long institutional history. But what they have been before assuming office, as well as the peculiar way in which the two of them react together, condition in their time the success of the BBC in meeting the public expectation which flows from

9

history. For that reason I begin this book about the philosophies and practices which are necessary for the successful conduct of the BBC, with an indication of what I brought to the office. At the end I shall offer some comments on how I thought my chemistry reacted with that of the two Chairmen under whom I served.

Traditionally, British institutions have paid a great deal of attention to family background. Looking back, in my own case I find much of credit and interest, but nothing of reputation, on which so many British judgements are based. My father was the son of a sergeant in the Royal Irish Fusiliers, who, in turn, was one of six brothers who had been evicted with their mother – my great-grandmother, and by all repute a formidable woman – from their tenant holding in County Cavan in the 1860s. My grandmother came from Halifax, Nova Scotia, the descendant of an English family who had settled there in the eighteenth century. She met my grandfather while he was on garrison duty there with his regiment. She died in 1892 in Ireland leaving my father, one of six children, an orphan of ten years of age. He was sent to the Royal Hibernian Military Academy in Phoenix Park to be trained for entry into the British Army, like many others in his condition. He joined the Army Corps of Schoolmasters in 1902, served the standard term in India; was refused permission to go with his holding battalion as a combatant to take part in the Battle of Loos, survived and finished the war at the depot of the Royal Scots at Glencorse near Edinburgh, where he met my mother.

She had joined the Women's Army Corps as one of its earliest volunteers after having seen both her brothers go off to the war – one in the Army and one in the Navy. They married in 1920, and since there were no married quarters at Glencorse, she went to the family home in Dublin, to await my arrival. Three weeks after I was born she left Dublin for Aberdeen, her own home. And so I acquired an Irish descent and an Irish birth without an Irish upbringing. But the family tie has been strong ever since, and I have always felt Irish by sympathy.

But alongside these Irish sympathies I was very much aware of my Scottish antecedents. In alternate years we would usually spend our holidays either in Dublin or in Aberdeen. My mother was born in the countryside of Aberdeenshire near Ellon on the River Ythan, and every other year we would visit the family farm, which had been in the hands of the Lowes or the Ingrams – her mother's side of the family – since the early seventeenth century. And she herself was a Bruce. It never seemed to me strange that the Scots should claim a special identity of their own. I had known it since childhood. Indeed, for anybody to think that the Scots were just a different kind of English would have seemed to me to be a most perverse opinion. They were, and always had been, recognizably different, both in the way they behaved and in the way they thought of themselves. They were not North Britons. They were not another part of the country. They *were* another people and they *were* in another country, just as the Irish were.

In 1924 my parents moved to the coal-mining district of South Yorkshire, where my father had found a teaching job under the West Riding County Council in the mining village of Thurnscoe. We stayed in South Yorkshire until my father died in 1945, though effectively I left there when I went up to Cambridge in January 1940. But my education, until I went to University, took place entirely in the environment of a mining community, first at the local elementary school, and later at what was, in name, a grammar school, but was, in fact, quite different from the institution which is brought to mind by the phrase 'grammar school' in the present climate of controversy about today's comprehensives. We had no ancient history of foundation or re-foundation under the Tudors. We had no 'direct grant' tradition. We were simply the secondary layer of education, established under the Acts of 1904 and 1918. It was

a hard and competitive experience, with little time for cultural
'frills'. But it was sound teaching by dedicated teachers, and I
remember especially my headmaster, who was himself a
Cambridge man, a historian, and brought up in the softer
traditions of the South-West of England. It is quite certain
that if it had not been for him, I should never have gone to
Cambridge, and that would have altered my whole life.

But the fundamental influence in my education was that of
my father. I learned from him – and it came to him through
twenty years of teaching ordinary soldiers how to equip themselves for promotion in the Army before the First World War –
the discipline of work. The precision of Euclidean geometry
and of analytical grammar were a pleasurable experience as he
taught them, though they would undoubtedly have been
condemned by his later civilian contemporaries as old fashioned
and retrograde. And for my mother, academic attainment was –
and is still – a supreme lodestar. Like so many country-born
Scots, she had a total reverence for formal education, and from
my very earliest days I remember being told that one cousin or
another of hers had been 'dux' of some Scottish academy. I am
not sure that such reverence is altogether in place, but there is
no doubt that it established a standard for emulation in our
family from which I do not believe that we suffered. And
above all, it was the discipline of work, established by my
father and confirmed by my schools, which constituted solid
bedrock for later life.

It was only when I reached the University and began to
encounter people from public schools who had had a broader
education, and had been encouraged to think more adventur-
ously than I had, that I began to see that work could be no
more than a means to an end. It was the object to which one's
work was devoted which really mattered. It sounds a banal
lesson. It was late in coming.

I think the first recognition of this truth came to me when I
presented to my tutor and supervisor, Frank Salter, an essay on
the significance of Luther. Was he more important as a

12

religious figure than as a political phenomenon? I had written the usual solemn judgements based on reading the standard reference books. Frank wrote one marginal comment at the end: 'What about the eschatological element?' And, whether by accident or design, he had blotted my page at that point. I had to confess that I did not know what he meant. And then he told me the story about Luther throwing inkpots at the Devil in his room. I am still capable of writing formal analyses of the problems which I face in the same style as I would have written that essay about Luther. But I should never now forget the unpredictable human element. I suspect the beginning of wisdom was my three-year contact with Frank Salter. He could always upset logical perfection by asking the forgotten question.

The principal academic asset from my University studies was the awareness which I acquired of constitutional law and political theory. I took a delight in the analysis of constitutional documents, which were a standard part of the course in history. The study of political theory, though baffling in its continuing failure to produce satisfying solutions to the problems it poses, was, nevertheless, for me an intellectual exercise which was disproportionately tempting when I put it alongside the political history which we were also required to study. Of course, the two go together. Political theory means nothing without a knowledge of the course through which political events develop. But it was the ideas which were fascinating. They have remained so for me throughout my life.

But the enduring character which was left in my mind after my academic studies, especially those at Cambridge, was the compulsion to look at every institution in which I found myself in historical terms. I wanted to see the perspective, and I never felt at ease until I knew how the situation in which I found myself had evolved. Taking a long view from the past was a natural state of mind.

Part of that long view, wherever I found myself, was my Catholic faith. Since my view of that faith underwent a considerable evolution, the outcome of which substantially influenced the way in which I thought as Director-General, I think it right to set down the story at some length. I cannot honestly say that our family life was one of continuous piety or of deep spiritual dedication. The customary Catholic family routines of morning and night prayers, Grace at meals, and the Crucifix in every bedroom were not a part of our life. But my father, through whom the Catholic strand ran in the family, had remained a regularly practising follower throughout his Army career. I remember him using a small leather-bound Tamil prayer book which he had acquired during his time in India (I still have it), which he read in order to retain a residual command of that quite difficult language. I should not have called him devout, but he was certainly loyal to his Church. My mother, who had been a Scottish Presbyterian before her marriage, was received into the Church and, like most converts, asked fewer questions than those brought up within it. From an early age we walked to church, about two miles away, every Sunday, and we rarely missed, even in the worst weather. But we did not go, as children, to Sunday School. An understanding priest accepted that my father was perfectly capable of teaching us the basic truths of our religion, and we were consequently never 'drilled' as many Catholics are. The 'penny Catechism' was an ephemeral experience, sufficient only to qualify me for confirmation by the Bishop. We simply learned to be, like my father, loyal and regular in our practice.

What made me ask questions and begin to argue with myself was the experience of being taught Reformation history at my grammar school. Those who taught us made Protestant assumptions about where the right of the argument lay when we were studying the embroilments of Luther or Calvin or Henry VIII with Rome. It was a natural response for me, feeling my own assumptions challenged, to go and find out whether the challenge could be resisted. I read a great deal beyond the strict requirements of the syllabus, and I suppose that this was the beginning both of my historical curiosity and of such training in apologetics as I have had. There is no doubt that this process inculcated in me a proneness to contention which has certainly shown itself in my later life. I am not sure that it deepened my faith, although it certainly hardened my convictions.

Alongside this process of apologetics through history I was considerably influenced by our local parish priest, himself a convert, and a former teacher of classics. His preaching, which was better than most I have heard from parish pulpits through my life, was strongly Dominican in flavour. He became a friend of the family through playing chess with us and it was not long before I found myself being taken by him through the Latin texts of the Thomist proofs of the existence of God in the Summa Theologica. So St Thomas Aquinas and the classical models of scholastic argument became a part of my mental furniture. The pretext for these exercises was that I had decided to take Latin as one of my three Advanced Level courses, and he was only too pleased to recall his classical skills and to practise on another pupil. (I also found myself copying out for him the text of his Libellus – his appeal to Rome against the alleged iniquities of the then Bishop of the Diocese, for he was a natural rebel, the vigour of whose case was enhanced by the elegance of his Latin style.)

My religious education continued at Cambridge. It had two aspects. One derived directly from my studies, and the other from membership of the University chaplaincy association for Catholic undergraduates, known as the Fisher Society. Here there was an opportunity to attend, every Sunday, a half-hour sermon by a series of distinguished preachers. The chapel was small and the atmosphere intimate. It was impossible for the preacher to offer dogma. He had to engage in persuasion. For nearly two years I was exposed to some of the best Catholic preaching in the country, and in the most favourable circumstances. The effect was undoubtedly a liberalisation and an extension of my understanding.

And my studies opened up for me, for the first time, the

richness of medieval Europe. I particularly immersed myself in the development of medieval theology. It was not so much that the philosophies I was studying had a direct relevance to the world in which I was living, as that they offered a mode of thought which combined analysis and contemplation. I was building a foundation, although I did not know it, for a truer understanding of the faith which I had inherited but had not properly understood.

This religious development was important, I believe, because when I came to occupy positions of authority requiring me to make moral judgements about people and programmes I had already had to bring myself from the acceptance and defence of dogma to a readiness to understand that the doctrinal formulae were not, on close examination, as severe in their demands as their wording seemed to imply, and that however firm my own beliefs might be, others would have thoughts to contribute to my understanding which I could not afford to reject. A Director-General cannot be arbitrary. He must allow for dissent.

Long after the years of my formal education were over I found myself steadily seeking to widen my understanding of my Catholic faith, and with every new study I found myself compelled to a new liberalism. We Catholics were, after all, a minority in Britain. We could not simply assert the correctness of our beliefs and insist that they should be accepted by others, in the tradition of the Holy Office and Rome. We were dissenters in a country with an established Church whose position was conventionally unshakable. That was no bad thing. It was better, I believe, to live in a country with a formal commitment to Christianity, however imperfect its practice might be. But it followed that all dissenters had a common interest in a freedom of discussion. This, I know, is the contrary of the view which people normally expect to be held by Catholics. But it seems to me to be wholly logical. When the Second Vatican Council made the final commitment to the principle of freedom of religious belief it seemed entirely natural to me that this should be the formal position of my Church. It was a far cry from the dogmatism of the accidental training in apologetics which I had acquired during my school-days.

My wartime activities were hardly distinguished. I had to serve somewhere. I volunteered to train as an officer in the Indian Army and went out as a cadet in the bottom deck of a troop ship. It was not agreeable, As we sailed in convoy round the Cape (we left Gourock on 4 December 1941) we heard, successively, the news of Pearl Harbour, the fall of Hong Kong and the loss of the *Prince of Wales* and *Repulse* in the developing attack on Malaya. At the time we landed in Bombay on 29 January 1942 we thought we could see our destination fairly clearly, and not very happily. But it did not happen like that. After four months' training in Bangalore I was posted to a battalion of the Frontier Force Rifles on the Frontier itself. During these months in India I experienced for the first time the sense of isolation which comes from not speaking the language of the surrounding people. My required studies of Urdu represented my personal response to this linguistic isolation, and I discovered, for the first time, that I liked language studies and found them not difficult. I went next to the Middle East, to finish up with a battered unit refitting in Cyprus. We stayed in Cyprus for sixteen months. I learned a fair amount of modern Greek, which I have, for the most part, forgotten. Then came Italy, with our Division (the Tenth Indian) holding defensive positions on the Adriatic while the attack was conducted at Cassino. We were static and I began to learn Italian. I continued my studies when I was shipped to Army Group Headquarters in Siena. After three months there I was reasonably fluent, and I have never lost the language. For the last five months of the Italian campaign I was posted to 8th Indian Division Headquarters. The Division had a tremendous record in Italy and worshipped its commander, General Russell. As soon as I joined them I knew what 'high morale' meant and I recognized how great could be the influence of a single leader. Russell was not showy. He was very quiet. But he was utterly competent and likeable. It was a long lasting lesson.

I returned to Cambridge as soon as I could, in October 1945, to complete my third year. It was by far the most fruitful I spent there. The sense of having a future again, and of being immersed once more in the world of ideas, was the best postwar resettlement I could have imagined. But I had no certainty of what to do for a career. I sat for the Civil Service resettlement examination and was not accepted, at which point I took the adjective 'temporary' describing my Civil Servant status in the India Office as meaning exactly what it said, much to the surprise of my Personnel Officer. And so I came to the BBC.

The story, told about anyone else, would be written down as yet another example of the working of the 'old boy network'. But in 1947 nobody, I think, would have listed me among its members. During 1943, in Cyprus, I had called fairly regularly on Colonel Harman Grisewood in Nicosia. He and his wife, who had retired there before the war, kept open house on Sundays for British officers. They were Catholics, and I would join them after the midday Mass. One day the Colonel asked me what I intended to do after the war. I told him I had some idea of trying to join the Foreign Service. If I found myself at a loose end, he suggested, I could do worse than ask his son, Harman, at the BBC whether they had anything for me. In late 1946, having failed to convince the Foreign Service that I was their man, I did just that. I was not a devoted listener to the BBC, but I was interested in politics, and especially in foreign affairs. I explained all this to Harman Grisewood, and one week later I was called for interview to Broadcasting House as a candidate for the post of Talks Producer for the Home Service. The interviewing board, of which Harman Grisewood was a member, seemed unduly impressed when I said in reply to a question about economic affairs, that I could read and understand the City column of *The Times*, but probably took more note of my two Firsts in History, in 1941 and 1946. Within a week I was invited to take the post. By April 1947 I was in the BBC as a Talks Producer.

Within six months I was producing the major weekly Home Service evening talk on world affairs and progressed to others on domestic and social questions. I also asked to be allowed to handle *Round Britain Quiz* as its second producer. And then I left the BBC. After three years I could not see any realistic prospect of promotion. BBC pay levels were depressed. I did not feel that talks producing was a profession for life, since it entailed no obvious professional qualification. And I found that the degree of detailed and compulsory scrutiny of every talk for which I was responsible was not only irksome to me, but difficult to explain to my contributors. I was a party to three-cornered arguments in which the third party never appeared. I left with respect for the BBC as an institution, a certain capacity for getting things done, a much improved English style (made more direct by the exigencies of the microphone) and a continuing journalistic interest. I had also acquired, although I did not know it, the firm stamp of the BBC ethos.

When I came back to the BBC a year later in the Monitoring Service I had certainly learned humility. My experience at the *Fishing News* – a weekly dealing with commercial fishing, had taught me a good deal about producing a periodical news-paper and the routine tasks of reporting and sub-editing, but a great deal more about the importance to an employee of having the support of a major institution as a background to daily work. It had not been easy to find the return path. At Caver-sham, as I have frequently explained to my friends in the Socialist countries of Eastern Europe, I became familiar with all the arguments and jargon of Marxist philosophy. Moreover, I acquired professionally the useful art of condensing masses of words into the shortest possible report.

I left the Monitoring Service to become the BBC's first internal selected Administrative Trainee. That really set the shape of the rest of my career. For twelve months – I was promised eighteen – I was sent around department after department to find out how each worked, and sometimes in doing so, to do some work myself. I spent six weeks in the Midland Region in Birmingham. It is possible only by working in a Region in the BBC to find out how much of their own identity each one has. They each form a perfect microcosm of the BBC operation. I learned a lot about how the BBC works, but above all, I learned that the BBC outside London mattered.

And later in my traineeship I helped a very experienced Personnel Officer to draw up the BBC's first Personnel Manual – an invaluable training. (Characteristically, it was then called the Staff Administration Manual.) I devised shift rotas in the Gramophone Department. I caused near panic when I was thought to have torn up the old rotas for announcers in the Overseas Presentation Department after devising new ones. I analysed patterns of work for Television Outside Broadcast crews to see whether they could be rationalized – and whether the pay rates attached to them could be made more sensible. I visited transmitting stations, and began for the first time to know about frequencies – especially those used in short wave broadcasting. I went round the various catering establishments and learned the essential lesson that profitability depends on turnover, and turnover depends on pleasing the customers. It had application far beyond the staff canteens! Naturally, I went to many of the programme departments, and talked to producers about what they did and how they did it. But the real advantage of this year of visits was that I knew how the machine worked, and where it was liable to stress. Perhaps more important than anything else – I made a lot of friends. They remembered me later.

After that it was a rapid progression – through a junior administrative post in the External Services looking after the overseas offices, including the relay station in Malaya; off to Canada as Representative for three years; back to run the External Services' budget under the eagle eye of Sir Beresford Clark. He was then in his final years as Director of External

Broadcasting, having originally joined the BBC as an announcer in Cardiff in the early days. He had been part of the small pioneer group which had started the Empire Service in 1936, and had subsequently been at the centre of all the wartime developments of the Overseas and European Services. His administrative experience was unique, and he had a formidable reputation for mastery of detail, and for subtlety in dealing with Whitehall. I had the feeling that he was taking me under his wing when I joined the External Services.

Of all this experience, Canada was perhaps the most formative individually. I saw a public organisation (the CBC) with a commitment to a general public service, in constant and debilitating competition with private commercial broadcasters having no comparable commitment. Much of the commercial competition came from south of the Canadian border, but much was internal, within Canada. And, of course, there was the public service of sustaining the Canadian identity – the issue of whether English-speaking Canadians could ever acquire a proper sense of respect for their French-speaking fellow citizens. The CBC was, moreover, a living example of the desperate problems of devolved management. Geography and language combined to make management virtually impossible. And everything had to be done under the central pressure of unremitting competition, in a social context which endorsed the competitive idea and generally under-valued public service.

I returned from Canada in 1959 to be responsible for the budgetary problems of the External Services. With a personally friendly but officially crusty accountant I devised the first cost analysis of the External Services, showing just what was saved and what was added by cutting or by creating a programme service. The deduction was basic to all broadcasting costs – that the invariable infrastructure is very large indeed. In the External Services something like half of the cost remains unaffected, however much services go up or down.

In 1963 I was selected by Hugh Greene, who had then been

Director-General for four years, to be Secretary to the Corporation. That meant being involved in formulating policy papers for the Board under his instruction. It meant drafting answers to the most difficult correspondence reaching the BBC about programmes. And programmes in Hugh Greene's day provoked a great deal of criticism. I became very familiar with the arguments about the freedom of broadcasters, and I wrote with conviction about them because I read, in the letters reaching us, a degree of intolerance which surprised me.

My final move before becoming Director-General was to Bush House to be Director of External Broadcasting, and for the first time I was faced with the problems of commanding very senior people. Many of them were older and far more experienced than I was. I wanted to change things because I thought that too much of the immediate postwar structure had survived for too long. It was not economical. It was not always as efficient as it should be. And yet it produced a marvellous programme service. How does one justify changing a structure which produces a good service? It is a permanent problem for the BBC. I found it in Bush House. I *did* change things, and I learned how much stress can fall on the man who tries to do it against well-argued opposition based on a good record, But I also learned that if the arguments are good, and the people who will carry out the ideas are also good, then there is no future in giving in simply because what is proposed is not liked. That means, of course, that you have to be very sure before you start changing things. It was a good training for the battles over 'Broadcasting in the Seventies', the policy paper published by the BBC in my first year as Director-General proposing changes in regional radio and television, and, much more provocatively, the disbandment of some orchestras and important changes in the then Music Programme and Third Programme.

When I became Director-General in April 1969 I was 47. I brought to the job, besides my educational history, nearly four years of wartime Army experience; a nine months' inoculation period as a temporary Civil Servant in the India Office; 21 years of work in many places in the BBC, broken only by my one year as 'Assistant Editor' of *The Fishing News*. Each of these aspects of my life added its own special flavour to my view of what I had to do and the way I did it. Some of that special flavour undoubtedly came from my family background, with its Irish sympathies, Scottish affinities, and Yorkshire childhood. The multiplicity of experiences and backgrounds matched the needs of the job. What struck me above all during the time I was Director-General was the impossibility of separating out any one strand of the job from another, and any one influence from all the others which were brought to bear. One started with programmes and one was led inexorably to politics and to money. One dealt in money and one was led to considerations of technology. One saw the prospects of a developing technique and one was led into problems of how to handle the people who were to apply it. It was impossible to disentangle, in the whole pattern, one thread from another. The evolution of broadcasting and its continuing operation, with every philosophy and practice emerging from it, did indeed present itself as a seamless robe. And the wider one's experiences and sympathies, the better one was able to cope.

Part One

Part One

CHAPTER I
The Origins

I HAVE OFTEN BEEN ASKED by professional colleagues from other countries how they should seek to organize their broadcasting systems in order to emulate the results which they admire in the BBC. My reply has always been that I do not believe that systems developed in one set of circumstances in one country at a particular period in its history are necessarily relevant or applicable to quite different situations in other countries and at other times. In order to assess how much of the organisation of British broadcasting, and in particular, of the BBC, may be relevant as an example for other countries, one has to know what were the circumstances in which the BBC system came into being. There were, I believe, certain special considerations which produced both the monopoly itself and the ethos of the monopolistic institution in the first instance, and which conditioned the subsequent emergence of the duopoly of BBC and IBA.

Nobody who writes on this early period of broadcasting in Britain can do other than depend totally on the work of Professor Asa Briggs, and I hope that in those parts of this chapter which refer to British experience in the 1920s I have correctly reflected his work. In so far as I take account in what follows of the European experience the analysis which I offer is my own. For the Canadian experience I have relied on my recollection of conversations with some of the pioneers (Donald Monson and Alphonse Ouimet of the CBC) and on the book by Frank Peers, *The Politics of Canadian Broadcasting*.

The institution of the BBC emerged in Britain as the product of certain historical factors which prevailed in the 1920s and 1930s. Those factors were technical, political and social. The technical factors related to radio frequency management in a densely populated continent of differing sovereignties. The political circumstances were the state of the British Parliamentary system at the time, and the condition of Europe as a system of nation States. The social factors had to do with views in Britain about possible institutional patterns in the 1920s and 1930s.

The technical facts were basic. The earliest broadcasting was based on radio transmission in the medium frequency band. It is a characteristic of transmission in this band that night-time range is very much greater than daytime. Transmissions at any significant power – and indeed, even at low power – may cause interference at great distances in night-time broadcasting. This means that the allocation of frequencies and their management by those to whom they are allocated must be a matter of high professional skill if chaos is to be avoided. It is also a matter of political significance. In both these respects there is a decisive difference between the Western hemisphere and Europe, although broadcasting comparisons are often made without any regard for these differences.

In North America, communities, even in the more densely populated Eastern seaboard, are, on the whole, fairly widely scattered. European communities, on the other hand, tend to be fairly closely spaced. This means that whereas in North America the broadcasting system can be based on the assumption that a transmission which serves a small community can be reasonably free of the fear of interference if it operates at relatively low power or on a highly directional aerial, the same is not true in Europe. Broadcasting in North America was originally developed on a pattern of primary service to small urban communities, with the rural areas being relatively neglected. Indeed, that was the very problem which the

Canadians faced when, in the interest of preserving the sense of national identity, they wanted to set up a national system serving the rural areas of each province. In the 1930s Canada had available for service to such wide, sparsely-populated areas only six clear channels (that is, frequencies which no other station in North America was using), operating on a maximum permitted power of 50 kW. National coverage across the Dominion was imperfect. The basic assumption had been that local coverage of the denser communities was what mattered, both in Canada and the United States, and the early frequency allocations had been made on that basis.

In Europe, on the contrary, the pattern of closely spaced areas of dense population dictated the use of frequencies in a way which would cover larger areas with higher power, and therefore from fewer transmission points. To have given each small community its own wavelength would have resulted in general chaos. But there was the additional factor of sovereignty and difference of language. Each nation in Europe, reflecting each linguistic group, wished to cover its own community as effectively as possible, and this was best achieved by a pattern of high power stations covering relatively large areas. That, at least, is my interpretation of the developments which took place.

By the time of the postwar Copenhagen Plan in Europe the effect of this pattern was quite clearly evident. Maximum transmitter power was 150 kW on medium wave stations, compared with the North American power of 50 kW which was still in force. Although there were subsidiary allocations at low power, the principal pattern was of high power medium wave stations giving wide area coverage, usually operating in a co-ordinated pattern as national networks. There were, it is true, two International Common Frequencies on which the maximum operating power was 2 kW, and then only if no harmful interference was caused to other users close at hand. And, most significantly, there were broadcasting allocations in the long wave band which were particularly suited for total national coverage in countries covering large areas. Europe, in fact, was the only continent in which such allocations were made. This general pattern was not materially changed at the Geneva Conference in 1976, although the multiplicity of stations operating at high power within interference range of each other by night seems likely effectively to reduce the coverage within countries and to degrade medium wave signals throughout the continent after dark. But this will not affect the basic structural pattern which was established as the standard broadcasting band slowly widened as a result of broadcasting pressures during the 1920s and 1930s. That was the formative stage, in which the institutional framework evolved.

Whereas in the Americas the pattern of broadcasting became one of local stations coming together to form networks, the European pattern was of national coverage on high power operation by national organisations. The frequency management problems of each broadcasting organisation in Europe had to be handled as an aspect of national sovereignty, usually by the postal administration of the country concerned. In the long run this meant that the European pattern, dictated by technical geography, resulted in the development of monopoly or near-monopoly organisations in each sovereign country.

The pattern is clear from the account given by Briggs of the technical history of early radio broadcasting in Britain and the United States. By 1924 some 530 stations were operating in the United States. A Post Office official from Britain who observed this situation came back convinced that the situation which had developed in the United States ought not to be allowed to develop in Britain. Out of some 1105 stations licenced up to August 1924 in the United States, no less than 572 had gone out of business by that date. There was considerable interference between all transmissions and the listeners suffered. The Post Office conclusion was that a greater degree of co-ordination should be applied in Britain. The observer recommended a single broadcasting organisation. No such solution would have been acceptable in the United States because, in addition to the commercial considerations affecting coverage which I have already explained, American anti-trust legislation and deep suspicion of any State intervention in commercial activity, including especially journalism, would have effectively blocked it.

The technical conclusion reached by the Post Office in Britain fitted in with the thinking of the British radio industry. The manufacturers, who had felt the need for some form of public broadcasting service to promote sales of equipment, had concluded, after much debate, that a single originating organisation would meet their technical need. They formed the British Broadcasting Company – the original BBC. Part of the impetus came from the ownership by the Marconi Company of a large number of patents essential to the operation of any transmitting station. Part came from the Post Office, under severe pressure from other parties interested in the use of frequencies – for example, Defence Departments. From the money point of view, the British Press feared a diversion of advertising revenue if broadcasting were allowed access to it. The licence fee therefore became the sole source of revenue, and, in consequence, the Post Office became the single collecting agency for that revenue. And this singularity of revenue was the more practicable because of the general acceptance by the British public, demonstrated by experience, of the obligation to pay properly imposed public charges. The Postmaster-General said in 1924, when asked about the possibility of extensive evasion, that he was confident that people would not only be willing, but anxious to put themselves right as regards the law and to contribute their quota towards the cost of a service which was affording them so much enjoyment. In general, that acceptance has stood the test of time as it has not done in many other countries. Indeed, the testing time for the licence fee came not in the early days, when the temptation to evade might have been thought at its greatest, but in the days of inflation in the 1970s when the amount became psychologically discouraging, though rather more so, as I think in the minds of the politicians who had to defend it than for the great majority of the public who paid it.

These, then, were the circumstances which led in Europe to the establishment of national broadcasting organisations, and in Britain to the concept of a monopoly financed by a public charge. These precise circumstances can hardly be reproduced again elsewhere, since no country will ever again be at the initial development stage of broadcasting, facing the same problems and blessed with the same freedom from precedent in solving them. But why did the constitutional form of a chartered corporation emerge as the British solution?

It did not follow from the technical arguments towards monopoly that this monopoly should be either non-commercial or publicly owned. In some European countries private ownership and commercial financing was the chosen pattern, though the Post and Telegraph administrations always served as a strong mechanism for state influence. In Britain the suggestion of public ownership came forward at a very early stage and caught on with astonishing rapidity. A combination of reluctances appears to have supported the positive idea. In the first place, as Briggs records, there was the Press reluctance to see a potential competitor for commercial revenues appear in the field. Nor, indeed, was the Press over-anxious to see a rival source of news established, though the early broadcasting experiments did not suggest that such competition in the news field would be overwhelming. It was not until the General Strike of 1926 that this argument became powerful, and that was after the main constitutional discussions had been completed.

Moreover, the politicians, who might have been expected to take an active interest in the development of broadcasting, had they foreseen that it might be a major element in the formation of public opinion, seemed, according to Professor Briggs, to show comparatively little interest in the future possibilities. The evidence suggests that in these formative years such expressions of interest as came from the politicians sprang from their reluctance to see the broadcasting medium fall into the hands of any Minister or any Government. Those in opposition – and two of the three principal parties were always likely to be in opposition during the 1920s in Britain – could all see that the broadcasting medium in the hands of their political opponents while in Government could be a distinct threat to a change in roles. The Conservative and Liberal Parties were in contention for power, according to the historical pattern, and the Labour Party was just emerging as a substantial third force in the House of Commons. None was particularly keen for the others to obtain the special advantage which Ministerial control of broadcasting might have offered. The Labour Party expressed the most coherent views, through Herbert Morrison. He told a Committee of Inquiry that the broadcasting organisation ought to be publicly owned and controlled. Other politicians seem to have been anxious only about complaints of bias in the reporting and discussion of political events. Their fears seem to have been stilled by an assurance from the Postmaster-General, who was the responsible Minister, that all kinds of political broadcasting were being prohibited. Had the discussion taken place fifty years later, it is only too likely that it might have resulted in the kind of minatory declaratory legislation which politicians are likely to produce whenever they are invited to consider the matter of regulating creative activities.

But if the broadcasting monopoly was not to be under Ministerial control, and yet was to be under public ownership, the constitutional pattern still had to be worked out. The earliest example of a public corporation managing a public asset in Britain must have been the Port of London Authority, set up in 1908. The Labour Party had, from the beginning, favoured the public ownership of national assets, but their view could hardly have been decisive at that stage in the Party's evolution in Parliament. The key suggestion, as I read the account by Briggs, seems to have come from within the Post Office and to have appeared in one of the early discussions which followed the report of the Crawford Committee in 1924. The device proposed was incorporation under a Royal Charter. This conveys a number of advantages, not all of which may have been fully appreciated at the time. The Charter is an act of the Royal Prerogative, and as such, it is not subject to debate in Parliament. The general terms of a Government intention to promote such a Charter, or to renew it, can, of course, be the subject of a normal debate, on a motion put before the two Houses. But the document itself is not subject to the detailed scrutiny before the House which is the fate of any proposed statue. There is, therefore, in the issue of the Charter, an element of removal from control by Parliament which has proved to be historically important ever since the BBC received its first Charter in 1927. This removal was clearly intended, as is apparent from the discussions reported by Briggs in his description of the formative stages.

Moreover, the incorporation of the BBC by Charter meant that the Governors, who formed the Corporation, were Crown appointments, and by that fact, themselves set apart from the normal run of political life. This constitutional device made it possible to set up a monopoly in a form in which the Governors could realistically act as 'trustee for the nation' in the use of the broadcasting system. The Crawford Committee phrase is key to the understanding of the thinking of the time.

The protective constitutional isolation of the body which was to govern the broadcasting monopoly would, nevertheless, have had no validity without a corresponding isolation from controversy over the funds which were to be administered by this governing body. Commercial revenues had not been entirely excluded from the Company's range of possibilities, and indeed, one or two commercially sponsored programmes had been accepted by the Company after its establishment in 1922 – for example, concerts funded by a London newspaper. Significantly, these projects were accepted by John Reith, then the Company's first General Manager, who was later to insist so strongly on the public service character of the proposed chartered Corporation. But the reluctance of the Press to see a competitor for commercial advertising revenue, together with the general concept of public service which evolved very rapidly during and after the enquiries of the Crawford Committee, suggested very strongly to those concerned that the licence fee ought to be the sole source of revenue. The Treasury seems not to have appreciated that what was being established was a permanently hypothecated tax – something to which they have always taken strong objection, but they do not seem to have pressed their objections on this occasion. But there is no doubt in my mind, looking back on history and at the present, that it was the establishment of the licence fee as a dedicated source of revenue, and one whose yield was potentially independent of annual Governmental scrutiny, which underpinned the constitutional independence of the new Corporation. True, the Government retained a specified proportion of the licence revenue, not only to meet collecting expenses, but as a specific precept, and did so for many years. But so long as the return to the BBC was related directly to the number of licence-holders, then a precedent had been established on which the independence of the BBC's revenue could be safely founded. That is a separate subject in itself, but in the consideration of the independence of the Board of Governors, this initial decision is an essential element.

Reith, who had at first been in favour of simple incorporation under the Companies Act, as had been the case with the original British Broadcasting Company, quickly saw the advantages of the Charter proposal and pressed very strongly for its implementation. His character and perception were undoubtedly the decisive final factors in the establishment of the BBC as a chartered public corporation and his nomination, in the first Charter, as the new Corporation's Director-General, guaranteed continuance of the broadcasting philosophy which he had developed as General Manager of the Company.

But it was the combination of circumstances which brought the Corporation into being in the form which it eventually took in 1927. It was the concatenation of technical necessities in Europe, lack of interest among the political parties in the possibilities of the medium for the future, a developing pattern of public ownership as the means of managing public assets, the availability of the constitutional device in the Charter, together with the character of John Reith, which determined the creation of the BBC. It did not come into being as an institution which represented the only logical solution, a priori, to the problem of how to manage broadcasting. It came into being because the circumstances were favourable, and because they existed in a particular country at a particular time. That is why attempts to recreate it elsewhere are unlikely to succeed if they ignore or under-value the relevance of local circumstances. There is no ideal pattern. There may be idealistic intentions. They are not enough without a realistic appreciation of the political, social and technical facts within the framework of which the problem is set.

CHAPTER II

The Charter

CRITICS OF THE BBC frequently refer to what is spelt out in the Charter. Those claims are so often inaccurate that a review at this point of the constitutional documents themselves may perhaps be useful. Such a study indicates how substantial is the genuine freedom of the BBC, and in particular, of its Governors, to do what they think is best in the interests of broadcasting, and properly to act, with full discretion, as trustees for the nation in broadcasting.

There are three documents. They are the Charter itself; the Licence and Agreement, and the set of Memoranda which are issued by the responsible Minister in accordance with the requirements of the two principal documents. The first two are published, and reproduced annually in the BBC's Handbook. The Memoranda are available in the Library of the House of Commons, but are otherwise not easy to come by. It is not that they contain anything secret or disreputable. It is simply that people do not seem to be interested in the constitutional documents, on the basis of which all the BBC's work must rest.

The Charter itself is remarkable for containing almost nothing about the making of programmes, and it is on this point that those who call the BBC to account for what it has not done, or for what it has done, representing these things as being in breach of the Charter, are most frequently wrong. In fact, the only allegation of breach of the Charter which I can remember in my time as having been conceivably related to the terms of the Charter was an action taken by the Periodical Publishers' Association, which alleged that the BBC, in agreeing that *The Listener* should publish other than broadcast material, was in some way in breach of Article 3 of the Charter, which sets out the 'objectives of the Corporation'. The argument was that to admit such articles to *The Listener* was to exceed the terms of Article 3(j) which empowers the BBC to publish and distribute such periodicals 'as may be conducive to any of the objectives of the Corporation'. The contention was not upheld, but it was at least related to the terms of the Charter itself.

The prime purpose of the Charter is to establish the Corporation and to say what it may do, as well as, in some respects, to say how it may do those things. It is only in the preamble that there is substantial reference to the programmes produced and the services provided. (There is one minor exception to this general statement, and it arises in the description of the character of the National Broadcasting Councils, whose functions are described in Article 10.) The preamble to the Charter refers indirectly to the popularity of the programmes provided by stating the number of licences issued in the United Kingdom. In the 1964 version of the Charter the number is given as 15¾ millions. Presumably the number of licences to be set down in the next Charter preamble will be of the order of 18 millions. The final paragraph of the preamble notes 'the widespread interest which is thereby and by other evidences shown to be taken by our peoples' in the services provided by the BBC, and goes on to speak of 'the great value of such services as means of disseminating information, education and entertainment'. Here is the famous trinity of values, but it is set down as an observation about what *is* offered – not as a precept that it *should* be offered. Like so much else in the constitutional conventions which surround the BBC, that precept was established by the BBC for itself in the earliest days of its existence. Of course, having been repeatedly set down as an observation of fact, this trinity takes on something of the character of a precept by precedent, but it is not more than that. The preamble also observes that it is 'in the interests of our peoples' that the BBC should continue to provide these broadcasting services.

And the end of the preamble stands firmly on 'our Prerogative Royal and our special grace, certain knowledge and mere motion'. The Queen in Council simply ordains and declares that there shall be a Corporation created as a legal person. From that character a number of beneficial consequences flow, as I hope to show in what follows.

In the first Article of the Charter itself the nature of that legal personality is set out. There is provision for a common seal; for power to sue and liability to be sued; to acquire and to hold property, with the reservation that the whole of the Corporation's income shall be applied solely to promote the objects set out in the Charter. And finally, Article 1 declares that 'the Governors of the Corporation shall be the members thereof'. That is the key to the whole structure. It is the Governors who are the BBC, in law and in fact. 'The BBC' is accused from time to time of expressing opinions. But whenever this is said it is almost invariably programmes made by staff who are employed by 'the BBC' proper who have done whatever is alleged. The Governors are the constitutional source of power and they are the ultimate source of authority, of approval, or of disapproval. This fact gives to the BBC a rather more than symbolic centre of authority, which could be said to correspond roughly to that of the Crown in the constitution as a whole.

Article 2 concerns itself with the duration of the Charter. This is a matter of considerable significance, since a reasonable guarantee of continuity is essential to the exercise of independent authority. The same is true of the IndependentBroadcasting Authority, and indeed, has a considerable bearing on the potential quality of their programme output. No programme company which cannot see a reasonable future before it is likely to invest either in programme facilities or in programmes of high quality, which involve high expense, unless it can see a possibility of return during its contractual period.

The first Charter of the BBC was granted for ten years from January 1927. So was the second, from 1937. The war intervened and the Charter was renewed for five years (in fact, by a new Charter, subsequently extended) in order to allow for postwar reconstruction in the BBC and for the further public enquiry which was foreseen. That enquiry, led by Lord Beveridge, gave rise to a further new Charter for ten years from 1952, which, in turn, was extended by two years to allow for the sitting of the Pilkington Committee and for consideration of its recommendations. Pilkington recommended a twelve year period for the next Charter, which took effect in 1964, and that Charter, in turn, was extended by three years, to expire in 1979. Annan recommended a period of fifteen years from 1979.[1] The general supposition has been throughout that, for the sake of stability and genuine independence, a reasonable period of guaranteed existence must be given to the BBC and the argument for stability has grown steadily more important as it became more evident through the years that change in the constitutional arrangements was likely to be marginal rather than major. Theoretically, each Committee of Inquiry has had substantial freedom to change the constitutional character of the BBC. None has done so, although there has been serious discussion of the possibility during each of the inquiries. The Annan recommendation of the fifteen year period seems at last to be approaching a point where the assumption can very nearly be made that no major change in the constitutional firm of the existing elements in British broadcasting is to be expected, and that what is wanted is a periodic examination of future possibilities, and a review of the existing institutions, rather than an assumption that their total re-casting would make sense.

Articles 3 and 5 of the Charter might perhaps be seen as its effective constituent parts, since they set out, respectively, the

[1] The 1964 Charter was extended yet again in 1978, to expire in July 1981, in order to give time for the approval of the new Charter and Television Act, and for their application.

purposes and activities, and the composition of the Board. In effect, the rest of the Charter is an amplification of aspects of these articles.

The first of the purposes set out in Article 3 is that the Corporation should 'provide as public services, broadcasting service ... in Our United Kingdom ... and elsewhere ...'. There is a statement that these services must be 'by the methods of television and telephony', which excludes the Corporation from operating in the field of cable distribution. It is also made clear in specific terms that 'elsewhere' means 'the British Commonwealth and other countries and places overseas'. That is the basis for the operation of the External Services. But the effective phrase is 'public services'. That carries tremendous implications.

In the first place, it is clear that the operation is to be on a non-commercial basis. Although the fact is not explicit, and has to be made so in the Licence and Agreement under the Clause dealing with receipt of money for sending programmes (Clause 12), the general intention is clear, especially when one takes into account the discussions which have accompanied the drafting of the various Charters. And the phrase 'public services' creates an obligation on the Governors to make no distinctions as between one part of the audience and another. The BBC's services are not simply for one part of the population, even though that part may be a very substantial majority. The requirement is general, and imposes an obligation, both in terms of geography and of taste, to serve the widest range of the British people. The external obligation is, of course, different, in that words empowering the BBC to provide services 'elsewhere' make it necessary for the location of 'elsewhere' to be more precisely specified. That is done under the prescribing power reserved to the Prescribing Departments in the Licence and Agreement.

The remaining sections of Article 3 call for little special comment since they simply empower the BBC to operate and construct the stations necessary for transmission; to do the same on behalf of other agencies; to carry on certain operations essential to broadcasting, such as the collection of news, the promotion of concerts, the publication of journals, the acquisition of copyrights, the making of films and recordings, the registration of patents, the negotiation of licences with municipal and other authorities, and similar matters. There is also a provision for the acquisition of stocks in companies which can assist the Corporation's business (Visnews is such a one) and to establish or support institutions, funds or trusts for the benefit of employees and former employees. It is under this Clause that the important pension fund provisions are made. Finally, in this group of miscellaneous provisions there is the usual 'catch-all' provision, the wording of which I quote in full:

> To do all such other things as the Corporation may consider incidental or conducive to the attainment of any of the aforesaid objects or the exercise of any of the aforesaid powers of the Corporation.

And here we come to one of the great benefits to the BBC of operating under a Royal Charter. The provisions of such a Charter are customarily held to be interpreted in the manner most beneficial to the holder of the Charter. The effect is to permit rather than to forbid actions by the chartered body, so long as they can be demonstrated to be 'incidental or conducive' to the attainment of its objects. It is therefore very difficult for a Corporation which is behaving at all properly to find itself acting *ultra vires*.

The provisions of Article 3 governing the BBC's borrowing powers are best understood when seen alongside the general financial provisions set out in Articles 16 and 17 of the Charter, Clauses 16, 17 and 18 of the Licence and Agreement, together with the Memoranda issued under those Clauses. I have therefore reserved a discussion of the issues raised in these provisions to a later Chapter.

In the general area of powers of the Corporation, Article

4 is important from time to time. It stipulates that the BBC shall not enter into any arrangement with other governments without having prior consent in writing from the responsible UK Minister. In itself, this is certainly a reasonable provision, since there would be no justification for the Corporation conducting, as it were, its own foreign policy with other governments in promoting its activities. (This is, of course, a very different question from criticisms that the Corporation may be accused of conducting its own foreign policy through the medium of material included in its programmes, especially those in the External Services. That is a criticism which I should regard as wholly unfounded, though some Conservatives at the time of Suez might have disagreed.)

Recent experience suggests, however, that the matter of relations with governments may not be quite as clear-cut as appears on the surface. In the early 1970s the Irish Minister of Posts and Telecommunications, Dr Conor Cruise O'Brien, was extremely anxious to inaugurate a second television service within the Republic in order to satisfy the claims of the population of the West and South to have equal access to British programmes with their fellow citizens in the East. He therefore opened discussions with Whitehall on the possibility of relaying live programme services from the BBC (and, indeed, from ITV, though he preferred BBC-1) to provide the substance of this second network. There were political aspects in this proposal in that he hoped that relays of RTE programmes would be made available in the North, and this would undoubtedly have provoked severe adverse reactions, unpalatable to the British Government. But the principal complication was that Dr O'Brien's proposal would have required a completely new set of copyright and performing right agreements between the British broadcasters and their contributors. These negotiations would at once have involved RTE, as the responsible Irish broadcaster, and discussions would have had to proceed as a matter of normal liaison between RTE and the BBC.

The active intervention of the Irish Minister in the plans of RTE for the development of the second network meant that the discussions were, in many respects, three-sided, involving the BBC, RTE and the Irish Government. At the same time, the political discussions were being conducted by the Irish Government and Whitehall. There was a point in the discussions when Whitehall took distinct umbrage at the possibility that the BBC might appear to be negotiating with the Irish Government about the new service. In fact, that was never so, and had the BBC not taken some precautionary steps to restrain the enthusiasm of the Irish Minister, some serious difficulties might have arisen with the owners of the rights in the broadcasts which it was proposed to relay. The episode does, I think, illustrate that when the question of overseas distribution of programmes arises, the distinction between what is a matter for the broadcasting authorities, and what is the point at which Governments become involved, is not entirely clear. My view would be that this responsibility is wholly within the jurisdiction of the broadcaster.

The second major constituent Article of the Charter – Article 5, taken with amplifications in Articles 6 and 7, describes the appointment of the Governors as a Board. In the immediate postwar period there were seven. The 1952 Charter – and that of 1964 – specified nine. But by an amendment approved when Edward Short was Postmaster-General the number was increased to twelve. There has been much discussion, within the BBC and in the Annan Committee, about whether the smaller number was more effective. In my own experience, as The Secretary from 1963, and with continuous contact with the Board thereafter until 1977, nine Governors represented a more cohesive force than twelve. It was always the case that new members rapidly acquired the corporate sense which is necessary for the effective functioning of this kind of a body. It did seem to be rather easier for new members in a group of nine to make an effective contribution at a rather earlier stage than new members in a group of twelve. And, of course, twelve is easier to split than nine when it comes to matters of difference. That could be a significant consideration for a Chairman or a Director-General who might wish to make less than scrupulous use of the play of politics within a Board. It might also be useful for a dissident faction in a Board which wished to block some particular change. These are facts of normal political life, rather than particular animadversions on specific incidents produced by the size of the BBC's Board of Governors. I think they have to be taken into account when considering whether nine is better than twelve.

Article 6, which sets out the terms of appointment, re-appointment, remuneration and departure of Governors from the Board, provides that, subject to the maximum appoint-ment period of five years set out in Article 5, a retiring Governor should be eligible for re-appointment. This has been useful from time to time in arranging for a sufficient continuity of experience within the Board at moments when a number of Governors appeared likely to leave at the same time. It has also been used at times when the length of the Charter has been adjusted, as it has frequently been, to take account of the reports of Committees of Inquiries and delays which have arisen from Government consideration of such reports. Re-appointment, however, is, on the whole, unusual, and I well remember the parting remark of Sir James Duff, when leaving the post of Vice Chairman in 1964: 'The rotatory principle', he said, 'is right'. He had been expressing the normal human reluctance to leave a pleasurable experience, but in that phrase he epitomized for me the essence of public spirit, in recogniz-ing that many talents go to make a successful Board, and that change is necessary to maintain that diversity of talents.

The terms on which a Governor may be required to leave the Board are of special interest in view of recent history. There is the normal provision for 'unsound mind' or bank-ruptcy, and for prolonged absence without permission from the meetings of the Board. But there is a naked provision (Article 6.3(b)) which reads: 'if his Governorship shall be terminated by Us'. I referred, in a Granada Lecture in 1977, to my knowledge that the recommendation made by the Annan Committee of a resolution of Parliament as the necessary prerequisite to the dismissal of the majority of the Board rested on a demonstration to the Committee of the practical necessity for some protection. This Charter provision was in my mind. I knew that at one point in Mr Wedgwood Benn's consideration in the 1960s of the appropriate response to pirate broadcasting and the public demand for pop music, together with the proposals for local broadcasting, he had had it in mind to require the BBC to devote one network to pop music, and to use that network as the revenue generating source for the BBC in general and for the proposed local radio system. At one moment there was a prospect that this network and the local radio operation would be split off from the BBC under a separate institution. But the difficulty was that any such arrangement would have required some degree of consent from the BBC, whichever course were to be followed. The Board, with its known opposition to advertising revenue, and its certain objection to being deprived either of a national radio network or of the prospect of local radio, would have been certain to resist. At some stage the question of possible dismissal of Governors, and substitute appointments, was raised, and although I do not know the precise details of how the discussions went between Ministers, what is clear to me is that the greater argument prevailed. The use of dismissal and substitution of Governors in a chartered Corporation was seen by senior Ministers to be so damaging to the general concept of independent appointment under the Queen in Council procedure that it ought not to be pursued in the case of the BBC. The convention was much too generally useful to be prejudiced by a particular political requirement. And so nothing ever happened. But it is clear to me that the Annan Committee was aware of this episode and made what they thought to be the necessary recommendation to prevent a similar instance in the future.

There is a special irony about Article 6(4), which stipulates that 'as soon as may be reasonably practicable after a vacancy arises in the Board' (or, it says, 'at a convenient time *before* such a vacancy') the attention of the appropriate Minister should be drawn to the vacancy, and the authorities should then proceed 'with all convenient speed' to the filling of it. This has been one of the most neglected duties in the whole of the Charter for many years. It is a regular occurrence that no successor will have been appointed immediately to succeed a departing Governor and that there will be a long interval before the appointment is finally announced. This is very bad indeed for the effective conduct of business in the Board, because one of the objects in the selection of Governors is to ensure an adequate spread of opinion within its membership. If vacancies are left unfilled for substantial periods that spread of opinion is improperly inhibited. It is true that the increase of numbers from nine to twelve has reduced the effect of these delays, but it has not corrected the imbalance of opinions which results from continuing vacancies. Moreover, delays in making appointments disrupt the sequence of change in the Board, which may have been carefully planned by one responsible Minister, only to be frustrated by the failure of a successor to observe the appropriate intervals. Thus, it has come about that the only times when a sensible rotation of office can be arranged have been when the Charter has been extended and the appointments of individual Governors then had to be correspondingly extended, and so arranged to produce a sensible pattern of retirement. In the normal run of appointments as they came to be made individually, the result of delays has been to disturb such sensible patterns of replacement.

Article 7 deals with the actual conduct of business within the Board, and only one or two points call for special comment. One relates to the question of voting. Sir Hugh Greene has made it clear, and so has Sir Robert Lusty, that voting was a rarity before the arrival of Lord Hill as Chairman of the Board. The maximum consensus was sought by the Chairman of the day and this was held by both of them to be a desirable state of affairs. On one occasion a particular Chairman was quoted to me as having said, on a difficult issue: 'One dissentient is too many in this instance.' I think that may be going a little far, but it is certainly the spirit in which the proceedings of the Board were carried on in the early 1960s. It did ensure that no extreme view prevailed on a split vote, and it did prevent the development of high feelings between factions in the Board. It may also, of course, have been held to inhibit action simply by the resistance of a few, but I think that must have been rare. The evidence of the early 1960s was not that the BBC was slow to move. If anything, many people felt that it was moving too fast, and the Governors were certainly behind Sir Hugh Greene in the changes he was making.

Lord Hill has described how he introduced voting to the Board and he has also explained how the Board seemed frequently to be divided between the old and the new group of Governors. This was certainly the case on many issues. For a Director-General, with his responsibility to the whole of the Board, it is very difficult indeed to deal with a group of Governors which is divided in its views. There is the temptation to play one group off against the other and I will not deny that this occasionally happened. But it is far better if the Governors seek zealously for extensive agreement so that the Director-General may have the fullest guidance and support for whatever action he is either proposing to take or being instructed to take.

The provision for the exercise by the Chairman, or, in his absence, the Vice Chairman, of residual interim power on behalf of the Board between meetings is very carefully expressed. The Chairman, in exercising this power of decision – and this can only be done in cases of urgency – is required 'so far as may be reasonably practicable' to consult with the other Governors, or those who may be accessible. He is also required to report, as soon as possible after taking his decision, to the Board on the question raised and the decision taken. He is therefore clearly acting in the place of the Board, and doing so, as far as possible, in a deliberative manner. The function described is not that of the day-to-day executive. It is of the constitutional authority operating in intervals between its full assembly. That is why, for me, the theory that the Chairman is a kind of superior Chief Executive of the Corporation, above the Director-General, is an incorrect view of what the Charter provides. The Charter is ensuring that there is a means whereby the executive authority of the Corporation is exercised in the presence of a proper regard for the ultimate constitutional source of authority. It is not seeking to provide an alternative executive.

The final section of Article 7 provides for the possible appointment of committees of its members to conduct particular aspects of business. There have been particular sub-committees to consider candidates for appointment when there was doubt in the Director-General's mind as to which of a number of people was the most appropriate for selection. This, at any rate, was the position until the end of Sir Hugh Greene's time. Subsequently, under Lord Hill, the practice of bringing candidates before the whole Board became more common – in fact, almost usual. Even when it seemed to me, as Director-General, that there was an obvious and outstanding candidate, I was sometimes required to bring others before the Board so that this view could be checked. I had considerable hesitations about this procedure because it sometimes meant that people who had little chance of being appointed even after seeing the Board, were drawn through the somewhat harassing process of being seen by a Board of as many as twelve people, and then being told – perhaps on more than one occasion – that he or she had not been selected. It is a very discouraging matter for candidates to be asked to appear and then to be repeatedly disappointed and it is an experience to which, in my view, staff with senior responsibility ought not to be unnecessarily subjected. I believe that under Sir Michael Swann this view began to prevail. I accept, however, that such interviews can be an occasion for the Board to see people with whom they may otherwise have had very little contact, and there have certainly been cases where one or two interviews before the full Board have resulted in the revelation to the Board of a personality whose subsequent advancement they were very anxious to secure. That is an undoubted benefit from this procedure. But I continue to have doubts about its indiscriminate use.

In Lord Hill's time two specific sub-committees were established, one to deal with financial matters and the other to deal with personnel policy. That on personnel policy found itself so rarely confronted with specific decisions on which it could offer sensible guidance to the Director of Personnel that it eventually fell into desuetude. That on finance, however, under Sir Robert Bellinger, was very active and from time to time, very useful. But it had one unfortunate effect. When those executives responsible for financial proposals had appeared before the Finance Committee it then tended to be assumed that all aspects of the matter had been fully considered by the Board and that little further explanation was called for. Sir Robert Bellinger, as Chairman of the Committee, would explain the matter to the Board and the decision of the Finance Committee would then be approved. But those members of the Board who did not attend the meetings of the Finance Committee undoubtedly felt themselves excluded from critical information. The long term result was that, although the Finance Committee met on some occasions to consider the annual budget after the departure of Lord Hill, it has since become the more common practice for the whole Board to take part in these annual deliberations, and for financial proposals in the normal run of business to be reported, as before, to the full Board, so that any one of the Governors could raise his particular points. For my part, I think that whatever additional time may be taken up in the full Board is worth the price. The Governors, at the end of the process, are all more fully informed than they were under the Finance Committee procedure.

The Charter of 1952 contained, for the first time, an indication of devolution to what became known as the National Regions – Scotland, Wales and Northern Ireland. The first provision, which resulted from the recommendations of the Beveridge Committee, was for three National Governors among the membership of the Board. There were to be National Governors for Scotland, Wales and Northern Ireland respectively, to be appointed for the 'knowledge of the culture and characteristics and affairs' of the respective peoples. They were to be in 'close touch with opinion' in their countries. The nature of their duties is more fully spelled out in Article 10 of the Charter describing the constitution of the new National Broadcasting Councils of which the National Governors were to be Chairmen. These Councils were set up only in Scotland and Wales. Provision was made for a corresponding Council in Northern Ireland if and when it should seem appropriate to set one up. It is easy to understand why the special problems in Northern Ireland should have deterred the Government of the day from suggesting the immediate establishment of a National Broadcasting Council there.

The Councils, which consisted, under the 1964 Charter, of between eight and twelve members, were nominated by an ingenious method which sought to secure a selection free from political influence, and yet outside the purview of the Board of Governors itself. The members were chosen by two panels of the General Advisory Council, each selected for that purpose from among the membership of the Council, and these panels were instructed to enter into consultation with appropriate representative cultural, religious and other bodies in Scotland and Wales. The choice of these representative bodies was left entirely to the appropriate panel of the General Advisory Council. In practice, the sounding of various representative bodies, including local authorities, was conducted on behalf of the panel by the National Governor and by the BBC Controller of the National Region in question. They were invariably consulted by the panel of the General Advisory

Council and on the whole, the system seems to have worked well to produce Councils of independent mind.

There was an interesting variant in the case of Northern Ireland. The establishment of a Council for that Province was deferred until a suitable time, but if and when such a Council were to be established, the Charter provided that its member-ship should be selected by a panel of the General Advisory Council, not from people whose names might result from the panel's own soundings of representative interests, but from a list of persons nominated for that purpose by the Northern Ireland Government. One can easily see what kind of a list that might have been in past years and how difficult it would have been to secure general acceptance of the names of a suitable list in the disturbed conditions which prevailed in Northern Ireland after 1970.

The members of the National Broadcasting Councils could be re-appointed, but, unlike the Governors themselves, such re-appointment could occur only if they had been nominated in the first place for a period less than the full five years. If they had served a full five-year term, then they had to leave the Council for at least a year before being eligible for re-nomination. The strictness of this ruling reflected and reinforced the principle of rotation which Sir James Duff so commended.

The functions of the National Broadcasting Councils were to control 'the policy and the content' of the radio and tele-vision services provided in the respective countries especially for audiences within them, and in addition to the services provided for those areas as part of the service for the United Kingdom as a whole. The Councils were also required to carry out such further functions as the Corporation might decide to devolve to them, and to advise on any other aspect of the Corporation's services which might affect the interests of the people in Scotland, Wales or Northern Ireland.

There were two provisos. The first of them protected from intervention by the National Broadcasting Councils a rather curiously assorted group of broadcasts – those by the Monarch, party political broadcasts, and broadcasts directed to schools. The second proviso was substantial. It provided that the Broadcasting Councils were subject to such reservations and directions as the BBC might think necessary in order to secure due co-ordination and coherent administration of its operations and affairs, or for reasons of finance. These were clearly potential major limitations on the freedom of action of the Broadcasting Councils, and they constituted the possible grounds of conflict over the respective jurisdictions of the Board of Governors and the National Broadcasting Councils, and between the national executive in London and the local executives in Scotland and Wales.

A further provision of the Article establishing the National Broadcasting Councils enabled them to appoint such staff as they might think necessary to exercise their functions – that is, in relation to the services of radio and television provided for their countries. The Corporation was required to employ these people and not to terminate their employment without the agreement of the Council. It was true that the Corporation might refuse to employ any such person who might decline to accept the current rates of pay or conditions of service, but the essential point was that the Council had the right to make appointments to the staff for the purpose of providing the programme services within their areas. Once again, there was a potential point of conflict, especially if the financial base was not provided for the employment of the staff and for the making of the programmes on which they might be employed. There was a curious proviso that in the event of a dispute between the Corporation and the Broadcasting Council, the Chairman of the General Advisory Council might be called in to adjudicate, along with the Corporation, on the desirability of the continuing employment of the person in question. There was no other point in the Charter at which the General Advisory Council or its Chairman was given any executive authority, and it seems an oddity that he should have been called in for this purpose alone.

There is no doubt that when these powers were first introduced in the Charter of 1952, the Corporation took a very
narrow view of them. Sir William Haley was much opposed
to the Beveridge proposals and thought that it would be
extremely difficult to operate the system because of the inherent
likelihood of conflict. In the event, conflict did not become
acute because a good deal of commonsense was exercised on
both sides. But the strength of the feelings which could
develop had been clearly indicated in the early days of the
Corporation, and particularly in Wales, which for years had
had to share a medium wavelength with the West Country
until, just before the Second World War, a re-arrangement of
frequencies was carried out which enabled Wales to have its
own separate radio service. Scotland had always exercised a
considerable degree of independence, opting out, as it was
called, from the national service from time to time in order to
provide specific programmes for the Scottish audience. What
was embodied in the Charter of 1952 was therefore, to a large
extent, a confirmation of existing practice – at least in radio.

But television was another matter. There had been no pre-
existing practice of opting out in television, and indeed, the
whole programme service and the technical distribution system
had been designed on the assumption that there would be a
single service throughout the United Kingdom. It is true that
contributions from regional centres were contemplated, but
for financial reasons these had not progressed very far, and it
was not expected that they would become a significant element
in the programme output until a much later date. The revision
of the Charter in 1952 to include National Broadcasting
Councils had two effects. First, it emphasized the necessity for
the provision of regional services, and it also made sure that
those regional services would be especially favoured in the
first instance in the new national regions. The consequences in
the English Regions can be imagined. There developed a good
deal of jealousy as between the English Regions and their more
fortunate brothers – as they seemed – in Scotland and Wales.

In retrospect, it can be seen that the 1952 provisions, although they appeared to be much in advance of the needs of the day, represented, nevertheless, an accurate foreshadowing of the devolutionary tendencies which were to become very evident by the end of the 1960s. Had there not been a constitutional framework of the kind provided by Article 10 of the 1952 Charter, it seems very likely that a good deal more tension would have developed in the internal affairs of the BBC over the nationalist problem than in fact occurred. Such difficulties as arose were matters of implementation rather than of principle. The questions were whether the money and the resources could be made available in time and in sufficient quantity to satisfy legitimate aspirations. They were not arguments about whether what was proposed was within the proper scope of the National regions as they saw themselves. And in my experience the tensions arose not from the inadequacy of Scottish and Welsh provision within the BBC allocation of resources as from the general inadequacy of provision for the BBC as a whole.

Having set up a Corporation, stated its powers and objectives, and elaborated it in its application to the national regions, the Charter, then in the form which has remained more or less constant, empowers the Corporation (Article 14) to provide the services which may be asked of it by way of a Licence from the responsible Minister. There is also a requirement (Article 15) that the BBC shall 'devise and make such arrangements as appear to the Corporation to be best adapted to the purpose' to bring the services provided 'under constant and effective review *from without the Corporation*'. The BBC is also required to provide 'sufficient means for the representation to the Corporation of public opinion on the programmes broadcast' and to ensure that this information is considered within the Corporation, together with criticisms and suggestions included in these representations.

Although there has always been a very full consideration of all representations from the public in the form of correspondence, dating back to the very earliest Reithian days, and although there has been a continuous study of audience numbers since the late 1930s, and a reasonable system of assessing audience responses to programmes, it could hardly be said that this constitutes the full provision for a review of the services which is required by Article 15. Although the standard BBC response to questions about the fulfilment of the terms of this Article has been to refer to the readiness to study correspondence, the provision of the audience research surveys, and the willingness to listen to representations from other quarters, particularly those expressed in Parliament, I always felt uneasy about the absence of any formal external review of the services. True, such review would have been difficult to devise. And at the end of the 1960s the McKinsey review of the method of operation of the services certainly did constitute a form of external review, just as the inquiries of the Public Accounts Committee and the Estimates Committee constituted an external review by Parliament. But the Annan proposals for a Public Inquiry Board, whatever its fate, did represent a form of external review which perhaps the BBC might have considered earlier in its history.

The objection can always be raised that complaints will always be made by the few and rarely by the many. Indeed, Reith made a comment to this effect in the earliest days, when he was writing about the matter of correspondence from the public. It is also difficult to devise procedures in which the professional response of the broadcasters can be as effectively presented as the complaints of the dissident few. Nevertheless, I remain convinced that earlier steps to seek the criticisms of the public in a public forum outside the BBC might have done a great deal of good in earlier years and might have served to diminish some of the accusations of remoteness and Olympian detachment.

Part of the deficiency is certainly made good by the various bodies under Articles 8, 9 and 11 – the General Advisory Council, Regional Advisory Councils and specialist advisory committees on any subject which the Corporation may seek to choose. The network of advisory bodies is now very extensive, incorporating some 800 people, excluding the Local Radio Advisory Committees, each of which consist of some 20 people, advising the 20 stations which had been established by 1974.

The Articles of the Charter dealing with 'organisation' (Articles 12 and 13) contain some important statements, and some which are made by implication rather than overtly. Thus, Article 12(1) says that the Corporation 'shall appoint such officers and such staffs as it may from time to time consider necessary'. In the first of the BBC's Charters Reith was specifically mentioned as the Director-General to be appointed. This was a matter of establishing continuity between the new Corporation and the old Company. But in the latest of the Charters there is no mention even of the Director-General, or indeed, of any specific chief executive. But it is more important that the power to appoint whomsoever they wish is allocated to the Corporation – in other words, to the Governors. The Director-General, and his supporting staff, are appointed within the organisation, and not by Government as in so many other countries. This mark of liberty has always seemed to me crucial to the argument that the editorial independence and operating independence of the Corporation are absolute. The Director-General owes his appointment, and looks for the termination of that appointment, only to the Board of Governors, and nowhere else. Similarly, he can guarantee to his supporting staff that they are in the equivalent position.

Other Charter provisions (Articles 12(2) and 13) require the BBC to fix rates of pay and conditions of service. Here again, there is an important statement by implication. Those rates of pay and conditions are settled by the Corporation and not by Government. It is true that in recent history national incomes policy, applying to many other institutions as well as to the BBC, has taken a good deal of the independence out of this power to fix rates of remuneration. But in the last resort it is the BBC's responsibility, and if the Governors were to say that they could not accept direction from a Government, they would be fully entitled to do so. Of course, they would have to take the political risk inherent in such a declaration.

The establishment of machinery for consultation and negotiation with unions, both within the permanent staff and outside it, is required under Article 13. In fact, this Article refers to consultation 'with any organisation appearing to the Corporation to be appropriate'. The injunction is not exclusive to the staff on regular contract with the BBC. These consultations and negotiations apply specifically to 'terms and conditions of employment' and suggest that there should be provision for a reference to arbitration in default of agreement. There is also a requirement for *discussion* of matters affecting safety, health and welfare of people employed, and other matters of mutual interest. There is a special reference to discussion of 'efficiency in the operation of the Corporation's services'. In these days of discussion of worker participation I suspect that this provision is as far as it would be wise to go in the case of a public Corporation dealing with the transmission of information, including political information of wide interest to the public. In a publicly-owned institution it seems to me not desirable that the employees should be represented in the management of the enterprise at the highest constitutional level and so constitute a special interest voice. But that is a subject which deserves discussion in its own right, and I shall deal with it at a later point in this book.

Again, in the light of current difficulties about incomes policy, there is a significant reference to the Corporation's obligation to report all agreements on rates of pay and conditions of service, both to the responsible Minister and to the Secretary for Employment. Should there ever be any question during a period of incomes policy of the BBC's obligation in this matter, doubters could be referred immediately to this paragraph in the Charter which is wholly binding.

CHAPTER III

Licence and Agreement

THE SECOND OF THE BBC's constitutional documents is the Licence and Agreement. Whereas the Charter is a Royal Prerogative document, the Licence is issued to the BBC by the responsible Minister as an authority for the body set up under the Charter to operate as a broadcasting system. In the last few years Ministerial responsibility has passed from the Postmaster-General to a short-lived Minister of Posts & Telecommunications, and finally to the Home Secretary. This move followed the successive restructuring of central Government by various Prime Ministers. It had always seemed likely that the Post Office, as one of the smaller Ministerial departments, might be absorbed in one of the 'super-Ministries' during one of these restructuring processes, and this became even more certain when the Post Office Corporation was set up as an autonomous body, not directly under the operational control of the Minister of Posts and Telecommunications.

It was important that the first Home Secretary to carry the responsibility for broadcasting, Roy Jenkins, was a politician of genuinely liberal and open sentiments. He took extreme care to ensure that in the formative days when the Home Office first assumed responsibility for broadcasting, the line between constitutional responsibility for general broadcasting policy and the responsibility of the broadcasting authorities for the day-to-day operation of the systems was very clearly observed. I remember being asked to see him on one occasion about some programme which had included references to the administration of the Prison Service. Before opening the conversation he began with an unequivocal statement that he was not speaking to me in his broadcasting capacity. It would have been very easy indeed for the Home Office, as the Department responsible for internal security, to have veered towards the exercise of an improper supervisory power over the content of broadcasting, but I believe that the presence of Roy Jenkins as the first Home Secretary to carry this responsibility was decisive in avoiding that development in the initial period.

The change carried another important incidental consequence. Broadcasting was now represented directly in Cabinet when occasion required, whereas previously the Postmaster-General or the Minister of Posts and Telecommunications had been only an occasional visitor, suffering all the disadvantages of that position when called in to take part in Cabinet deliberations. The Home Office was always bound to be held by a major political figure, and to that extent broadcasting was likely to benefit. It was equally possible, of course, that political considerations might adversely affect broadcasting, for political advantage is always likely to swing the thinking of a senior Minister, especially when such matters as raising the licence fee – considered to be electorally disadvantageous – come into question.

But the effects of the change of Ministerial responsibility went wider than those which could be formally recorded. During the years after the war there was a continuing informal contact between the Director-General and the Lord President of the Council, under whose general surveillance matters of broadcasting policy had come. Thus, Sir William Haley was, from time to time, in touch with Herbert Morrison, particularly at the time of the renewal of the Charter immediately after the end of the war. There were also contacts between Sir Hugh Greene and Herbert Bowden (now Lord Aylestone), as well as with R. H. Crossman. Sir Hugh Greene's contact was with Rab Butler in the last four years of the Macmillan administration 1959–63. In my own time I had most constructive exchanges with Fred Peart and William Whitelaw. In all these exchanges there was an opportunity for the professional chief executive to convey both information and anxieties to a senior interested Minister in a way that was not entirely possible in the formal exchanges which took place with the immediately responsible Minister – the Postmaster-General. I believe that informal exchanges of this kind, provided they rest on a foundation of complete frankness, are parts of the necessary lubrication of the processes of Government. With the change of senior responsibility in the Cabinet from the Lord President to the Home Secretary these exchanges became no longer possible, because for the Home Secretary to accept private conversations with the BBC's chief executive would have amounted to a very obvious by-passing of the Minister of State to whom direct day-to-day responsibility for broadcasting had been allocated in the Home Office. The relatively informal supervisory role which the Lord President played in relation to the Postmaster-General, and later to the Minister of Posts and Telecommunications, made it more possible for personal conversations of the kind I have described to take place. That line of communication is now no longer available.

The first two clauses of the Licence itself are formal, containing definitions and dates. The next nine clauses are entirely concerned with the regulation of the technical operation, siting and authorisation of transmitters. Amongst other things, they bind the BBC to observe the standards which are imposed on the United Kingdom as a result of international agreements, and they require both the BBC and the IBA to accept directions to co-site their television transmitter systems. Since this is clearly an advantage to both, in that viewers need only provide themselves with one aerial for UHF reception of both services, this is not a matter of contention.

The first constitutionally significant provision is contained in Clause 12, which provides that the BBC must not accept 'money or any valuable consideration' for any broadcast unless it has received the consent in writing of the responsible Minister. There is also a prohibition on the broadcasting of

61

'any sponsored programme' – which is defined in Clause 1 as material 'provided at the expense of any sponsor' . . . and 'is the subject of a broadcast announcement mentioning the sponsor or his goods or services'. The essence of sponsorship is therefore that the programme should be provided by some-body other than the BBC, *and* that attention should be drawn to the identity of that sponsor in an announcement. There are therefore two elements in the prohibition – the receipt of money or programme material by the BBC from another party, and the identification of that party in the programme.

There has been a good deal of ill-informed comment on the inclusion of commercial material in BBC programmes without sufficient regard for the terms of what the Licence actually says. Thus, advertising material placed round sports venues is not a contravention of the Licence, though it is embarrassing because whenever such material becomes prominent on the screen those who see it are likely to ask whether the BBC receives any payment, and whether, if it does not, it should not seek to do so in order to reduce the strain on the licence fee. Since the BBC attaches fundamental importance to the licence fee as the source of the overwhelming proportion of the revenue which sustains its domestic services, and is particularly opposed to advertising revenues for its programmes, any phenomenon which tends to weaken the case for the licence fee and to suggest advertising as an option is felt by the BBC to be damaging to its long term independence. That is why there is reluctance to see a proliferation of obtrusive advertising at venues of major public events and why careful lines have to be drawn about what incidental advertising is permissible within programmes and what has to be excluded. It is not, as is often suggested by Press critics, a question of BBC old-fashioned stuffiness. It is at the very heart of the BBC's argument for financial independence.

The other aspect of the prohibition of commercial sponsor-ship for BBC programmes which deserves comment is the requirement of consent from the Postmaster-General. It was on that issue that the argument about possible dismissal of the Governors arose among Ministers in the 1960s. The clause, as worded, would require the BBC to *seek* the consent of the Minister for such an arrangement, but if it does not seek that permission then the question does not arise. The problem for the Minister who raised the matter in the 1960s was that the BBC did not intend to make any such request, and he wished that it would.

The instruction to the BBC to carry on the broadcasting services for the home radio and television audiences and for the radio audiences overseas is contained in Clause 13. In addition, the clause requires the BBC to broadcast 'an impartial account, day by day, prepared by professional reporters, of the proceedings in both Houses of the United Kingdom Parliament'. Like so many other elements in constitutional practice affecting the BBC, this arose from a voluntary act of the BBC itself, which started these reports in 1945. The practice was incorporated, on the suggestion of Herbert Morrison, in the Licence which was then being prepared for renewal. In my view, it is an aberration from the principle that the constitutional documents should contain no instruction which relates to the content of particular programmes. Its omission would make no difference whatever to the practice of the BBC. So far as Parliament is concerned, the reporting of its affairs is far more likely to be changed by decisions which the members of both Houses make about the direct coverage – whether by radio or television, or both – of their proceedings. Now that the day has arrived, there ought to be a re-consideration of this provision in the Licence. Once the microphones and the cameras are admitted to Parliament I can see no possibility that proper daily reporting by that means will not automatically take place.

Within Clause 13 there is also contained the provision for the Ministers to require the BBC either to broadcast or to refrain from broadcasting particular material. In either case the BBC is free to announce that such a direction has been received.

The power to require the BBC to broadcast material has never been used to direct the BBC to put on programmes, and indeed, the text of the Licence refers to 'any announcement', rather than to a programme. There are regular broadcasts of public service announcements which are accepted by the BBC as a voluntary act, but in an emergency there would be no doubt that Ministers could require the transmission of particular announcements.

The power to require the BBC to refrain from broadcasting particular material is the famous 'unused' veto. This arouses immense suspicion in the minds of those visitors to Britain, who are not accustomed to the force of convention in British society. The fact that the power exists leads them to suspect that it must be used, or that its use must, at times, be threatened in order to secure desired objectives. This is simply not the case. There was an original prohibition in the 1920s against the broadcasting of any controversial matter, which was very soon abandoned. There was a subsequent prohibition on the broadcasting of programmes which dealt with subjects which were to come before Parliament within the succeeding fourteen days – the so-called 'fourteen-day rule'. That collapsed after the war in the face of the commonsense necessity for broadcasting to cover matters of public interest and to do so at the time when they were of interest to the general audience. The provisions of the fourteen-day rule either ensured that discussion of a subject took place long before the major issues had been identified, or was so frustrated by uncertainty of the Parliamentary timetable that it never took place at all. That situation clearly could not last – and did not. The only other use of the veto was the rather peculiar one designed to prevent the BBC from broadcasting party political broadcasts by the newly-developing Nationalist Parties in Scotland and Wales. A direction was issued by the Postmaster-General in 1955 which required the BBC not to broadcast any series of party political broadcasts other than that arranged between the BBC and the political parties. Since that series made no provision for the Nationalist Parties, the effect of the prohibition was to prevent them from taking part in the annual series of party political broadcasts. It was an ingenious use of a power of veto provided for quite other purposes, but hardly a serious restriction on the editorial independence of the BBC – which nevertheless continuously protested against the prohibition, until it was removed in 1965.

The final section of Clause 13 states the terms on which the BBC operates the External Services. It sets out the power of the Government to prescribe the languages and hours of operation of Services, and establishes the concept of 'Prescribing Departments', as they are called, to specify those languages and hours. The clause further provides for the operation of the Monitoring Service. Finally, it requires the BBC to 'consult and collaborate' with the Prescribing Departments, and to 'obtain and accept from them such information regarding conditions in, and the policies of, Her Majesty's Government towards the countries prescribed and other countries'. This flow of information is intended, as the Licence explains, to 'enable the Corporation to plan and prepare its programmes in the External Services in the national interest'. The points of interest here are that while the BBC is required to seek information – and would be foolish not to do so in the case of closed countries – it is left with full discretion as to how that information should be applied. And while it is required to broadcast 'in the national interest', there is no definition of what that phrase implies, or indeed, of who should define it in the normal course of broadcasting operations. It is, in fact, left to the BBC to judge the matter in the light of its own broadcasting principles, of the information it receives, and of the natural wish of those serving any public institution to work in the best interest of their country as perceived by a broad concensus. That leaves open the possibility of the peculiar operation of individual conscience. But that is a matter best left to the editorial judgements of honest men, and that discretion has proved to be the basis of long term success for the BBC's External Services, and, in turn, for the country.

The regulation of the hours of broadcasting is provided for in Clause 14 of the Licence. It is now virtually obsolete. The judgements about hours of television broadcasting were handed over entirely to the discretion of the broadcasting authorities during the Conservative administration of 1970–74 and the use of regulatory powers would seem unlikely to be restored. As for sound broadcasting, although there are still limits, they derive, in practice, more from the financial and operational necessities of the BBC than from the intention of the responsible Government Department to maintain them. There is consultation about the extension of hours of sound broadcasting, but more from the point of view of the possible consequences on the BBC's financial requirements than from that of maintaining Government control. It is still possible that at a time of emergency – such as that which occurred during the miners' strike of early 1974, when electricity supplies were endangered – for the Minister to curtail the hours of broadcasting under the powers reserved to him under this clause, and that, no doubt, is a necessary safeguard. In fact, the limitation of hours in 1974 was a voluntary limitation by the BBC. But for the rest, the power to define the hours of broadcasting seems to be a relic of the past.

The ultimate power for the Government to take over the operation of the BBC, which conceivably could occur in wartime, is set out in Clause 19. The remaining clauses of the Licence contain a miscellany of precautionary provisions, such as the requirement for the BBC to observe the principles of the original Parliamentary 'fair wages' resolution; to refrain from any form of bribery of public servants, and not to dispose without proper consent of property acquired at public expense through the External Services Grant-in-Aid. There are also provisions for reference to the responsible Minister of any question of failure to fulfil the requirements of any of the constitutional documents, and for the winding up of the Corporation, should that become necessary.

Finally, Clause 28 stipulates that the Licence and Agreement, which, as I have explained, is the operative document, is not to come into force until it is approved by resolution of the House of Commons. Parliament, therefore, retains the ultimate key, and it is on the Licence and Agreement that debates take place, the Charter being a Prerogative document, and not subject to debate – though, of course, proposals for changes in broadcasting policy which might be reflected in the content of the Charter can always be the subject of debate on a White Paper, and, therefore, of Parliamentary debate.

CHAPTER IV

The Prescribing Memoranda

THE PRESCRIBING MEMORANDA, which are issued by the appropriate Minister (at the moment the Home Secretary) under the terms of the Charter and the BBC Licence and Agreement, although little known, contain much of what is frequently referred to as being 'in the Charter'. The contents of the Memoranda are, in many cases, observations of existing BBC practice rather than prescriptions by the Minister to the BBC. It is important that they should be so, because, as I have explained earlier, the general intent of the main constitutional document – the Charter – is to establish the BBC as a body having discretion to conduct broadcasting in the best interests of the nation, and not to prescribe exactly in what manner those operations should be conducted.

The only Memoranda issued under the terms of the Charter are those relating to the quorum of the Board of Governors (which is four); the appointment of the BBC's auditors; and the manner of presentation of the Annual Report and Accounts, which is prescribed as being that at present followed. The Charter, in other words, is substantially a self-sustaining document.

The Memoranda attached to the Licence and Agreement are more substantial. As I have noted, the document is a Licence and *Agreement*, so that what it contains is a form of treaty between the BBC and the Government of the day. In the last instance it would be possible, I suppose, for the BBC to refuse to accede to the Agreement, and although discussion has not reached that acute point in the times which I have experienced, there were certainly occasions during Reith's negotiation of the original instruments when his dissatisfaction with the proposals of the Government representatives was not far short of a total rejection. Once established, the terms of the Licence and Agreement have tended to vary very little. Perhaps the outstanding change was the issue to the Corporation in 1952 of a 'non-exclusive Licence' implying that the new Conservative Government which issued it was contemplating the possibility of a parallel system of broadcasting.

The detailed prescriptions raise some points of potentially major significance. That issued under Clause 13(1) simply confirms that those stations from which the various services are transmitted are those which 'at present' do so – not a very onerous imposition. There is, however, another clause in the Licence under which no specific prescription has been issued. It also relates to the placing of transmitting stations, and seemed recently to be capable of causing problems to the BBC in the planning of its capital expenditure programme. The relevant section – Clause 4 – states that 'if, and whenever, with a view to extending the coverage or to improving the strength or quality, either generally or in any areas of transmissions in the Home Services the responsible Minister, after consultation with the Corporation, requires the BBC to set up and use additional stations anywhere in the British Isles, the Corporation shall do so'. This had always been interpreted as part of the normal process whereby the BBC, in planning extensions to its coverage, sought and secured Government approval. Such extensions raised issues of money and of service to the public. It was therefore something on which the BBC would have expected to seek political confirmation. There was a stage, however, during the financial difficulties of the early 1970s, when the UHF television networks were being developed, at which it seemed that it might be necessary for the BBC to restrict the speed of installation of further transmitters to complete UHF coverage of the country. Home Office officials at this point felt the BBC would not be free to vary its capital expenditure plan by this means because it was Government policy that the networks should be expanded as rapidly as possible. They suggested that they might arrange that directions were issued which compelled us to continue the installation programme without reduction.

The BBC argued strongly that this removed the discretion which it had hitherto exercised over the content of its capital expenditure programme, so long as that programme was contained within the limits of the national capital plan. The BBC would be compelled, under the Home Office proposal, to spend money on one purpose rather than another to which it would prefer to give priority. This was quite different from the exercise of the general power to control total capital expenditure, under which the BBC can be prevented from spending money on capital projects which it wishes to undertake. But the priority within that total in such cases is set by the BBC. In the end the dispute did not come to a head because the maintenance of the UHF installation programme proved to be possible within the financial restraints of the time. But an important issue had been raised, and it is to be expected that on a future occasion adequate prior consultation would prevent the imposition by the Home Office, roughshod and by purely technical instructions, of expenditure directives which might conflict with the BBC's fulfilment of its programme service objectives.

The major injunctions to the BBC which are commonly supposed to exist under the Charter are, in fact, imposed under the remaining sections of Clause 13 of the Licence and they do not go so far as is generally supposed. Under Clause 13(4) the BBC is required 'to refrain at all times from broadcasting matter expressing the opinion of the Corporation on current affairs or on matters of public policy'. There is an addendum to this paragraph in which the Minister 'takes note' of assurances given by a former Chairman of the BBC about programme standards and 'relies upon the Corporation' to carry on its services in accordance with the assurance given in that letter. In general, the letter, originally written by Lord Normanbrook, reaffirms the BBC's duty to ensure a high editorial standard, and programmes which, 'so far as possible', do not offend against good taste or decency. The letter also contains the longstanding assurance noted in the Memoranda attached to previous Licences that the BBC will 'treat controversial subjects with due impartiality'. The key to the understanding of this exchange of assurances is that the BBC is acting of its own volition, and that the assurances are being noted for the record by the Minister. The Minister is not imposing anything. He is accepting what the BBC has imposed on itself in the past. That policy was enunciated by Reith as early as 30 November 1923, when he wrote in *Radio Times*: 'Great discretion has to be exercised in such matters, and the question of expediency considered, but if on any controversial matter the opposing views are stated with equal emphasis and lucidity, there can at least be no charge of bias.' He made a similar statement to the Sykes Committee.

Lord Normanbrook's letter represented, in fact, the concluding phase in a long history. From the beginning the Corporation had devised and followed the policies outlined in it. In the early 1960s there was pressure from the Potsmaster-General, Reginald Bevins, to see imposed on the BBC, in its Charter or in the Licence, or the Memoranda, formal obligations similar to those which were contained in the Television Act, at that time being considered by Parliament. The Board of that day took the conscious decision to make a voluntary statement so as to maintain the principle of acting on its own initiative in carrying out its role of trustee for the nation in broadcasting (at least, in BBC broadcasting).

There is an incidental but important reference to the BBC's undertaking to ensure that a 'proper proportion' of the BBC's programmes should be of 'British origin and British performance'. When the BBC is asked whether it operates a quota system in relation to imported programmes, the answer is, quite properly, in the negative. The BBC would be technically free to vary the proportions which it applies at any time. There is no instruction that particular proportions should be observed. As in all British institutions, however, practice becomes sanctified, and changes have to be negotiated with those who are affected. And it has always been argued by the BBC that those proportions of imported material which are included in programmes are for the benefit of the audience, in that the best of what is available is selected. If it were ever to be the case that finance was to be the sole consideration then the proportions might considerably increase, and to the detriment of the audience. I think that is very unlikely to happen.

But it is necessary to return for a moment to the inhibition on the expression by the BBC of its own opinion on current affairs and matters of public policy in general. This is an understandable prohibition, if the broadcasting medium is to be seen as a means of conveying facts and opinions for the benefit of the audience, and not in the interest of those who are conducting the service. That is the premise on which the BBC is built. But there is one serious restraint which follows from the particular form of direction which has so far been imposed. It is that the BBC cannot directly decide to use its own programme services to express its own point of view about a matter of broadcasting policy. The difficulty here is that too few people understand the practicalities of broadcasting policy for there to be a sensible discussion about it unless representatives of the BBC – and indeed, of other broadcasters – take part. I should argue that it would be in the public interest for there to be a relaxation of this total prohibition so as to permit the BBC to put forward spokesmen in discussions on broadcasting policy. The principle of due impartiality would still apply, because it is an inherent part of the BBC's philosophy, and necessary, if it is to justify its own performance. That ought to be a sufficient safeguard against the improper use of the air by the BBC to advance its own purposes. But so long as there is a technical exclusion of BBC representatives from public discussion of broadcasting policy on the air, so long will the public be deprived of what it has a right to have – a full explanation of the problems, informed as well as opinionated.

In practice, the BBC has not felt itself prevented from accepting requests from its news services for normal interviews with responsible staff in a position to make authoritative statements about policy. There is a well established practice of access for the press to BBC spokesmen, both of the anonymous official variety and named senior representatives, including the Chairman. It was thought quite wrong for the BBC's news services to be put at a disadvantage against the Press when it came to the reporting of broadcasting issues. The public has therefore had access in programmes to the minimum requirement of basic information about the BBC. But this does not resolve the problem of how to secure the presentation of a BBC case in controversial discussion, and it never seemed right to me that when broadcasting policy became controversial the most interested and informed party should be excluded from the discussion. The result could only be the kind of unbalanced discussion which the BBC would seek to avoid in any other area of public debate.

During the arguments about the proposals made in 'Broadcasting in the Seventies' in 1969 and 1970 I took part myself in both television and radio discussions with some of the critics. Later I twice appeared in 'phone-in' programmes on radio when important BBC questions were in the air – notably the raising of the licence fee. Similarly, I appeared in broadcast interviews, both on television and radio, when the BBC's coverage of events in Northern Ireland was being attacked. But in the early stages of the Annan Committee Home Office officials indicated informally to the BBC that Ministerial eyebrows had been raised at the frequency with which the Chairman and I were appearing on the air. In fact, we had made comparatively few appearances, none of which could have been said to be invitations to the audience to pre-judge the issues being studied by the Annan Committee. Nevertheless, in response to the indications we received from Whitehall, we followed a course of substantial self-denial, to the point where our programme producers felt that they were unable to present fair programmes about broadcasting at times when they were certain that the issues ought, on the normal criteria of programme selection, to be debated before the public. I am sure that this is an undesirable position, and that changes in rules and attitudes should go rather further even than the Annan recommendation that representatives of the broadcasters should be enabled to appear on the air in controversial programmes about broadcasting policy, provided that the other parties to the debate were always represented either in the same programme or in a series devoted to the same subject. There are occasions when the public needs a critical evaluation of some proposal, and when a determined interviewer is a better servant of that interest than the most ardent advocate of a contrary point of view.

The restraints on broadcast appearances by broadcasting spokesmen does not, of course, prevent the dissemination of BBC views (or, indeed, IBA views) through the normal channels of public reporting and discussion. The Press has always taken a lively interest in broadcasting affairs, and both formal and informal contracts with the Press are a regular part of the life of any broadcaster. Furthermore, it is easy to arrange occasions through which broadcasting points of view can be expressed. Most societies are glad to welcome speakers on broadcasting matters, and indeed, the difficulty is to select, from among the invitations received, those to which proper justice can be done. The difficulty is not that there are too few outlets for the expression of broadcasting points of view. It is simply that the forum which is available for all other controversy is unreasonably limited when broadcasting excludes discussion of broadcasting itself.

There is a minor prohibition in the Memorandum issued under Clause 13(4) which relates to the use of subliminal techniques to convey messages to an unsuspecting audience.

This reflects a particular anxiety prevailing in the early 1960s that advertisers, then testing the use of subliminal techniques for conveying commercial messages, might perhaps be pointing the way for other messages to be used in non-advertising contexts. It always seemed to us in the BBC so much in contradiction to the BBC's basic philosophies that anyone should think of using subliminal techniques to convey messages through our programmes that we felt this prohibition was unnecessary. Nevertheless, it exists as a piece of historical dross, the sense of which would be as closely observed if it did not exist as it is through its inclusion in the formal Memoranda.

The Memorandum issued under Clause 13(5) which specifies the prescribing Departments of Government which may state the extent of the activities of the External Services lists what one would expect – the Foreign & Commonwealth Office and the Ministry of Defence. But interestingly, it includes also the Board of Trade. It would be encouraging to think that the Board of Trade might take the initiative and require a particular service to be broadcast, but so far as I know, it has never done so. It has, however, given support to the activities of the External Services insofar as they serve to support the activities of exporters. Unfortunately, the content of the Grant-in-Aid which sustains the External Services falls entirely on the Foreign Office vote, and the Board of Trade, in the material sense, has no money to give effect to its wishes. Would that it had!

The Memoranda issued under Clause 14, relating to the hours of broadcasting, are, to a great extent, now a dead letter, in that those governing the hours of television broadcasting were completely revoked under the Conservative Government of 1970/74 as part of the process of giving complete freedom of hours to the IBA, in the absence of the allocation to them of the so-called 'fourth channel'. The prescribed hours of broadcasting on radio, although still in existence, are anachronistic in that the BBC now broadcasts for fewer hours of the day than was once prescribed and would no doubt have no

75

difficulty in securing an extension of the hours if it could prove that they were within its financial capacity. The political probability seems that no re-imposition of restrictions is likely, although there could be a residual use of the power to prescribe hours of broadcasting in order to impose particular obligations on those who might eventually have to operate the fourth UHF network. It would be possible, for example, to envisage a restraint on the use of particular hours of television on the fourth network so as to ensure that the Open University could be contained within that network at peak times. That, at least, is the theoretical possibility, and it could be operated so long as the power to control the hours of broadcasting remained in Clause 15 of the Licence and in the parallel Licence issued to the IBA.

Taken together with the Charter and the Licence and Agreement on which they depend, the Prescribing Memoranda have proved an instrument entirely adequate to the tolerant control of broadcasting to the extent that it is proper for Governments to seek to exercise that control. The BBC has always felt strongly that the Charter, as the basis of its existence, is a constitutionally important form. It represents the deliberate use of archaic instruments of government in order to set aside from the direct political interventions of Parliament certain activities which are considered best left autonomous. The Charter, as such, cannot be debated or amended in Parliament. The Governors cannot be dismissed simply by a Minister. The BBC is, to that extent, substantially cushioned by the force of tradition against ephemeral political intervention. Proposals to extract from the present constitutional documents certain elements of control which appear to be common to the BBC and to the Independent Broadcasting Authority, and to embody them in statutes, to be put before Parliament, ignore the importance of symbols in the British constitutional machinery of checks and balances. The fact of operation under a Charter is an important protection for the BBC, as it is for a university. The intention is that a Charter should create a body of self-sufficient authority, subject, like an individual, to the general laws of the State, but not to particular statute law invented for the particular activity conducted by the chartered body. To place the obligations included in Lord Normanbrooke's letter about the content of programmes within a statutory framework, held in common with the IBA, is to throw away the priceless asset of the spontaneous origin of those restraints within the authority of a chartered body. They are the outcome of voluntary choice, not of external imposition. That is the peculiar value which comes to the BBC programme services through the fact of the BBC's incorporation under a Charter. A statute embodying the same obligations would not be merely a tidying-up operation. It would be an intervention in the symbolism of the instrument whose character guarantees the autonomous character of the BBC. And similarly, the use of a statute in this way to regulate one chartered body would imply the possibility that similar statutory powers might be used to control other chartered bodies in matters relevant to their activities.

It is a conservative argument, hallowed by tradition, to argue that if what exists works well, it should be left alone. And it is not always a well sustained argument. But successive inquiries have been convinced that in the case of the BBC the choice of a Charter rather than a statute as a source of authority does make an important difference to the character of the organisation itself. Free will is the characteristic of the free man. It is an appropriate characteristic for a free institution like a broadcasting corporation, and freedom is best secured at a distance from Government rather than in subjection to it.

CHAPTER V

The Financial Framework

THE CONSTITUTIONAL FRAMEWORK for the financing of the
BBC is laid down in three Articles of the Charter (Articles 16,
17 and 18), three clauses of the Licence and Agreement
(Clauses 16, 17 and 18), and in some fairly extensive memoranda issued under both documents. The financial provisions
of the Charter state the general powers of the Corporation to
receive and apply monies, and the general character of those
monies. The relevant sections of the Licence set out the
detailed nature of the revenues, their mode of payment to the
Corporation, and the limits which apply to the spending of
the money. The Prescribing Memoranda relating to finance set
out such specific rules for the administration of the monies as
are appropriate to the Home Services and the External Services
respectively, and they go into much greater detail than the two
general documents.

Under Article 16 of the Charter the Corporation is empowered to receive and apply funds received from the
responsible Minister, subject to whatever conditions may be
attached to their grant. They are also empowered to receive all
other monies, with the sole proviso that borrowings for
capital purposes, authorized by the Minister for that purpose,
may not be applied in any other way. Apart from this restraint,
and those which may be attached to any particular grant of
monies (such as the External Services Grant-in-Aid), the
Corporation is given, under Article 16, discretion to apply its
revenues to capital or revenue purposes as it may think fit.
There is an exclusion, naturally, of any payments other than

fees to the Governors of the Corporation. Nothing by way of profits may be distributed.

There is one section of Article 3 of the Charter which has to be read in conjunction with Article 16. It is that which deals with the borrowing of money. After providing that the Corporation may mortgage or charge its property, or issue debentures or stock in order to raise money – something which has never been done – there is a provision that the BBC is allowed to raise temporary banking accommodation not exceeding £10 millions at any time, and money to defray capital expenditure up to a maximum of £20 millions. These capital borrowings require approval by the appropriate Minister (now the Home Secretary). The temporary banking facility can be exercised without reference elsewhere. Before the present Charter, the amounts of these borrowing powers were, respectively, £1 million and £10 millions and there was considerable argument about whether it was right to increase the permitted amounts. On the one hand, it was suggested that inflation and expansion of the Corporation's activities in themselves justified an increase in the figures. It was further argued that major new capital expenditure, as, for example, on a new service, should be spread over future licence-payers, and not loaded onto the present generation. On the other side of the argument, it was held by the rigorists that the increase in the amount of the Corporation's borrowing power simply created a temptation for Governments to delay a decision to increase the licence fee. In other words, the effect of borrowing was simply to alter the political timetable. This case was strengthened by the fact that there have been very few times in the history of the Corporation when substantial capital investment has been the means of increasing the Corporation's income. One of those periods might have been the first installation of colour television transmitters, when the provision of a service in the highly populated areas undoubtedly resulted in a substantial and relatively rapid increase in income from colour television licences. But that phase very soon passed, and additional installations did not have the attraction of bringing in more money than was being committed in their provision. And in any case, so the rigorists argued, the first phase was such a rapidly profitable investment that it did not need any borrowing power to finance it. It could be better done from current revenues since the amounts were not alarming. The same argument will no doubt be conducted every time the Charter is renewed, and on the whole, the argument that borrowing powers represent a danger rather than an easement seems to me to be the more valid.

Certain precautionary restraints are set out in Article 17 to ensure the repayment of sums borrowed for capital purposes. The Corporation is required to set aside, for the repayment of such capital borrowings, sums from its revenue according to whatever agreement may be reached with the responsible Minister. The expectation implied when this provision of the Charter was drafted must have been that when, for example, the BBC first began to use its capital borrowing powers in 1976 a repayment schedule would be set up. Since, however, the use of the capital borrowing powers was, in effect, no more than an additional means of postponing the need for an increase in the licence fee, and therefore, in practice, if not in form, an extension of the temporary borrowing facility, no conditions were laid down by the Home Secretary as to the reservation of repayment funds. It is perhaps a matter for question as to whether that should not have been done. I believe it would be better for the BBC's current revenue to be under the pressure of such a requirement than for Governments to be allowed to use capital borrowing facilities, dubiously desirable in themselves, as a substitute for new licence revenue.

The remaining sections of Article 17 and Article 18 provide for the normal depreciation of capital assets, applicable in any business; empower the Corporation to hold reserves and to handle them in whatever way it thinks best; and require the submission of an annual statement of accounts through Parliament to the Minister. The general character of what is to be included in this statement of accounts is indicated in the Charter, and the Minister has the power to direct the Corporation to publish in it whatever information may be required. He also has the power, at all reasonable times, to require the Corporation to supply 'all forecasts, estimates, information and documents' which he may feel necessary to him in considering the financial transactions and commitments of the Corporation.

The terms of the relevant clauses of the Licence and Agreement state that the Corporation is to receive 'out of monies provided by Parliament' sums 'equal to the whole of the net licence revenue' or such percentage of it as may be decided by the Treasury from time to time. The effect of this section of Clause 16 is that although the revenues of the Corporation are a subject of a Parliamentary grant, under the annual vote of supply, the amount of that grant is fixed in terms of the numbers of receiving licences taken up by the public, and the value attached to each licence by Government decision from time to time, after consultation with the BBC. In other words, although there is an annual vote, the calculation of the amount to be included in that vote is predictable according to certain elements fixed in advance. The reduction of that amount to a percentage of the 'net licence revenue' has not been practised since 1962, for the simple reason that the amounts provided by the prevailing licence fees have been barely sufficient to develop and operate the service according to policy decisions reached by the Government on the recommendation of the various committees which have studied broadcasting.

Indeed, the significance of Clause 16(2), to the effect that the net licence revenue is to be paid to the Corporation by instalments at intervals 'not longer than one month', has greatly increased in recent years because of the tightness of the funds available. The incidence of renewal of licences is quite sharply seasonal, with a peak in the autumn. Consequently, if the Post Office were to pay to the BBC those amounts which were actually received in a given period, there would be ample funds at the peak licence fee renewal times of the year, but an embarrassing deficiency in the earlier months. Since the Corporation has been running for substantial periods on the basis of borrowing, it has been necessary, in order to adjust the cash flow to conform to the borrowing limits, to arrange for the payment of the licence revenue by equal instalments each month, even though that does not conform to the pattern of funds actually received from licence holders by the Post Office. It is, nevertheless, a pattern which is fully compatible with the voting of an annual Parliamentary grant and the provision that it may be paid in such instalments as may seem to be convenient and acceptable to the Corporation and to the Post Office. The phrase 'net licence revenue' takes account, naturally, of the cost to the Post Office of collecting the sums and enforcing the licence fee system. It also provides for the funding of the interference investigation services of the Post Office, whether they are carried out to protect the signals of the BBC or of other broadcasters.

The brevity of Clause 17 of the Licence, which provides for the payment to the BBC of the Grant-in-Aid sustaining the External Services and such amounts as may be made available for the provision of other Government services, is indicative of the final control of the Treasury in fixing the total amounts and their administration. The clause in the Licence refers simply to 'such sums as the Treasury shall authorize'. The degree of control over the financial administration of the funds is also reflected in the extent of the Prescribing Memoranda on this subject. Nothing, however, in these documents suggests control over the content of the broadcasts – not even Clause 18 which stipulates that the sums paid to the BBC are to be applied 'in accordance with any terms and conditions which may be attached to the grant by Parliament or by the Treasury'.

Under Clause 17 of the Licence there are extensive Memoranda relating to the principles governing expenditure 'both in the Home Services and in the External Services'. So far as the Home Services are concerned, the key phrase appears in the second paragraph of the Memorandum which reads: 'The

Corporation is empowered to spend the income granted to it ... according to its own judgement in forwarding its approved objects (subject to such controls as operate in respect of the provision of foreign currency and Government control of capital investment)'. That is the legal buttress of the day-to-day managerial independence of the BBC. It becomes substantially inoperative, of course, if the finances provided are insufficient to forward the 'approved objects'.

So far as capital controls are concerned, the BBC is subject to the operations of the Public Expenditure Survey Committee,[1] and has been ever since the war (whether those capital controls took their present form or their old form of 'Plowden limits'). This control is a serious matter, because it was this which effectively prevented the BBC from developing its Television Service as rapidly as it would have wished in the immediate postwar years, and which gave the opportunity for critics to say that the BBC was lagging behind the needs of the moment. It was always an unfair criticism to say that the BBC had failed to develop its television service because of lack of enthusiasm on the part of its senior management. It was, after all, Sir William Haley who had the foresight to buy the White City site and to plan the Service on the basis of an output which was substantially electronic. It was even more unfair to suggest that what could have been done was not done. The truth is that the BBC was never permitted to do what it wished to do, and Government capital control was decisive.

Since that time capital controls have continued to hold back the development of BBC television, particularly outside London, and there has been little understanding in the country of this factor. It is true that absolute financial stringencies also had their effect, but even had money been available to the BBC, the planning constraints attributable to the national economic restraints would have prevented the BBC from exercising to the full the theoretical discretion to spend according to its own

[1] The Public Expenditure Survey Committee *formal* control was lifted in 1978.

priorities within its total income. The fact is that these priorities were simply not open to the BBC for choice. The IBA is subject to the same restraints, but the programme companies who are considered as being in the private sector, are not limited, as is the BBC, in capital investment in studio facilities.

The Memorandum relating to the finances of the Home Services requires that the responsible Minister shall be given forecasts of expenditure and income so that he 'may be fully informed as to trends of expenditure and development and may be in a position to make recommendations to the Treasury regarding the financial provision to be made for the Home Services'. There has been plenty of forecasting but not enough recommendation in recent years. Indeed, BBC managers reading this clause in the Memorandum may be forgiven a certain wry disbelief in its utility.

There are extensive provisions in the Memorandum at this point about the financial management of the External Services, which is much more closely under Government control than that of the Home Services. Thus, current and capital expenditure are required to be specified in the estimate and these limits have to be observed. Specific projects, either for operating or for capital expenditure, are subject to strict limits, for which the BBC does not have delegated power and must refer to the Prescribing Department and thence to the Post Office and the Treasury. Increases in expenditure due to rising costs are permitted without reference to Government, but only 'provided the totals of the Grants-in-Aid will not thereby be exceeded' – a provision unlikely to be met if salary increases in the present inflationary age are in question. The definition of the term 'rising costs' as given in the Memorandum covers 'increases due to the excess cost of normal increments or promotions over savings due to retirements; rising prices of materials; and increases in rents, rates, taxes, etc.' What the Treasury describes as *abnormal rising costs* are not included – and those abnormal rising costs are, of course,

84

negotiable salary increases. The consequence is that every salary increase for BBC staff, for which External Services' staff, as members of the BBC's complement, are eligible, is liable to provoke a new discussion on policy. Every such increase gives rise to a debate as to the need for all the languages and hours for which the Services are broadcast, and becomes the occasion for a new policy discussion as to whether some Services ought to exist at all. It is not a sensible approach if one considers that the benefits of broadcasting in the field of information and opinion come from trust established with the audience over long periods – benefits which are in danger of being nullified by a programme prescription which operates on the principle of the switchback railway.

There is one final element in the Memorandum on finance which is worthy of comment. It is contained in the sentence 'The principle governing the apportionment of common services expenditure between the Home and External Services will be that any expenses which would remain in existence if there were no External Services will be charged to the Home account and additional expenses due to Overseas broadcasts, and other services performed for Government Departments will be charged to the External Services account'. This is the so-called 'extra definable costs' formula, which gives to the External Services all the benefit of the BBC's infrastructure, paid for from the Licence income, without any charge whatsoever. Nobody in the BBC would question this, because there is a general acceptance that the inclusion of the External Services within the BBC structure is of general benefit to the Corporation. But it does make nonsense of any suggestion that the External Services represent an unduly expensive operation for the State. They are an astonishing bargain, simply because the rest of the BBC exists and gives to the External Services the financial benefit of that existence.

The general picture which emerges from these financial provisions in the constitutional documents – even allowing for the appearance of detailed restraint which is evident at certain points in the Licence and in the related Memoranda – is nevertheless one of real managerial independence. And this is massively reinforced by the established convention of respect for the BBC's editorial independence whenever issues of content come under public discussion. Given that respect, it is hard to see how the limited financial restraints set down in the formal documents could ever be seriously inhibiting. The danger comes from inadequate funding, not from the rules about the management of the funds provided.

Part Two

CHAPTER VI
A BBC Ideology?

THE CONSTITUTIONAL DOCUMENTS establishing the BBC and authorizing it to operate a broadcasting service bring into being the body of 'trustees for the Nation', as the Crawford Committee described them, and set forth, also in very general terms, what they are empowered to do. But, as I have explained in my examination of the documents themselves, there is no suggestion whatever of the ideological base from which the trustees are to work, and no definition even of the identity of 'the Nation' which it is their trust to serve.

No body of this kind could be expected to set out on its task without having some idea of its attitude to the society in which it is to operate. Where can they start?

The essence of broadcasting is to communicate ideas, concepts and pleasurable experience, and that act of communication is bound to produce effects among those to whom they are addressed. It would be normal for the people responsible for these communications to want to be able to assess the effects of what they were doing, in order to adapt their activities to beneficial rather than damaging effects. But it has been a characteristic of broadcasting from the very beginning that the assessment of effects has been virtually impossible, at any rate as an exercise which could offer contemporary guidance to those responsible for the conduct of the service. Studies of effects were bound to be long term in character if they were to be worth respect, and by the time the results were reported the good or the harm would have been long established in the past. Broadcasters and those responsible for broadcasting, therefore, have to operate not in the knowledge of known effects, which would make their responsibilities relatively easy, but against expected or probable effects, and more often, against the even lesser standard of a possible effect. The result of taking account of every possible effect of a mass communication, without knowing precisely what it was, would undoubtedly be to inhibit any freedom of decision, and to discourage the act of intelligent communication. So the responsible bodies can, at best, judge their decisions by what they think may happen in the minds of their audiences, and, more often, they will be proceeding by the light of their own intelligence and nothing more. How, in this vacuum of information, can they proceed? How can they gauge what should be their moral responsibility to society?

The communications researchers would say, no doubt, that they ought to seek to establish what the effects of broadcasting operations might be. Research should be commissioned into the pre-existing state of the potential audience, and the change resulting from broadcasting – or, at least, taking place after broadcasting started – should be measured. That would be the theoretical ideal. But development does not proceed in that way. Communications researchers come into being because communication is already going on. They are inevitably concerned with a state of affairs in society which has already changed by the introduction of that which they wish to study. And however regrettable this may be, this order of historical development will always mean that research will be retrospective rather than prospective. The Board of Governors of the BBC fifty years ago could not have committed themselves to finding what the effects of their actions might be before embarking on their task. No more can their successors today wait for the answers from the sociologists to tell them what they must do tomorrow, or even next year. They would be right to seek information on the ways in which communication operates in society, with a special interest, naturally, in broadcast communications. But such research is hardly likely to offer them an acceptable guide in identifying the philosophy according to which they should proceed.

As the philosophy of the BBC has evolved it has become evident that those responsible for programmes, in whatever capacity, do not interpret the phrase 'moral responsibility' as carrying an obligation to preach a particular form of conduct. They do not see it as their job to adopt a particular morality as their own and then to use the broadcasting medium in order to persuade everybody else to follow that morality. The question arises in a particularly acute form when the BBC is asked whether it supports the Chritian morality or not. I think that the question can best be answered after considering some alternative positions which might be adopted by the BBC. Could the Governors, as a collective body, endorse as their morality, for example, that which derives from the Muslim or Buddhist faiths? Or could they commit themselves to a profession of atheism? The answers to these questions must be that they could not. It would not be conceivable for the BBC to preach the morality of the Koran to the British people as a whole. I doubt whether, even if the Governors as a group thought it right to commit themselves to an atheist profession, that they would carry the British public with them – and that would be an important consideration for them in deciding what morality to adopt. We are living in what is, in many ways, a post-Christian era, and I think that just as the BBC could not commit itself to the endorsement of the moral positions of other beliefs or unbeliefs, so they could not commit themselves to the direct preaching of Christianity – given that the content of 'Christianity' could be agreed between them. They would find themselves, in a very real sense, acting for the whole of the public and yet endorsing a morality which, in its full sense, was accepted by only a minority, even though a large one.

What, then, is the position of the BBC about the Christian faith, which has been the basis of established institutions in Britain for centuries past? It is a fact that the traditions of the

country were formed in a Christian world, and that its literature, past and present, its criteria of public conduct, and its
public symbolic activities all reflect that fact. Whatever the
BBC presents of that literature, that conduct, and those
activities in its programmes is therefore bound, as a reflection,
to present a Christian aspect. To that extent the messages
communicated by the BBC are Christian, and are inevitably so.
The BBC cannot reflect the country without reflecting its
Christian origins and continuities.

Long before I ever had to consider this question, Sir
William Haley, in speaking to the British Council of Churches
(2 November 1948), said much the same thing. Commenting on
the question as to whether the BBC's commitment to the free
expression of serious opinion meant that British broadcasting
was neutral where Christian values were concerned, he
observed that it was not. 'There are', he said, 'many demands
of impartiality laid on the Corporation, but this is not one of
them. We are citizens of a Christian country and the BBC – an
institution set up by the State – bases its policy upon a positive
attitude towards the Christian values. It seeks to safeguard
those values and to foster acceptance of them. The whole pre-
ponderant weight of its programmes is directed to this end.'
That observation has often since been quoted as an indication
of how far – so it is alleged – the BBC has slipped from Haley's
standards. But it is clear, from what he said in the passage
which immediately followed that much quoted observation
about the BBC's commitment to Christian values, that he was
making substantially the same statement as I made in Edinburgh, and which I have just set out. Haley said: 'Purely
Christian considerations would not prevent the BBC broadcasting any particular item. Some of the world's greatest
dramas for instance can be held to be anti-Christian but we
must certainly broadcast them. But our regard for Christian
values and the *great weight of Christian literature and Christian
tradition* [my italics] insensibly regulate the number of such
plays broadcast.' He argued further in reply to the suggestion

that the BBC 'should make not only Christian values but the Christian faith itself the criterion of everything it does', that such a commitment could lead to clericalism and intolerance.

This, then, is the position of the Board as it must look to an outside observer contemplating the task of the Governors in seeking a moral ideology. But let us contemplate it from the point of view of an individual member of the Board. When I conduct this exercise, as I have done for myself on a number of occasions, it has seemed to me useful to suggest the problems which would arise if the BBC were to accept a specific responsibility for promoting a particular morality which might be held by an individual member of the Board. Whatever the individual beliefs of its members, the Board as a collective entity would still have to reach some collective conclusion as to what was the acceptable morality which should represent the BBC's standpoint. Pursuing the point of individual commitment, and taking myself as a hypothetical member of the Board, I need only mention, as I have done in the prologue of this book that I am myself a Roman Catholic for it to become self-evident that an arrangement whereby the moral course of the BBC was determined according to the wishes of an individual would be unacceptable to many. It makes no difference whether that individual is the Chairman or the Director-General or an individual Governor. If he or she is an adherent of a faith outside the latitudinarian Protestant tradition, great difficulty is certain to arise for the Corporation in speaking, on the assumptions of that faith, to the mass of the British audience. As for the collective identification of the public morality to be promoted, it seems to me impossible that the diversity of a pluralistic society such as that in which we live should not be represented in its different opinions in the Board itself. That has certainly been my experience in witnessing the Board as a group of people over some fifteen years. I cannot see that any of the Boards I have known would ever have agreed on which particular morality should be espoused by the BBC. Nor do I know by what authority they would have committed themselves

93

to a chosen morality, even if they were able collectively to agree on one. Those people of good will who suggest that other men of equal good will assembled in a Board of Governors, should be able to establish and apply generally acceptable notions of decency or belief are presupposing as practical what has not been a probability in my experience.

I cannot believe that it is the business of people chosen to protect the public interest to dictate to the public a particular canon of public morality which many of their constituents might reject. The Governors could not, like Moses, go up the mountain to bring down the Tablets of the Law because neither they among themselves, nor their people, on receiving the Tablets, would agree when they came down from the mountain about the authority of the God who had been responsible for the engraving of the law which they had brought back. Their only resort, therefore, must be to judge cases according to their best lights, taking account of the general climate of opinion in which we live, assessing what is within the bounds of a widely tolerant amalgam of views, and what, reluctantly in extreme cases, must be held to exceed those limits.

As I wrote this passage I turned with interest, and for the first time, to what Haley had written some thirty years ago in that address to the British Council of Churches. 'It seems to me that one of the BBC's highest duties', he said, 'is to preserve tolerance. I am not a metaphysician, but I do not see why conviction and tolerance cannot co-exist. Without the one, there would be no values. Without the other, no liberty or thought and free discussion whereby those values can be established.' And he added: 'It does not seem to me an inherent duty of broadcasting to make people join the Christian faith.' That parallels almost exactly my own phrases when I spoke in Edinburgh in 1971: 'We are not, in the last resort, a moral weapon. We are a means of conveying messages which may be moral, according to the criteria which each of us in the audience applies.' And, as I said on another occasion, speaking to representatives of the Religious Press in 1970: 'We are concerned reflectors of the world we live in, responsible in our freedom and balance because we live by balance and by perspective, and we are lost without them. We do not seek to usurp the spiritual and moral authority of the Nation's leaders, ecclesiastical or temporal. We put our microphone in the pulpit and on the platform but do not seize it ourselves except when we talk, as I am now doing, about broadcasting.'

To people who like to think in terms of the leadership of society this doctrine of tolerance as the basic philosophy for broadcasters often seems weak-kneed and evasive. They criticize it as neutralism – what old style theologians would call 'indifferentism' and would have condemned because there was no commitment to faith. But tolerance assumes an enthusiasm for the active circulation of ideas, with many of which it might be possible to disagree, but which nevertheless merit publication. Neutralism would imply a lack of interest in the ideas, whether they were acceptable or not. Tolerance is a more positive virtue.

The BBC's position is one of quasi-judicial impartiality. Just as most public law reflects the general will of the public, and just as some law reflects not simply that minimum standard which the public wishes to protect, but also what it would like to see as an ideal, so the BBC's programme philosophy seeks to display what the world is like, and to present what might be. Our judicial role is perhaps more like that of the Supreme Court in the United States than that of the courts in this country. Judge-made law here tends towards conservation of what is written within the statute. Judge-made law in the Supreme Court, especially under a Chief Justice like Marshall, tends to expand the philosophy which led to the writing of the Constitution. In that respect, I suggest, the parallel with the BBC is to be found more in the philosophical attitudes of the Supreme Court.

If this is the true position for the BBC's Board of Governors, then it follows that the general character of the programme services will be decided by the cumulative effects of many particular programme judgements made by individual producers and editors. The question of how to identify the role of the Board therefore leads to a further consideration of the way in which producers and editors exercise their individual responsibilities, and to a discussion of the conscience of the programme producer.

Once again, Sir William Haley, in that same lecture, put his finger on the central point. The BBC, after twenty-six years, under the guidance of its first generation, had built responsibility into a tradition. 'Today', he said, 'it is not one man's will but the obligation laid upon a thousand. I would like to lay great stress on this diffusion of responsibility. It is something we have sought more and more to encourage. It is a strength and a safeguard. It may lead to individual vagaries, but the awareness of moral responsibility delegated to every possible member of the Corporation's staff means that there is now a live weight of tradition which would be automatically exerted against anyone who tried to pull that responsibility out of true.'

CHAPTER VII

Good Taste

LORD NORMANBROOK'S LETTER OF 1964, which is now associated with the Prescribing Memoranda, undertakes that 'so far as possible' the BBC will not broadcast programmes which are likely to 'offend against good taste or decency ... or be offensive to public feeling'. Lord Normanbrook also said that in judging what should be included in programmes the Governors would 'pay special regard to the need to ensure that broadcasts designed to stimulate thought do not so far depart from their intention as to give general offence'. There was a recognition in the letter that it would be 'impossible to ensure that every member of the public will always be wholly satisfied with the programmes' because of the difficulties inherent in the broadcasting medium and in the fact of a changing society. (There was an additional undertaking not to put on programmes 'likely to encourage crime and disorder', but that is a rather different matter from undertakings about taste.) The letter specifically noted that 'the placing of particular broadcasts at appropriate times' was a significant factor in achieving these ends.

The wording of the letter is appropriately cautious, in speaking of what was possible and of the problems of plural opinions within the audience itself – for that was the significance of the references to the inherent problems of broadcasting and of the changes in society. Indeed, the Board of Governors is faced, in the matter of taste, with exactly parallel problems to those which arise when they have to consider what moral standpoint they should adopt. For the same reasons they are bound to take a latitudinarian view. From a personal stand-point, I realized, as soon as I was appointed Director-General, that, as a practising Roman Catholic, I should have to formulate a view about these matters of taste and I therefore had to answer for myself the same questions as each Governor no doubt had to pose for his own enlightenment when invited to join the Board. Matters of taste, in my experience of reading correspondence from the public, are often discussed as though they were the immediate consequences of judgements of substantive morality. It is possible that criticisms of taste in programmes may indeed be symptoms of the wish to ask a deeper question about the underlying moral assumptions which may motivate the responsible producer. But in my opinion it was absolutely necessary to distinguish between the concept of morality, which is a fundamental matter, and the judgement of taste, which seems to me to be ephemeral. I was forced to the conclusion that the BBC's judgements about taste were likely to be based on wholly pragmatic considerations. To take one example, there would be no sense for a producer in administering such a shock to the audience by some lapse from taste at an early point in a play that his intended audience would switch off – either mentally or physically – and thus exclude themselves from seeing the rest of the performance which the producer wished them to witness. If the object of the programme were to be communication, then a rupture of that communication made no sense. If the attitude of the BBC as an institution, and of the Governors as its constitutional rulers, must be one of tolerant latitudinarianism, then there is at least an equal responsibility on the producer so to handle his work that it will fall within the bounds of tolerance of his intended audience, for tolerance is a phenomenon with two aspects – that which is claimed by the presenter of a programme, and that which is exercised by his audience. It follows that a producer must have a clear brief about his intended audience, and an intelligent concept of the nature of that audience. This was the problem to which Sir

Hugh Greene directed his attention in his Rome lecture (February 1965) on 'The Conscience of the Programme Director'. He expressed the basic guideline for the producer in these words:

'Relevance is the key—relevance to the audience, and to the tide of opinion in society. Outrage is wrong. Shock may be good. Provocation can be healthy and, indeed, socially imperative. These are the issues to which the broadcaster must apply his conscience. But treatment of the subject, once chosen, demands the most careful assessment of the reasonable limits of tolerance in the audience, if there is any likelihood of these limits being tested by the manner of presentation of the material. As I have said, however, no subject is (for me) excluded simply for what it is.'

I agree entirely with that view. Indeed, the wording is substantially that of a draft which I wrote myself, after having discussed the matter at some length with Sir Hugh. The important factor remains the judgement of what constitutes offence, and on this subject John Robinson, the former Bishop of Woolwich, offered, in his book, *Christian Freedom in a Permissive Society*, what seemed to me to be a very constructive analysis. He suggested that the 'offence susceptibilities' were changing constantly, and he argued that 'where there is a reasonable likelihood of serious offence it is proper that society should exercise restraint so that people can be free not to be damaged if they cannot take it'. In other words, it is incumbent on the presenter of material which might be regarded by some as offensive, but by others as justified exploration of new thinking, to give proper advance warning of his intentions to the general audience. It has always seemed to me that there is a need to create general expectations of what may normally be seen on the screen or heard on the air, and to give specific warnings about what is to come if we have reason to think that some people may wish to avoid it. The judgements have to be made both by the producer and by the audience as individuals. And I should add a further qualification. It was well expressed by my former colleague in the

Canadian Broadcasting Corporation, Eugene Hallman. He wrote: 'Freedom to see what you do not like or enjoy, freedom to hear what you do not agree with or approve, is a freedom jointly shared by the audience and the broadcaster. It is essential to both parties to preserve that freedom if the medium is to fulfill its real potential.' I take that as an injunction not merely towards freedom to see and hear opinions which are not acceptable, but also to see and hear portrayals of manners and behaviour which may diverge from one's own standards. That reflects very closely the view expressed in the Pilkington Report about the responsibilities of broadcasting:

> Broadcasting must pay particular attention to those parts of the range of worthwhile experience which lie beyond the most common; to those parts which some have explored here and there, but few everywhere. Finally, and of special importance: because the range of experience is not finite but constantly growing, and because the growing points are usually most significant, it is on these that broadcasting must focus a spotlight.

The issue of taste is to me, as it was for Hugh Greene, one of relevance. It is not a matter of principle. What is needed is a doctrine of limits, and those limits are, in principle, the same as those which are imposed on us by the need for courtesy in personal exchanges. There must be a restraint of courtesy in the attitude of the producer towards his audience. But I cannot accept as a relevant argument in the matter of taste the existence of those who may switch on a programme in order to experience the sensation of not enjoying it, or of being offended by it. That seems to be a misuse of the rational faculty of choice. It is too common a phenomenon, if one studies the correspondence which reaches broadcasters from the public.

Nor do I believe that 'commonsense' is a sufficient guide in deciding what is in appropriate taste at any given point in the programme schedules. The whole centre of the problem is that judgement of taste is not common over the whole range of the audience. There is no commonsense in this matter. There is a demonstrable plurality of opinions, and it cannot be ignored.

Moreover, despite re-assertions of so-called 'traditional' standards of taste, the general evidence seems to be that the plurality of moral standpoints seems to be moving further from uniformity, or even consistency. Within a single family, viewing in the same home, there will be different opinions about whether the same programme is in good or bad taste. There is no resolution for the broadcaster of that problem in any statement about common decency or commonsense. The only available resolution to the broadcasters' difficulty is not in making the choice for others, but in providing them with information about the programmes offered which will make it possible for each to make an informed choice of whether to view or not.

One aspect of the question of taste which has always proved particularly sensitive is the use of so-called 'bad language'. The Annan Committee found that the complaint which most frequently came up in response to their general appeal for evidence was that television programmes in particular made excessive use of language which the respondents clearly regarded as being unsuitable for introduction into the home. That reflects exactly my own experience of correspondence reaching the BBC. I identified in these letters three separate elements. Many writers objected to what might be described as 'coarse' language – the normal expletives commonly used by the inarticulate in the search for emphasis. The words themselves have long lost any meaning in their own right and could hardly be taken as offensive in that sense. The second category of words to which objection was taken was the so-called 'four letter word' – the use of primitive Anglo-Saxon expressions for the various bodily functions, sexual and excretory, with the words still retaining an explicit meaning, though frequently used allusively. And the third group of objectionable words involved the various names of God, often used in an expletive sense, rather than with the deliberate intention of identifying the Divine.

The nature of the objection to the first category, as I

understood it, was that the use of such language was a departure from the normal standards of courtesy within the home, or within polite society. This objection seemed also to apply to the second category, though here there was also a sense of outrage among those who felt that the concept of sex was being degraded. But the bitterest protest came from those who resented the use of the name of Christ, because they quite clearly felt that such interjections were a form of blasphemy, offensive to the deepest religious feelings.

It was always possible to defend the very occasional use of such language in plays, or indeed in programmes portraying real life. The response to the critics always came down in the end to a question of degree and intent. Were the words included gratuitously in the programmes, either in circumstances where they were not necessary to a true portrayal, or with a frequency which exceeded the needs of truth? To me the use of merely vulgar language, put in the mouths of the inarticulate for the sake of emphasis, rarely seemed as offensive as it frequently was for those who wrote about it. But since courtesy is a general requirement, their representations had to find some acknowledgement in the practice of the broadcaster. The matter of four letter words seemed to me to raise the same question, but in a more acute form, since the shock was greater. I can only suppose that the relative rarity of the use of four letter words in polite society sets up a kind of taboo response. And taboos have to be respected because they always reflect the deeper need of society for a degree of restraint in certain areas of conduct. The protection of bodily privacy from even verbal assault is a reasonable claim on the broadcasters.

For the last category of bad language – the invocation on the name of Christ simply as an expletive – always caused me to hesitate before accepting the claim of dramatic realism. It was sometimes sustainable, but something more than the needs of courtesy was being infringed. The complaints reflected more than distaste. They were objections to the casual casting aside – as it seemed to the critics – of deeply held and centrally important beliefs. It is one thing to offend a man's sense of what is proper. It is a much greater thing to offend his conscience.

The question of the use in programmes of bad language provokes great differences among the audience, whose responses range from admiration for realism, through indifference, to outrage. The variety of that response reflects the plural condition of modern society in Britain. There is no agreement on moral standards, and that lack of agreement is reflected in the language in which people choose to express themselves. The disagreement is characteristic of a society in which moral commitment is fragmented into a whole series of shades of opinion about proper conduct.

But what is the function of the Board of Governors in this sea of uncertainty? If they cannot lay down a uniform standard of taste, then they are bound to take a particularist view of their responsibility for the assessment of programmes. They must offer criticism when evident errors of judgement and lapses from good taste occur, but it is at least as important that they should offer encouragement and praise when excellence presents itself. The judgement of excellence has to be made in professional rather than moral terms because of the moral uncertainties which project themselves from the condition of pluralist society into an equally pluralist group of Governors. But professional excellence is at least recognisable. And if the objection is raised that professional skills do not make the pernicious less objectionable, but only more so, then my comment would be that any artistic work which laid itself open to that attack would, at best, be a flawed masterpiece, because it would lack the sincerity which must be the test of true professional excellence.

The Board of Governors of the BBC cannot rule simply by negative objection. It cannot seek arbitrarily to limit the freedom of the programme planners and producers. It has a responsibility to encourage as well as to guide, and never to diminish by the restriction of a purely negative censorship.

This responsibility is, on the whole, little understood by the general public, and least of all in the world of politics. There is a feeling that positive instruction is possible, and that the the shape of programmes can be dictated to producers. The practical experience of the BBC argues conclusively, on basis of programmes seen and heard by the public, that this is not true. As Lord Normanbrook said, 'the initiative in breaking fresh ground and making new departures must remain with the producers themselves and their immediate superiors'. In the last resort, judgements of taste rest on that level, and it is only in the exceptional situation of crisis that judgements will be made at a higher level. The norm lies in the conscience of the producer.

CHAPTER VIII

Political Attitudes

THE DIFFICULT QUESTIONS which arise for the BBC's Board of Governors over their general moral stance, and in matters of good taste and decency, present themselves in a more specific way in the matter of politics. As I have explained, there is a general BBC commitment to impartiality in matters of public controversy. There is also the formal injunction to the BBC not to express its own view on such subjects. These are no more than particular applications of the general principles which I have outlined in the previous two chapters. They become the subjects of special mention in the constitutional documents, I suspect, only because political controversy is the main interest of those who are responsible for drafting the formal framework within which the BBC operates. If government were nowadays conducted, as it used to be in medieval times, largely by clerics, then no doubt similar injunctions would have been given to the broadcasters about the treatment of religious subjects. But the direct injunctions in the constitutional instruments point to the need for the BBC to evolve much more specific policies for the coverage of public affairs than suffice for the more general fields of morals and taste.

There is one potential confusion which I think should be removed at the very beginning. 'Objectivity' is frequently mentioned as the guiding principle for the BBC in its handling of current affairs. But objectivity describes the position of an observer looking at events, and seeking to detach himself from them so as to give a wholly externalized account of them. That is the position of the classical reporting journalist, and when such a man works for the BBC he is expected to take precisely that position. But objectivity is not a sufficient description of the position of the BBC itself. If the BBC were to be objective, and nothing else, it would seek to exclude in its account of the world every expression of debatable opinion. That would not conform to the requirement to be impartial, which must consist in the presentation of the range of differing opinions about the interpretation of events. The objectivity of the BBC as an institution is not towards the facts which it seeks to report. It relates much more to its attitudes towards the various interpretations of those facts, all of which must at some time be given access to the air, and the result is better described as 'impartiality'.

The underlying assumption of the BBC is that of liberal democracy. The BBC as an institution is the child of parliamentary democracy. And the whole concept of its establishment assumes its support of that system. I once heard one of the BBC's senior editors admit that we were biased. 'Yes', he said, 'biased in favour of parliamentary democracy'. And he was absolutely right. That form of democracy depends on there being a plurality of opinions, on the freedom of their expression, on their public dissemination, and on the resolution, in circumstances of tolerance, of the differences of view which will then arise. The resolution for the time being of those differences is embodied at any given moment in the current policy of the prevailing government. It is a matter of accommodation, of tolerance, not of principle. No public policy is 'right'. It is simply accepted for the time being. Democracy allows for the possibility of change and for the possibility of argument for it. That possibility is the concern of the broadcaster in a democratic society. That is why BBC programmes are as they are. The news programmes are intended to provide the participants in the British democracy with the material which forms the ground of the variety of their opinions. The programmes of opinion – and the division, I know, is somewhat arbitrary – are intended to provide an opportunity for democracy to express itself in public argument. The BBC reflects in this way the requirements of the parliamentary democracy by which it was created and for which we must operate.

BBC news and current affairs broadcasting has attracted a particular form of criticism of late. The people responsible for these programmes are said to be so conditioned by their upbringing, the society within which they live, and the precepts of professional journalism as established over the years, that they are unable to give a truly objective view of the world. Their search for what they call 'objectivity' is frustrated from the beginning because their concepts of what is objective are distorted by their previous and prevailing environment. I ought to be the last to deny the importance of environmental factors in the shaping of a man's mind. As a Roman Catholic, and as a member of the proletariat conditioned by the education of the Establishment, I must accept that environment is important. But such conditioning does not prevent one from looking for the nearest approximation to the truth, and from making a contribution, along with others, to the construction of a total picture of the truth. So long as we admit the principle of constructive argument about the validity of the picture once constructed, nobody should be too alarmed about the threat to due impartiality.

Recent critics have suggested that news and current affairs editors and reporters are so pre-conditioned that what they present to the world is determined in advance. The critics argue that this is part of the process of the continuing dialectic of the Marxist class war. The broadcasters are not presenting to the world real choice of opinions because their pictures are so distorted by pre-determined attitudes that they exclude such choice. They dictate the answers which have to be given. That philosophy reflects directly the ideas of the determinists, and to me those ideas are wholly incompatible with the operation of a parliamentary democracy. Such a democracy assumes as a possibility a reality of choice. It rejects the exclusion of choice which is implicit in the determinist view of history, and it accepts that those who report and comment on social developments are capable of bringing to public discussion the element of personal independence, to which their environment is a contribution rather than a limitation.

It seems to me that there is no point in burking the fact that Marxist determinism is incompatible with parliamentary democracy. Since the BBC is the expression of that democracy, and the means of its maintenance, it cannot accept that its thinking and policies should conform to the determinist philosophies which underlie some recent sociological research into broadcasting.

The best Marxist-based analysis I know of the present structure of broadcasting in Britain is contained in a lecture given by Stuart Hall to a seminar at Leicester in 1976. It is difficult to select for quotation from what he said, but I choose as central this passage:

> 'In a system – that is, a political system – where "power" in the abstract rests, finally, with the sovereignty of the "popular will", it [the broadcasting system] reproduces the already-structured disposition of the popular consensus . . . Broadcasting reproduces, through the independence/impartiality couplet, not this or that position or interest within the field of the contending classes as expressed in the political system, but rather the whole structured field of political ideologies and forces.'

He rightly adds that to question this structure 'would force us away from broadcasting in particular to an examination of the nature and character of the liberal democratic state itself'. Quite right. And he goes on to state the opposing alternative. He says that such a broadcasting system 'not only raises particular interests to a general or universal level; it fragments the antagonistic unities of the struggle between the classes'. That analysis indicated the nature of the alternative struggle as the basis for political development. I do not accept the class struggle and Marxist determinism as the basis of British broadcasting. Clearly, however, despite its incompatibility with liberal democracy, a presentation of the Marxist arguments amongst others is a proper part of the BBC's editorial duty, because in the end it is for British democracy to choose its own course – not for the BBC to choose on behalf of all.

The primacy of discussion as the essence of parliamentary democracy is a guiding principle for the Board of Governors of the BBC when they consider their attitude towards the presentation of issues of current public interest. It was well expressed by Shirley Williams in a speech which she gave in January 1977 about the need for open discussion within the Labour Party. She said:

'No question is more important for the Left than the compatibility of individual freedom with socialism. . . . The Labour Party has always been as devoted to the method of democracy – progress by persuasion rather than by compulsion – as to the objectives of socialism.'

And then analysing the problems which faced Socialists, she identified one which she regarded as central:

'It is the problem of consent. We cannot always expect everyone to be enthusiastic about the changes that we socialists propose' – and she listed several examples. 'But,' she added, 'it is vitally important that people consent to these changes, that they accept that the changes, whether they like them or not, are the result of the workings of a free democratic process through the agency of a sovereign Parliament.'

One of the problems of the public discussion of political issues which is implicit in the approach to the business of government of liberal democrats like Shirley Williams who commit themselves to party platforms is that the various parties proclaim their intentions in somewhat rigid terms, leaving little apparent room for compromise. This rigidity is, in part, a consequence of the complexity of managing a modern society. The solutions to problems have to be closely worked out in advance in order to ensure their practicability, and it is, in part, a political consequence of public disclosure itself. Although the democratic process assumes compromise between differing views, the politics of democracy tend to make compromise more difficult because of the need to enlist popular support for apparently conflicting solutions. Both Government and Opposition develop rigid positions as a result of the resolution of internal arguments within the parties which respectively represent their support. The compromises which have already taken place within groups contending for power make further compromise with external interests more difficult. It is these inhibitions to compromise, often expressed in the hyperbole of election manifestos, which can place substantial difficulties in the way of a broadcasting organisation which is committed publicly to the task of informing and educating its audience.

They are, in effect, barriers of emotion. I accept that the simple provision of information will not break them down. Information is not some kind of pure gold which can readily be identified and separated from the dross of opinion. Beyond a very simple level, every piece of information incorporates an attitude of mind. But I believe it is possible to present information and opinion in a way which will generally be recognized as fair.

And so I argue a general position, in the light of experience, that it is possible for a body like the BBC, engaged in journalism about public affairs, to present a view of the world – or rather a series of views – which, in their totality, will be regarded by most people for most of the time, as reasonably balanced. That is the BBC's principal role in sustaining the democratic system. The BBC is trying, as I see it, to reduce the extent of incomprehension of the basic facts about our society. I remember vividly the number of misapprehensions entertained by many people about the intentions which we in the BBC had in mind in publishing the policy statement 'Broadcasting in the Seventies'. That experience gave me some fellow feeling with other authorities – even governments –

seeking to carry out a declared policy. The BBC, expert in communication, sought to explain its policy as carefully and as skilfully as it could. It was as misunderstood as everybody else. The fault was not in the formulation of the published paper, nor in the intelligence of its critics. The complexity of the practical problems underlying the proposals, together with the suspicions of the critics of the motives of BBC management, combined to inhibit rational public discussion. The barriers to understanding are very strong and very high. The difficulty is a general one. It is the duty of the BBC to try to overcome those barriers for others as well as for itself, with all the skills at its command.

It is useful to look at this task in a longer historical perspective, recalling, for example, how the electorate has grown in the past century and a half. At the beginning of 1832 the electorate of the United Kingdom was half a million. About one person in fifty had the vote. The Great Reform Bill of that year doubled the electorate. The Reform Bill of 1867 more than doubled it again. The Bill of 1884 again doubled the electorate, and by this time more than one in six had the vote. In 1918 the enfranchisement of women over thirty meant that nearly half the population had the vote. The Flapper Vote in 1928 continued the process, and the 1969 Act, enfranchising the eighteen-year-olds, brought the electorate to forty million out of a population of fifty-four million.

This is an enormous rate of growth, and I do not find it surprising that even 150 years should not have been sufficient time for the expanding democratic electorate to accustom itself to what Antony Jay has acutely diagnosed as the change from 'government by private words' to 'government by public words'. The latter is a far more difficult task.

I find it enlightening to look again at Bagehot's *The English Constitution* on this point – and particularly at the introduction to the second edition, written after the passing of the second Reform Bill. He restated his thesis that 'Cabinet Government is possible in England because England is a deferential country'. And he looked somewhat gloomily at the consequences of an electorate which had reached the figure of two-and-a-half millions. The real question, he suggested, was whether the new voters would 'defer in the same way to wealth and rank, and the higher qualities of which these are the rough symbols and the common accompaniment'. It seems almost comic today, but it was a serious statement in its time. For statesmen he gave this warning: 'If they raise questions which will excite the lower orders of mankind . . . (and) on which the interest of those orders is not identical with, or is antagonistic to, the whole interest of the State, they will have done the greatest harm they can do.' In other words, public debate on awkward matters should not be encouraged. And as for the electorate, Bagehot could not expect that 'the new class of voters will be at all more able to form sound opinions on complex questions than the old voters'. Again, it is unwise to raise awkward questions in public! The electorate is incapable of understanding them! I am not with Bagehot. He did not allow for the parallel development of general education.

One year after the first Reform Bill, Government made its first grant – of £20,000 a year – to voluntary educational societies. In 1870 Foster's Education Act brought elementary education within the reach of all children, though not all could enjoy it. By 1901 elementary education had become virtually free, and was compulsory from age five to twelve. And in the following year Balfour's Education Act introduced the Local Education Authorities and public secondary education for the first time. This looks like a story of steady and substantial progress. But by 1906, when the Liberals took office – twenty years after the last of the three great electoral enfranchisement acts – the number of Local Authority scholarships for working-class children at secondary grammar schools was less than 25,000. By comparison, the electoral roll in 1906 contained over seven million names.

The expenditure figures tell a similar story. In the twenty years between 1832 and 1852 Government expenditure on education increased tenfold to reach £460,000 a year. In the next thirty years it increased tenfold again. And in the following thirty years there was a further tenfold increase, if one takes account of Local Authority expenditure. But even so, the total expenditure was only about £50 millions in 1914 as compared with the present expenditure of well over £2,000 millions. Even allowing for inflation, the increase is gigantic.

The scale of the task which had to be tackled in educating the new democracy can be measured by what is now being done. In 1971 there were more than ten million children and young people in full-time attendance at schools, universities, colleges of education, and technical colleges, and amongst that number were 234,000 university students. And there is still said to be not enough educational provision to match the need. Given that background, is it surprising that Aneurin Bevan thought that democracy was only just coming of age? It is only recently that the task of educating the people for democracy has been tackled. And the effectiveness of the education given is hardly perfect.

That is where the media find their role. Once again, a historical perspective is useful. W. T. Stead, the Editor of the *Pall Mall Gazette*, wrote to his father in 1883, only a year before the establishment of adult manhood suffrage, 'Here am I, not yet thirty-five, and already the most influential man in England'. To measure the force of that comment, one needs to remember that the sales of Stead's paper rose in 1889, as a result of his famous campaign against the prostitution of young girls in London, from just over 8,000 to just over 12,000. It is fair to add that the *Daily Telegraph*, at the same period, had a circulation of some 300,000 among the middle classes. The young Harmsworth was supposed to have been the first to see the opportunities which were offered by the growth of literacy. The first edition of the *Daily Mail*, published in 1896, sold just under 400,000 copies. That was a large figure. But it was not until after the First World War that the national press circulations began to attain the levels which we now regard as common – a total daily circulation of fourteen millions or more with a readership which might be double that, depending on the number assumed to see each copy. So there have been about fifty years of communication of public information by the genuinely mass circulation newspapers to an electorate whose formal education has only just begun within that period to reach the level necessary for the absorption of the printed word.

That period coincides exactly with that of the development of broadcasting. The foundation of national broadcasting – that is, broadcasting reaching almost every home in the country – was laid during the first fifty years. But the foundation was more than material. It included the concept of the obligation to balance and impartiality as part of the obligation to inform. That was of fundamental importance. But balance is essentially a negative approach, which tells broadcasters to avoid being used in the service of particular interests. Can they be more positive about what we must do, or try to do?

I think they can, and without taking political authority from its proper place. It is the broadcasters' role, as I see it, to win public interest in public issues. The organisation of political consent is more difficult in a complex society than it has ever been before. If broadcasting can arouse public interest, it can increase public understanding, and in this way make the organisation of political consent to the actions of government more possible. It is emphatically not the broadcasters' job to persuade their audiences about the truth of particular propositions which may be put forward by one interest or another – including by one party or another. But it *is* their duty, for the sake of the successful government of society, to persuade their audiences to feel themselves involved in the issues which have to be debated. As Reginald Maudling said in a notable article in *The Times* in 1973 there is 'a long term national interest in proceeding by agreement rather than by conflict'. Agreement can only come out of understanding – and many of the issues that have to be understood are so complex that it takes the greatest skill to present them in such a way that they will hold the interest of the audience.

When one looks back it is extraordinary to see how slow the progress has been – not how slow and how little the effort has been, because that has been formidable, but the effects. And yet I think it is possible to say that for the most part young people in Britain today have the means, as a result of the present educational system, of acquiring basic information. It is the broadcasters' function to bring to this population the facts about the world in which they live once they have emerged from the process of formal education. Some of them, of course, acquire the habit of turning to broadcasting for these facts from an early stage during that formal education, but it is, I think, a fairly general experience that the wish to know about the world does not make itself manifest in any intensive way until late in the secondary educational stage.

Broadcasters have a responsibility, therefore, to provide a rationally based and balanced service of news which will enable adult people to make basic judgements about public policy in their capacity as voting citizens of a democracy. That is not very much. It is a complicated thing to do, but the result is often small. Broadcasters must add to this basic supply of news a service of contextual comment which will give understanding as well as information. It is there that they begin to run into trouble. The selection of news of a factual kind is difficult enough. The selection of people to comment on it, or even simply to explain it, and the identification of which are the important views to place before the public is much harder. But it has to be done, and the only practical guideline is to try to ensure that every view which is likely to have a lasting effect on public thinking is at some time reflected in the public debate on the air about any particular subject.

In their efforts to achieve a fair presentation of the range of opinion it is, in my view, a cardinal error for broadcasters to plan the presentation of one view of a subject without a specific intention to return to it in order to present the other views which may be in circulation. It is impossible to guarantee that the treatment of any subject will be comprehensive at any one time. It is possible to come very close to that ideal over a period, given an initial intention to do so. The moral responsibility of the broadcaster is not simply to keep the ring open for all opinions, but to see that everybody has a chance to appear in it. Thus it would be quite wrong to present the case for higher wages for low-paid workers without at the same time presenting the other arguments about the need for proper relationships between one kind of skill and another in the rewards they receive, and the general effect on the economy of higher wages at a time of inflation. And in speaking of inflation it would be the broadcaster's responsibility from time to time to bring home to the audience the ultimate effects of a financial phenomenon which, until recently, none of them can ever have experienced personally, but of which there are many examples in recent history.

Merely to cite these examples indicates the complexity of the subjects which can be raised. It is self-evidently impossible to present these issues comprehensively enough to satisfy academics and yet in a form simple enough for people to form basic opinions about public policy. But there is no escape from the need to present the bare essentials. One comes to accept, in running a broadcasting organisation, that the truth can never be complete in the day-to-day exchange of opinion and one has to be satisfied with less than the whole. In accepting that inadequacy, the broadcaster has to try to make sure that he is simply smoothing out the seasonal variations, so to speak, and not distorting the underlying pattern, The broadcaster has to make the complex comprehensible and the routine interesting. That calls for considerable ingenuity and imagination, and neither of these capacities flourish except at the level of the individual. I believe that the broadcasting approach to these problems of public education must rely on initiative at the programme periphery and discard the thought of direction from the management centre. There may be a general stimulus from the centre from time to time to encourage the exercise of imagination in a particular direction, and sometimes a check on particular enthusiasms in the interests of fair dealing. The guiding principle must be that programmes are not the outcome of a central management process, but of the efforts of one man or of a very small group thinking, in the context of a studio, about a script. When a broadcasting organisation considers its stance in handling political subjects, therefore, it must seek the reconciliation between its general duty of impartiality and the need, nevertheless, to present the widest range of interpretations and policy views in the variety of imagination which will be displayed by its programme staff when faced with the professional challenge of presenting issues to the public.

If broadcasters accept these limitations they can enjoy a limited success in this field of public education. That limited success is far greater than anything attainable in history so far. They ought not to be attacked for not doing better when nobody has ever done as well before. In return they must give an undertaking to society that their consciencies will be applied to a determination to stick to the facts so far as they can honestly establish them; not to present one aspect of the facts with undue advantage over others; not to exploit programme capacities in the directions which are suggested by technique rather than by the intention to enlighten. Those are the obligations on the broadcaster. When they depart from them they must expect to be the target of legitimate criticism.

I have been in broadcasting for more than a quarter of a century. When I first started, as a radio talks producer, I was responsible for putting on talks about inflation by Graham Hutton and others. The results, in terms of audience size and evident movement of opinion, were not, on the face of it, very encouraging. But I think, with my first hand knowledge of what had been done over the last twenty-five years, that broadcasters are at least beginning to show that these questions can be made intelligible and interesting, and that public understanding benefits from persistence by the broadcasters. Clear and ingenious exposition is the aim, and it can be aided – not hindered – by argumentative conflict. Political clap-trap on the air can be the death of understanding, and the BBC's postbag and telephone log show that audiences are quick to resent political gladiators who prefer phrase-making to persuasive argument.

I believe that this reflects the present temper of our modern society in Britain. And here I should like to take up a social development whose significance was described by the Catholic sociologist, Anthony Spencer (in an article published in *The Listener* on 20 December 1972). His then recent experiences of living in Northern Ireland suggested to him an interpretation of the reasons for the deep differences of opinion which existed there – an interpretation which seemed to me to have relevance to the rest of the United Kingdom. He had noted, in a particularly striking form, the effects of the steady change in society from a substantially rural population – which would still have been a fair description of the United Kingdom population at the turn of the century – to a predominantly urbanized population, as it is now. Spencer's Northern Irish experience suggested to him that 'community identity is far stronger in the country than in the city'. His deduction was that 'the individual is therefore much freer in the city to make his own decisions, without regard to the social pressure of the community, than he is in the country. The social and cultural diversity of the city brings a toleration of difference, a readiness to negotiate and compromise'. To summarize his continuing argument, he suggested that the city dweller is more likely to interpret events in terms of truth, the universal standard, and less likely to interpret them in terms of his own group or family, a particular standard. And further, that this contributed to the greater tolerance found in the city. Progressive urbanisation, in short, leads to a more active and more tolerant circulation of ideas. That is the fact with which broadcasters in Britain have to deal. The requirement which follows is that the span of opinions which they present should be broad and the choice within that span recognisably impartial. If it is not, they will over-strain the tolerance of their audiences, whose respect they will consequently cease to enjoy.

The seventeen years which covered the service of Hugh Greene and myself as Directors-General saw massive changes in the handling of current affairs by the BBC, particularly in the matter of election coverage. From a complete absence of campaign coverage the broadcasters came very close to the point where the charge of excess might have been justified. I do not doubt myself that those changes would have come in due time, as the normal extension of the process of liberation which had been resumed after the war by Sir William Haley. But the process was undoubtedly speeded up by the competitive element. The recurrent disputes between the BBC and Harold Wilson during the 1960s were a reflection of this gradual extension of freedom of political comment on television as much as of the personalities involved. By the end of Hugh Greene's regime the assumption that reporting and comment on broadcasting should be, in principle, as free as they were in the Press had been established, at least among the broadcasters. The special test for broadcasters in my time as Director-General was to discover how that freedom could be exercised with responsibility in the face of the threat to the identity of the State which was posed by the Northern Irish insurrection. The issue was not simply that the unity of the State was being threatened. It went further. How far was it possible for the assumption of unity to be debated? At the end of my time the debate on Scottish devolution seemed to suggest that constitutional unity was a legitimate topic for broadcasters to discuss quite freely. I believe that that is where the debate about the scope of broadcast discussion should end. But it was the element of violence in Northern Ireland which made it difficult for many to accept that this degree of tolerance represented reasonable ground on which broadcasters, politicians and the public might agree.

The long argument about the proper role of news and current affairs broadcasting will never be decisively concluded. But it seems to me, in 1978, that the broad principles – editorial freedom, impartiality in its exercise, and balance in the presentation of views – are now solid assumptions which will not again be challenged, so long as Britain continues to be a living parliamentary democracy. When Haley spoke to the British Council of Churches in 1948 he concluded by quoting Pascal:

> 'There is but one absolute position for which it is right to look at a picture. Others are too near, too distant, too high, too low. Perspective dictates this position in matters of painting. But who will assign it in matters of morality and truth?'

He might well have added politics to morality and truth. But just as no broadcaster can give an absolute answer in those spheres, none will seek, I hope, to give one for politics.

CHAPTER IX
Dissent

THE OBLIGATION OF IMPARTIALITY certainly presents problems for the broadcaster, but if it is accepted that his basic assumption is one of tolerance, with an active care for the circulation of ideas, then the problems are soluble so long as the arguments proceed within the general consensus about the nature of democratic society. Liberal opinion tolerates the expression of a very wide range of opposed views, and although the proponents of each view will dispute fiercely among themselves, they will all accept the Voltairian dictum that each may detest the views of the others but will defend to the death their right to express them. In the same Bristol speech from which I have already quoted several times Sir William Haley said that, having seen the BBC exercising its independence for some five years, he had been 'more and more struck by the fact that the only requirement upon it all the time, from which it has no independence, is the requirement to do the right thing'. He went on to say that there would always be more than one view of what constituted 'the right thing', and in subsequent amplification he spoke of the duty of tolerance required of the BBC as being 'toward liberty of expression for serious thought' – of 'allowing all relevant and sincerely held convictions a fair say in a given context, including those that are opposed to the Christian religion'.

In Edinburgh in 1971 I said much the same thing, but I went a little further. It was easy, I said to arrange for a general balance in programmes between those ideas which fell within the broad consensus which exists in all normal Western society. But, I added, 'the difficult and courageous thing is to make sure that there is also room from time to time for those new ideas which fall outside the consensus but which have a rational justification or an emotional base, and which therefore ought to be examined by an informed public'. I argued that it was one of the duties of the BBC to add to the presentation of a balance of ideas within the consensus 'a presentation of those ideas which fall outside it and which may eventually serve to change it'.

The principle is easier than the practice, and the resistances come more frequently and fiercely from the audience than from within the BBC. In January 1955 Mrs Margaret Knight, a lecturer in Psychology at Aberdeen University, was invited to give three talks from the point of view of a humanist. They were to set out her approach to the problem of morality. She chose to do this in a way which led her into some critical comments on conventional religious views. The public's reaction was fierce. It was argued that such views had no place in the programmes of a BBC whose Director-General had, for example, committed himself to views like those which Haley had expressed about the BBC's support for the Christian religion. But the BBC, in inviting Mrs Knight to give her broadcasts, was doing no more than allowing a sincerely held point of view to be expressed. If she had used a more conciliatory tone towards other beliefs nobody could have argued – at least in my view – that her views were to be excluded from programmes for being what they were. I am fairly sure that the outcry would have been much the same, though the attack would have been much less easy to sustain.

Some eleven years later, after reiterated representations from humanist spokesmen, addressed both to the Pilkington Committees of Inquiry and to the BBC itself, the BBC broadcast a series of six interviews with leading humanists under the title *An Enquiry into Humanism*. These interviews were broadcast in the Home Service on Saturday mornings. There had already been a series of talks by distinguished philosophers and theologians on the Third Programme under the title *Religion and Humanism*. This had produced no hostile reaction, but the Home Service was another matter. Hence the Saturday morning placing. In the event, the hostility aroused by Mrs Knight's talks was not repeated, and for anybody who wished to see how a once controversial subject can be introduced in an acceptable manner I commend the study of those six programmes as they were published at the time. Something of this acceptability was, I believe, due to the interviewer, Kenneth Harris, but much came from the decent humility of those interviewed. Once again, it was a matter of no subject being inadmissible, provided that the manner of its presentation was carefully considered. But the Mrs Knight incident of 1955 was a reminder that when the boundary of consensus is crossed the limits of tolerance are very severely strained. It is not the tolerance of the BBC which is in issue. It is that of the audience.

Any institution like the BBC which depends fundamentally on the general assent of the public for its continued existence, even though that assent is formally signified only at fairly long intervals, will inevitably reflect the society which it serves. It cannot be the instrument of total revolution. It will most often be the vehicle of conformity. But just as a generally conforming society, if it is democratic, must be open to question, so the programme-maker in the BBC must be free to probe and to explore. Free exercise of the programme-maker's conscience and of his commonsense – the one rebellious and the other conformist – must be the foundation of BBC programme policy. On this matter the Pilkington Committee made an important point about the freedom to err. 'All broadcasting', they said, 'and television especially, must be ready and anxious to experiment, to show the new and unusual, to give a hearing to dissent. Here broadcasting must be most willing to make mistakes, for if it does not, it will make no discoveries.'

In reminding an audience of the religious press in 1970 of this Pilkington comment I recalled an opinion which I had recently seen attributed to Pyotr Kapitsa, the Soviet physicist who formerly worked at the Cavendish Laboratory in Cambridge. He had recently written, in the Soviet youth magazine *Yunost*, that an authoritative and healthy public opinion could 'only be formed in an atmosphere of liveliness and active thinking; in an atmosphere of seeking and of productive creative work. An indispensable prerequisite of such an atmosphere is the clash of differing opinions, exchange of disputed ideas, discussion and debate. . . . Whenever science has no upsets, no struggles to show, then it is on the road to the cemetery'.

When I read now the condemnations by those who claim to be upholders of orthodox Christian belief that the BBC has gone too far in some particular programme decision, and has outraged the ordinary people, I cannot help but recall that the original Christians were a people of protest, for whom the imperative of conscience was the reason for rejecting a politically advisable conformism. The essence of their stand was an assertion of conscience. Those who claim now to speak for the orthodox Christian standpoint may find themselves, in due course, a minority in a society which less and less accepts the normality of religious commitment. When that day comes it is those who now consider themselves orthodox who will be claiming the right of dissent to be heard. When they consider the opportunities given to dissenting views in current broadcasting they ought perhaps to be more conscious of the continuing argument in favour of giving dissent a hearing.

But in arguing the case for dissent it is very easy to assume that those who claim the right to be heard are all in the 'progressive' camp. Thus, for example, over the years since the war, the advocates of humanist ethics, birth control, the abolition of capital punishment, abortion, and homosexual reform have campaigned, with substantial success, for the reflection of their viewpoints on the air, and as the social climate has changed more and more to accept their claims, so the problem of the broadcaster has eased. But, in principle, the case for allowing expression for the views of 'reactionary' dissent is no different. Thus, the traditional evangelistic religious position, given special expression by, for example, the Festival of Light, is as much entitled to a place on the air as any of the more 'progressive' expressions of dissent. The same case could be made for the National Front, or for advocates of South Africa's policy of apartheid. The criterion of admission to the air is not whether the consensus of producer opinion – or, indeed, of audience opinion – would accept that the views of advocates of these causes were reasonable. The principle must be that general disagreement with a view is not sufficient ground for excluding it. Thus, when the Editor of *The Times* published a substantial case for a return to the Gold Standard it would have been difficult to find support for him among the ranks of the orthodox economists. Nevertheless, his contribution was certainly, in the words of Haley, a 'relevant and sincerely held conviction'. His case for an invitation to broadcast, had he made it, would have been a good one, however antediluvian other economic thinkers might have held his thesis to be.

For a brief period in 1949 the Third Programme recognized the theoretical force of this argument for the admission of dissenting views by presenting a somewhat unfortunately named series – *Crankcase*. But, despite its name, the idea behind the series was theoretically well justified. It was a deliberate attempt to give to ideas well beyond the then existing consensus an opportunity to be heard. Thus, at a time when fleets of bulldozers were being deployed in Tanganyika on the ground nuts scheme, Geoffrey Pyke, one of the originators of the wartime idea for the Habakuk Iceberg aircraft carrier, was given the chance to argue the case that the best means of helping the developing countries was not by the massive application of American agricultural technology, but by the production of a better designed shovel. Muscle power, he said, was more relevant to their needs than machines. And who would as easily dispute his thesis today as they did then?

It is one thing, however, for the social forces of inertia to be reflected in a resistance among broadcasters to the projection of unorthodox technological ideas. There is a worse phenomenon. It is becoming more and more common for more people positively to try to stop broadcasters – and others – from publishing ideas of which selected minorities disapprove. One example in recent years, of which I have had personal experience, is the Festival of Light movement. I am like any believing Christian – and indeed, like most thinking humanists – in supporting the maintenance of high moral standards. In this respect I am at one with those who support the Festival of Light. But there was an element in the Festival of Light propaganda which I found unacceptable, whether I looked at it from my individual point of view, or from my position as a responsible official of the BBC. The efforts of the Festival's supporters were directed not simply to the advocacy of their own ideals, but to the suppression of those ideas of which they disapproved. Thus, plays which presented sexual irregularities as a human problem were denounced because they presented the problem at all. Most recently the Festival of Light supported Mrs Mary Whitehouse in her initiative in prosecuting *Gay News* for the publication of an allegedly blasphemous poem. I should never suggest that the BBC should broadcast such a poem, and my judgement would be based both on the quality of the poem and the unacceptability of its theme to most listeners. But the proposition that the poet and the publisher should be the subject of penal sanctions imposed by the State for uttering views which are intensely objectionable to other citizens, without regard for the intention of the publishers, does not strike me as being in the true liberal tradition which sustains the generally civilized atmosphere of British society. The torches of faith which are carried by the Festival can too easily be seized by others only too ready to follow the example of Savonarola in starting a bonfire of books. The darkness of intolerance begins to close in when the torch-carriers begin to want to burn the sinners, instead of to forgive them.

I have mentioned the argument for a hearing to be given to

the National Front, and I have argued that the case rests on the fundamental principle of giving room for dissent to be heard. I do not see how democracy can be selective against ideas, although I accept that action to preserve public order is as absolute a requirement in a democratic society as the willingness to hear every argument. Intervention to that end, as I see it, is the critical decision in the treatment of a group which challenges public order by its behaviour rather than refusal to listen to what it has to say. After all, the right to know what the critics of democratic action are saying is inherent in the condition of being a democrat. That is why, over several years, I refused to accept demands that spokesmen for the Provisional IRA would never be interviewed. Decisions about such interviews were always referred to me. I took the view that the public which was going to judge the issues raised by the insurrection in Northern Ireland had a right sometimes to know from the men of violence why they had chosen that course. There was nothing in the history of British democracy which could lead me to fear that the exposure of the arguments of the Provisional IRA would make them attractive to the vast majority of those who heard them. And if it is argued that to present them at all on the air is to give them a spurious respectability and glamour which will attract recruits among the less sophisticated, I should still argue that the right of the great majority to know is more important than the risk that the few may be deceived. The first is the fundamental argument in democracy, and the second the argument of all those who seek to 'protect the weaklings among the flock', which is always the case presented by authoritarians.

There are two qualifications which I should make in advocating access to the air for the spokesmen of movements in Britain which would be regarded by many as anti-democratic and therefore doubtful candidates for such access. Both relate to the principle that the audience must not be deceived. It has sometimes been the case that determined minorities will consider it reasonable to advance only a part of their case in order to attract support, while holding back on those elements in it which would be likely to arouse resistance. Thus, classically in Britain, the Communist Party has emphasized its interest in individual right against institutional power. But there has been less emphasis in Communist presentations on the revolutionary aim of dictatorship of the proletariat. Indeed, West European parties claim now not to pursue this aim. But it remains a part of the classical Communist approach, and any opportunity for Communists to explain themselves on the air should be accompanied by an awareness, brought home to the listener and viewer, of this aspect of Communist philosophy. Similarly, the National Front stresses the 'patriotic' element in its programme and claims to speak for 'Britain'. But there is less emphasis on their intolerance of those who express views in favour, for example, of full civil rights for all immigrants. It would be quite wrong for broadcasters to admit National Front spokesmen to the air without reminding the public, by questioning such spokesmen, of these other aspects of their policies.

My second reservation relates to the tendency of extremist movements to resort to conspiratorial tactics. An example was the use by Communists of ballot-rigging in the Electrical Trades Union in the 1950s, and the current practice of the National Front in disseminating propaganda in schools shows similar characteristics. The use by the Socialist Workers' Party of the Anti-Nazi League is open to the same criticism, and there have been many examples, notably in the motor industry, of action inspired by the International Socialists and by the Workers' Revolutionary Party. The claim is always made that these privately inspired activities coincide with the interests of the workers who are being represented, but the essence of the tactics used is the avoidance of overt attributions of responsibility to these extreme political movements. Broadcasters have a responsibility to make plain in these instances what is being concealed, or at least not too openly discussed.

But, given these two caveats I have mentioned, which relate

more to the relationship of trust with the audience than to the principle of access to the air, I find it inconsistent with democratic thinking when arguments are presented against inviting spokesmen from these minority interests to give their views from time to time. Their appearances ought to reflect the relative volume of support which these movements attract, but their lack of mass support is not an argument for avoiding discussion of their views and their direct presentation. The ground of objection to their appearances is not so much one of disagreement on rational grounds as repugnance on moral grounds. It is a powerful consideration, but not enough to justify exclusion.

Occasionally the BBC will find itself confronted with the same problem of how to be fair in the treatment of minority views when questions of politics outside Britain have to be presented on the air. A particular instance is that of South African racial policies. Sir Hugh Greene said in his 1965 lecture in Rome that the BBC was not obliged to be impartial about racialism. I think that declaration, which is incontrovertible as a statement about the attitudes which must be adopted by any liberal democrat, has been over-interpreted, in that it has been held to exclude from BBC programmes any objective explanation of the policies of apartheid. I do not believe that Hugh Greene would have intended that to be the effect of his statement. There are a number of levels on which the question of relations between the races in South Africa could be discussed. There is the simple factual level, which describes the relative capacities, opportunities and situations of the various communities as they can now be seen in South African society. In itself such description is a useful and thought provoking activity. It leads to a presentation by the component elements in South African society of the patterns of behaviour which are followed by each towards the others. That must include a justification of those policies.

Up to that point I am sure that Hugh Greene would share the views which I have expressed from time to time about the reflection on BBC programmes of apartheid as a philosophy which is in dissent from the views generally held in the rest of the world about race relations. Neither of us would go beyond that point of accepting justifications of apartheid on British air without the addition of some critical appraisal of those justifications. It is impossible to believe, as a liberal democrat, that in discussing apartheid, to understand everything is to forgive everything. But it is not possible to form a sensible view about a policy like apartheid without understanding it. That is why I should argue that such explanations are necessary to the British audience, and certainly not matters to be wholly excluded from BBC programmes.

The extreme case in the consideration of the airing to be given to dissent is that of the admission to the air of spokesmen of the Provisional IRA. The reporting of movements which depend on violence for the change of the existing order is a difficult editorial question wherever it arises. The activities of the Baader-Meinhoff group in Federal Germany are the subject of general disapproval in the West because they attack the principle of consent through the ballot-box, with no saving grace in the shape of widespread public support. Yet, retrospectively, the Sinn Fein movement in Southern Ireland during the struggle for independence has acquired certain admirable qualities. They would not have been self-evident throughout the observing community at the time when the struggle was being conducted. 'Terrorists' become respectable in history as their activities recede in the memory, and as they succeed to power in the countries in which they have fought for independence. It is possible for Menachem Begin, as the leader of Irgum Zvai Leumi, to argue the legitimacy of 'murdering' British soldiers at the end of the mandate and to protest as Prime Minister against the murder by Palestinian terrorists of Israeli citizens.

The broadcasting organisation which is required to report on the activities within its own State of these 'freedom fighters' or 'terrorists' – the name depending on the point of view – is faced with very special problems. The people concerned are expressing dissent in an extreme form. The broadcaster must ask himself whether a voice should be given to the ideas which underlie the physical expressions of dissent. The State authorities will undoubtedly say that to give such expression to physical dissent is to join in the attack on civil order in society. And yet the maintenance of civil order will depend on an understanding of the reasons for revolt – and presumably on a rejection of those reasons. One argument suggests that to give air time to the rebels is to make available to them the instrument of publicity and recognition. The contrary argument suggests that the presentation of their case will in itself reveal the inadequacies of their argument. The broadcaster is caught in an impossible dilemma. I have identified one limitation only which ought to be applied in this difficult situation. The BBC is a corporate citizen of the United Kingdom. It is not looking in an abstract way at the troubles of some other country and reporting them to the home audience. If it were, it would follow without question the canon of independent objective and detached journalism. But in reporting in one's own country on the internecine quarrels of one's own fellow citizens there must at least be a difference in manner. There has to be an awareness of the emotional response among the audience, some of whom will be suffering, directly or indirectly, from the actions of the rebels. It is necessary to behave in one's own community in a way which respects the feelings of others. The broadcasting reporter has to accept this as an important limitation on his freedom of action. It is not a limitation on the *scope* of his reporting. He cannot expect, as a human being, to be wholly detached. But, as a reporter, he must still be objective. He has to present his report in terms which will enlist the interest and understanding of the audience rather than its rejection of his explanation of the ideas which he is seeking to report.

But dissent is not simply a phenomenon of politics. It can appear in the artistic field, when issues of taste arise. There will be disagreement about what is acceptable, both between broadcasters and among their audiences. Thus, when BBC Television decides that Dennis Potter's play *Brimstone and Treacle* should not be shown on the ground that some of the scenes in it will disgust some of the viewers beyond tolerance, the decision is one which defines the limit of dissent by a dramatist from the generally accepted canon of taste. The decision went in favour of *The Return of Roger Casement's Bones to Dublin* – a play by Rudkin which dealt very openly with the matter of Casement's homosexuality. I heard it myself before it was due to be broadcast and judged that it could be broadcast, as proposed, on Radio 3. It would not have been acceptable on Radio 4, and if it had been capable of visual presentation, it would have been wholly unacceptable in either of the BBC's Television Services. On another occasion, when it was suggested that Hochhuth's play *The Soldiers* might be broadcast by the BBC, I went myself to see the play in the theatre because it seemed to me that it raised the issue of how far, even in a dramatic presentation, the BBC could stretch the limits of probable truth. I thought, after seeing the play, that the probability of the truth of its central accusation – that Churchill arranged for the assassination of Sikorski – was so small that the BBC's reputation for truth-telling would be damaged by presenting even a play on this thesis. Had the question arisen as a practical issue, I should have decided against a BBC production.

Questions of the limits of tolerance in matters of taste frequently arose during the so-called 'satirical' programmes of the 1960s. The attribution to Sir Wavell Wakefield (as he then was) of participation in the singing of a particularly bawdy song which was parodied in *That Was the Week* . . . seemed to me to go beyond the justifiable limits. And there was a further objection. The joke, bad as it was, was understandable only to those who knew the original words, and, in effect, the authors were inviting those in the secret to enjoy a joke at the expense of those who were not, while suggesting quite clearly that something distasteful was being proposed. In another case, in one of the programmes in the series *Not So Much a Programme* . . ., there was a satirical sketch on Catholic attitudes to birth control, as demonstrated by the visit of a parish priest in Liverpool to a mother with a very large family indeed. At that time I was the Secretary, and responsible for drafting answers to protests against such sketches. As a Catholic, it seemed to me that the subject was legitimate for satire, but that the manner of its presentation was unacceptable because it depended on a false representation of Catholic doctrine and practice. The suggestion was that priests encouraged the production of large families regardless of other considerations, and were interested only in the 'rights' of the husband. I concluded that satire, to be effective, must be based on an essential truth, even though that truth may be exaggerated. On that account I argued that the sketch, depending, as it did, on untruth, was offensive because it was not good satire. On the whole, it is bad programmes which offend. Good programmes on difficult themes avoid offence because of their sheer quality.

When the question arises of how far the limits of tolerance in the audience can be stretched by what might be regarded in some quarters as a departure from good taste, the first consideration must be the seriousness and honesty of intention of those proposing the programme or the episode. If there is good reason to think that they are honest, and if the subject justifies the risk, then practical considerations of timing and prior warning have to be considered. The audience should not be taken unawares by material which, given the choice, it would positively have wished to avoid. This is not simply a matter of viewers or listeners turning away from a subject which perhaps they ought to be brought to consider. It is a question of whether they would have made an active choice not to view or to listen and they ought not to be deprived of that choice.

Whether the discussion is about dissenting views about morals, politics or taste, there will always be a case for risking some degree of offence in the audience. The basic issues are the importance of the subject matter and the preservation of the right of the audience to choose, with knowledge, whether they wish to be present when the broadcasters offer what may stretch their tolerance to its very limits. The question for those who plan broadcasting when such tests of audience tolerance are being proposed is 'Who will be viewing or listening?'. In the end, the matter of broadcasting dissent comes down to the issue of respect for the audience by the broadcaster.

Whenever I have considered this subject of the liberty to be given to dissent on the air I have returned again and again to the advice given by Burke in his letter to the three Sheriffs of Bristol in 1777. I have not found a better expression of the treatment of dissenting views. 'The extreme of liberty', he says, 'obtains nowhere, nor ought to obtain anywhere, because extremes ... are destructive both to virtue and enjoyment. Liberty, too, must be limited in order to be possessed. The degree of restraint it is impossible in any case to settle precisely. But it ought to be the constant aim of every wise public council to find out, by cautious experiments and rational, cool endeavours, with how little – not how much – of this restraint the community can subsist. For liberty is a good to be improved and not an evil to be lessened. It is not only a private blessing of the first order, but a vital spring and energy of the state itself which has just so much life and vigour as there is liberty in it.' That seems to me to represent a proper philosophy for the BBC in considering the matter of how much to reflect dissenting views.

CHAPTER X
The Delegated Ideology

IN THE CHAPTERS describing the constitutional authority of the the Governors of the BBC I emphasized their unique quality as source of editorial authority. In the chapters describing the ideological choices facing them, moral and political, I said it was impossible for them to choose any particular stance as their own, and I suggested that tolerance of the whole range of ideas must be their preoccupation. It must be clear that their tolerance cannot be selective. But this abstention from commitment on the part of the Board of Governors has to be seen alongside the facts of programme production. There are two aspects to their problem when they contemplate these facts. First, there is the sheer volume of production. And second, there is the inescapable recognition that each programme is the particular responsibility of a producer whose work cannot, in the last resort, be controlled in detail. It can be guided only by the general philosophy of the organisation, and by the producer's recognition of that philosophy.

When Lord Normanbrook spoke in 1965 about the output of the BBC he noted that the schedules offered some 150 hours a week on television on two channels and nearly 400 hours a week on radio on four channels. The hours of television have since expanded marginally, and in radio the whole dimension of local broadcasting has developed. Yet even in his day, without these additional programmes, Lord Normanbrook said quite firmly that 'no Board of Governors, whole time or part time, could possibly control this vast output in detail in the sense of approving all programmes in advance before they were broadcast'. Some five years later I pointed out myself that in a single year the BBC broadcasts some 6,500 hours of television and 23,000 hours of radio on national networks alone. I added that there were less than 9,000 hours in a year in any man's life, including the nights. I was reinforcing Lord Normanbrook's conclusion that it was impossible for one man to supervise the whole of the BBC's output in detail. Indeed, it would be impossible for several men to carry out such supervision and still do the other things which are necessary to run a broadcasting organisation. It follows, from the sheer volume of output, that management of its content has to be selective, and the argument put forward by the BBC since the war has always been that selection for special scrutiny should take place as the result of reference from the producer to his superior of points about which he was in doubt. The skill of the producer lay in his capacity to produce programmes, and also to identify the points at which further consideration was necessary. The problem of control is to reconcile this system of 'reference upwards' with the ideological considerations which must govern the outlook of the Governors of the BBC when they consider the programme output.

The importance of the individual producer in this task of reconciliation has long been recognized. Sir William Haley spoke of a 'duty laid upon everyone in the Corporation'. The responsibility of the BBC to itself and to the public had been built into a tradition which was 'not one man's will but the obligation laid upon a thousand'. Sir William stressed the diffusion of responsibility as something which should be encouraged as a strength and a safeguard.

Haley's successor but one, Sir Hugh Greene, carried the philosophy a stage further in his address in Rome on 'The Conscience of the Programme Director' (February 1965). He had said that the freedom of producers was not 'total licence'. Lines had to be drawn. 'But', he added, 'in an operation as diverse in its output as broadcasting the only sure way of exercising control is to proceed by persuasion and not by written directives; by encouraging the programme staff immediately responsible to apply their judgement to particular problems, within a framework of general guidance arising from the continuing discussion of individual programmes by themselves, by their seniors – and, when necessary, by the Board of Governors. In Sir Hugh's view there was 'nothing to be achieved by coercion or censorship, whether from inside the Corporation or from outside – nothing, that is, except the frustration of their ideas in an atmosphere of freedom'. This is still the definitive statement of the BBC's current philosophy of creative responsibility resting on confidence in the conscience of the producer. The effectiveness with which that philosophy is applied in practice is the foundation on which the Board of Governors can have confidence that its own role of fostering tolerance can be reflected in the production of programmes without the risk of undue abuse or error.

Lord Normanbrook, speaking later in the same year about the functions of the Governors, suggested that codes written in advance in order to regulate what was permissible and what was not would be found, in practice, to be of very limited value. 'When all the necessary exceptions and qualifications have been included', he said, 'they tend to end up as general expressions of intent which are of little practical value as guides to action. They tend also to concentrate attention more on the letter than on the spirit of the advice which they are designed to convey.' He went on to emphasize that the nature of the broadcasting operation was such that a large measure of discretion must inevitably be left with individual producers and with those exercising immediate supervision over their work. 'What can be done', he noted, 'is to encourage producers to refer upwards for guidance in any case of doubt: to reinforce that encouragement by adverse comment and criticism when mistakes are made: and to ensure that heads of output departments and the controllers above them are vigilant in passing guidance downwards, as and when it is required, as well as encouraging those below them to refer upwards for advice.' And at this point Lord Normanbrook came to a conclusion of crucial importance to the manner in which editorial control is exercised within the BBC: 'This process is essentially one of editorial control by *retrospective* review [my italics]. It is a constant flow of comment and criticism, praise and blame, which goes on continuously at all levels within the Corporation. This constant exchange of views and ideas is, through its continuity, designed to develop among producers a sense of what is right. Programme staff are required to apply their own judgement to particular problems, but they do so within a framework of general guidance arising from the continuing discussion of individual programmes by themselves and by their seniors up to and including the Board of Governors itself.' Lord Normanbrook's use of Sir Hugh Greene's own words must have been quite deliberate.

Nearly ten years later, Sir Michael Swann, speaking also as Chairman of the BBC, took the matter a little further. He spoke of the way in which the Director-General from time to time sought the view of the Board, or of the Chairman, on some difficult programme matter, and of how the Board itself, at its meetings, discussed programmes already broadcast, and sometimes those which might still be to come. Having first seen this as 'a courtesy exchange getting nowhere in particular', he had come to the conclusion that it was an effective means of ensuring that the senior management of the BBC had a reasonable idea of the thinking of the Board. He had been encouraged to see this thinking 'emerge and spread down the line, not very often as a clear-cut request, not necessarily even as an opinion attributed to the Board, perhaps, indeed, unconsciously, but nonetheless emerging'. His view was that in an organisation like the BBC this was 'the only way it can happen'. The process made it possible for the Board to 'express an attitude and help to create a climate of opinion in broad matters of programme policy'.

My own view of the matter is set out in a lecture which I gave in March 1975. I noted that the internal discussion of programmes which had been the background to the comments made by Lord Normanbrook and Sir Michael Swann had become more formalized in recent years, but I believed that its effect remained broadly the same. 'A climate is deliberately created, and it is a critical climate. And out of all this discussion, the conclusions of which are widely communicated, there is slowly developing a series of documents which tend to be described outside the BBC as codes but which are, in fact, the synthesis of experience collected as guidance for the future, but not as instructions for the future'. The essential base for this programme philosophy is the theory of reference upwards, which enables the necessary public positions of the Governors to be reconciled with the fact of the individual programme decisions which have to be reached by programme editors and producers operating on their own.

The final endorsement of this theory of broadcasting control, running from the public body represented by the Governors to the individual producer, is contained in the conclusions of the Annan Report (Chapter 9, paragraph 17). After full consideration of this issue – I believe for the first time by a Committee – they concluded that on this matter there should be 'no ambiguity'. 'This procedure', they say, 'does more than resolve possible conflicts. It is the way in which the BBC evolves programme policies and the way in which those with longer experience guide those in the formative stages of their careers.' The Committee noted that the problems could be artistic or political. The purpose of reference upwards was not simply to give warning of controversy, nor to share problems, but to bring additional experience to bear on specific issues and to apply case law with the resulting working principles which could apply to similar problems in the future. 'The method of reference upwards permits producers to be free to decide for themselves on whether to take further advice, and at the same time to be publicly fully accountable for the decisions they take for themselves. Everything depends on the honest acceptance by producers of the obligations of the system and on the communication of particular decisions throughout the organisation.' The Annan Committee concluded that 'there should be a chain of confidence rather than a chain of command between the Director-General and the individual producers'. That is the fundamental philosophy on which the system rests. It is also the basic requirement on which the theory of control by the Governors must depend.

There are several reinforcements for the system. One of them is the now very complete system of formal programme review conducted every week by the senior programme staff of the Television and Radio Services, under the chairmanship of the Director of Programmes, frequently in the presence of the Managing Director. These discussions, which are conducted in an uninhibited fashion between professionals sharing the same experience, and never ready to let slip what ought to be criticized or to fail to notice what ought to be praised, began to take shape in the Television Service in 1964. The process was later adopted in Radio in its full formality in 1970. At these meetings it has proved possible to communicate effectively, though not always with attribution, significant views expressed by Governors in the Board, during its regular sessions with the Managing Directors and Directors of Programmes in Radio and Television. Sir Michael Swann noted that although these discussions in the Board rarely led to a clear-cut request 'not to repeat this, not to make any more in the same idiom as that, or to encourage the other', they did constitute an effective means of conveying the Board's general wishes.

As always in the BBC, news and current affairs programmes have been the subject of special attention. Every since the first creation, in 1958, of the post of Director of News and Current Affairs, there has been a regular weekly meeting of the senior news and current affairs staff throughout the BBC to discuss both practical day-to-day questions and issues of journalistic principle. That there was more of the former than of the latter simply reflected the way in which journalism operates. This regular discussion continued through the period when the 'Director' became 'Editor' of News and Current Affairs, and has been maintained under the restored Directorate. It is an essential part of the working of editorial control and responsibility in an operation which has no galleys and no page proofs for the senior editor to approve before publication. As in every other phase of programme production, the responsibility lies with the producer or editor handling the programme, and depends absolutely, in the last resort, on his capacity to recognize a problem and his readiness to seek advice about it. The system depends also on an awareness of the kind of problem which requires advice to be sought. It is easy enough, when the recorded minutes of such discussions – necessarily telescoped – occasionally become public property through some breach of confidentiality, for critics to poke fun at the workings of an editorial bureaucracy. But bureaucracy, like news, needs to be seen in its context, and in broadcasting that context is one in which public accountability is impossible without a careful recording of events and the meticulous analysis of arguments. For those tasks record-keeping bureaucracies are essential. They are, indeed, the indispensable accompaniment of accountability.

Internal and professional discussion within the BBC is accompanied by a constant stream of public comment. Some of it arises in the course of Parliamentary debate and question. No member of the BBC's programme staff can afford to be ignorant of what has been said in Parliament about his programme activities. Whether or not what is said is true and justified, the salutary effect is to produce a precautionary vigilance. It is true that ill-founded criticism can produce a vigorous resentment which can usually legitimately be seen as a healthy independence, but can turn into a mood which rejects even justifiable criticism if it comes from a source which has been unreasonable in the past. There is a responsibility on public critics of broadcasting to remember that excess in what they say reduces the authority of external criticism.

Professionals are only too ready to discount criticism on the
ground that it is ill-informed.

Press criticism is certainly read within the BBC, but it has
been a matter of regret to me and to others that only a few of
the broadcasting press corps have earned the respect of the
professional broadcasters over the years. This has been partly
because the popular press has tended to be preoccupied with
the more ephemeral aspects of programmes, and few of the
writers on broadcasting have managed, until recent years, to
acquire a sufficient knowledge of the political and logistic
background of broadcasting policy to make effective criticism
possible. There have been notable exceptions; their efforts
have been welcomed by the broadcasters. I do not think that it
can reasonably be said that the journalist genuinely in search of
information about broadcasting has been denied the means to
inform himself. Now that the number of serious studies of
broadcasting policy and programmes is becoming significant,
the standard of journalistic comment on broadcasting matters
seems to be improving, and the time could be coming when
press comment will be seen by broadcasting professionals not
as something which can be accepted if it is approving and
rejected if it is not, but as a contribution to the continuous
discussion of values and standards which is essential if the
responsibilities of the Governors in guiding the programme
course of the BBC is to be adequately reflected in the responses
of the programme staff.

Correspondence from the audience is also part of the
atmosphere within which the professional broadcaster works.
The volume is immense – some 500,000 letters a year – but
much of it is concerned with simple enquiries or comments on
points of fact. A relatively small proportion is about standards,
and much of that, as the Annan Committee found, is on
predictable lines, directed against what is called 'bad language'
or disapproved behaviour. From time to time, however,
correspondence will generate a furious debate about some
genuinely important issue, as it did about the bounds of

tolerance at the time of the satirical programmes in the 1960s. In the end that correspondence was part of the mechanism which enabled the BBC to set its long term course. But the interesting fact was that all of what was said in letters from the public had already been said much earlier in discussions among the professionals and in the Board. And that, I believe, is proof that the Board is a sufficient instrument for its task. It is not formally representative, but in fact, it acts in a representative way.

Finally, in the relationship between the Board, with its imposed responsibilities, and the production staff, who have to reflect an awareness of those responsibilities, history has a significant part. Broadcasting is a very public act, and produces strong reactions when anything new is attempted. On such occasions the BBC is bound to make some public statement about its attitude to the new development. Every such proclamation dictates to the BBC a little more the nature of any future pronouncement on a related subject. That is good reason for the BBC to avoid making too many such pronouncements. They all become part of the reciprocal process, operating between the producers and the audience, which establishes the standards of tolerance within which the BBC has to operate. The wider those standards can be kept, the richer will be the programme service. And discretion in testing the tolerance of the public is the best way of avoiding the drawing of lines in places which may well seem later to be embarrassingly restrictive. In the last resort, the decision on how far to test the tolerance of the public at any given moment rests with the producer in the studio. If, in making his decisions, he remembers the accountability of the Board to the public, he will be ensuring that the constitutional structure which gives him the means within which to exercise his professional skill is working properly, permitting and encouraging the production of programmes which will interest the public, and of a programme service which will be in the public interest.

Part Three

Part Three

CHAPTER XI
Wavelengths

THE FIRST PHASE in any consideration of a broadcasting development must be an examination of the frequency picture. What wavelengths are available to serve what purposes, and what coverage will be achieved if they are deployed in the different possible ways? The basic elements in the problem are simple. Before any radio transmission can take place a frequency has to be chosen to carry it. Once a frequency is in use for a given transmission the fact of that transmission precludes the use of that same frequency for any other transmission within interference range. The extent to which that exclusion holds good depends on, for example, the strength of the signal, the direction in which it is propagated, and the propagation characteristics of the frequency itself – in other words, whether, by reflection, absorption, or obstruction, the range of the transmission is extended or curtailed. Because of this exclusive character of the use of frequencies the radio spectrum is divided up by agreement, necessarily international, into bands which are devoted to specific purposes. Within each of those bands the frequencies it contains may be used for the purposes prescribed up to the levels of mutual interference which are accepted as tolerable by the various users.

About 50 per cent of the frequency spectrum up to 1000 MHz is allocated internationally to broadcasting. That is a very high proportion, and it has to be conceded that broadcasting is an expensive user of frequency space. Telephone traffic, for example, is incomparably more economical – and therefore potentially more profitable – than broadcasting as a user of frequency space. The restraints on the availability of frequencies for broadcasting use are, therefore, real and inevitable. This, in turn, leads to the conclusion that whatever frequencies are available for broadcasting should be used with the greatest certainty possible about priorities. Mistakes in the allocation of priorities constitute an absolute waste, and they are virtually irreversible, because once frequencies have been allocated to a particular use, and once the users have equipped themselves for that purpose, the inertia which is built up is formidable indeed. That is why, for instance, it is proving immensely difficult in Britain to clear for broadcast use that part of the VHF Band II, internationally allocated to radio broadcasting, but in practice used in Britain for the mobile services – fire, ambulance, police, taxis, and so on.

During my time as Director-General there arose three major problems which rested on decisions about the allocation of frequencies. They were the problem of the fourth network for television, which occupied so much of the time of the Annan Committee; the disposition of frequencies for local radio, both BBC and commercial; and the re-arrangement of the frequencies allocated to national radio coverage which was decided on during the last part of my eight and a half years of office. By the end of my time the question of satellite channels had begun to be discussed, and seemed likely to produce major policy problems in the late 1980s. The question of the fourth network aroused the most public controversy and offers the most striking illustration of the key importance of decisions on wavelength allocation in any consideration of broadcasting policy.

The frequencies available in Britain for television broadcasting are, respectively, the very high frequency channels – VHF – in what are known as Bands I and III of the spectrum, and the ultra high frequency channels – UHF – which are grouped in Bands IV and V. It can generally be said that the higher the frequency the shorter the range of the signal for a given power, unless some form of reflection of the signal occurs. By 'reflection' I mean the phenomenon of ionospheric reflection in which ionized layers in the upper atmosphere reflect certain radio frequencies. Such reflections occur as potentially useful phenomena in the medium waveband, where night-time transmission is very considerably enhanced by the reflected sky wave. The disadvantage is that the extended transmission range also means more extensive interference with the signals of others using the same channel. It is these reflections which enable short wave transmission to cover such very long distances and such very large areas. But when we come to the VHF channels, and particularly to Band I, used for television, reflection of the signals, which is sporadic and unpredictable, is, in fact, a hindrance because it produces interference between signals which, according to the planning predictions, would normally be clear of each other. It is, fortunately, a comparatively rare occurrence. The risk of interference is balanced by the fact that of the bands available for television, Band I is that which, for a given power, will cover the largest area. Its penetration over uneven land surfaces is greater. Its susceptibility to physical obstruction is less.

The UHF channels in Bands IV and V are much more susceptible to surface irregularities and are, in fact, limited virtually to line of sight transmission, so that the areas covered by a given transmitter will be less than in the case of a VHF-based system. The practical consequence is that in order to cover this country with a network of UHF transmitters there have to be far more of them. The comparative figures for Britain, as worked out in practice, have been for Band I, twelve main and ninety-five relay transmitters, and for Bands IV and V, something like fifty main, and anything up to 800 relay transmitters of varying powers.

Once the physical basis of the transmission network has been explored in terms of coverage for individual transmitters, the siting of such transmitters, the inter-connection between them, and the filling-in of the holes left by the basic pattern represent a formidable investment, both of frequencies and capital. The position in Britain is that the physical base exists for three UHF networks with identical conformation, and that room is available for a fourth network which follows the same conformation and does not call for further exploration. Anybody who secures the use of such a network has acquired a public asset of inestimable value.

The precise nature of the asset calls for a little elaboration. First there is the question of working out frequency distribution. This requires some extremely intricate planning. There are available to Britain some forty-four UHF channels. According to the most economical plan these have to be used in groups of four – the four networks. Each one of these groups will have to be used about seventy times over in order to produce four networks with virtually national coverage. The effective powers of the transmitters involved will range from a maximum of 1000 kW to a minimum of 10 W. Each type of transmitter involves a different design of equipment, sometimes entering into the range of completely new technologies. The plan itself constitutes a formidable investment of ingenuity. There is also a formidable investment of straight-forward geographical knowledge. The coverage of the country has to combine the choice of sites which are suitable from a technical point of view, and which also cover the areas of population. Technically, because of the line-of-sight characteristic of UHF transmission, the highest points must normally be used and above all those which give access to large groups of population. Ben Nevis is not useful in this sense. The ideal, for example, is the top of The Wrekin because it is high, in a relatively unobstructed area, and with fairly large populations accessible to it. But in building a station on The Wrekin there must be a risk of damaging a feature of great natural beauty and there will be objections from those who have the amenity of the countryside at heart, and quite reasonably so. The BBC needed about five years to secure final permission for the Wrekin site, which was one of several investigated in the same area.

The building finally erected was below the crest, except for a part of the mast, so that there should be the minimum interference with the visual beauty of the skyline, and yet the maximum exploitation of the height of the geographical feature itself. The costs, of course, were high because it was necessary to dig into the hillside in order to conceal the buildings. As soon as the BBC secured permission to operate with a mast on this site a number of other birds settled in the branches – because everybody operating a communication system is looking for the same kind of transmission facility.[1] The Wrekin transmitter covers the population concentrations of Shrewsbury, Bridgnorth, Oswestry, Whitchurch, Market Drayton, Telford, Wellington – a total of 165,000 people, none of whom could receive adequate signals in any other way.

The investment of time, patience and planning effort in the establishment of the physical base is very great, but justifiable in that the result provides, not merely for one network but, for four, because each of the sites identified takes all the four channels which make up the potential four UHF networks for the country. The investment in the transmission potentiality of the fourth UHF network with access to over 90% of the population is already formidable. The asset is priceless. But in any investment, a major factor is time. How long is it before the investment becomes effective and yields a total return? It is worth looking back for a moment at the history of the construction of television networks in Britain, and then at how long it might take to install the fourth UHF network.

Effectively the construction of the national transmission

[1]Mast shared by:
  Automobile Association
  Ministry of Defence
  Radio Society of Great Britain
  Salop County Council Fire Brigade
  Severn/Trent Water Authority
  West Mercia Police Authority
  West Midlands Gas Board
  Salop County Council Roads & Bridges Department

system began only with the reopening of the Alexandra Palace transmitter in June 1946. The network which is now BBC-1 took about fourteen years to reach its maximum coverage. Beginning in June 1946 with nearly 25% of the population (11½ millions) who could be reached from Alexandra Palace, the network took in, by December 1952, some 81% of the population of the United Kingdom, served by Sutton Coldfield (7 millions); Home Moss (13 millions); Kirk o'Shotts (4 millions); and Wenvoe (4½ millions). From 1952 until late 1957 there was a programme of installation of medium power stations – seven in all – which brought the total coverage to 97% of the population. Then, from 1957 until 1970, a further 2.5% of the population, making a total of 99.5%, were brought within range of the 405-line transmissions by the addition of no less than ninety-five low power relay stations.

The striking facts in this story are the length of time which it takes to achieve virtually saturation coverage, and the very high proportion of that time and the high expenditures which are involved in taking the coverage beyond the first 80% through the last 20%. That is true of any network, whether it be VHF or UHF. The same sort of time scale would apply to the story of the IBA network on Band III, though the early stages were quicker because the political course was clearer.

When Britain entered into the UHF bands, with the authorization of BBC-2 after the Pilkington Report in 1962, the same pattern repeated itself, but rather more rapidly as soon as the pioneer network, BBC-2, had shown the way. By December 1971 the BBC-2 service, which had opened seven years earlier in April 1964, covered 90% of the population. As in the case of the earlier two VHF networks, it was a question of finding new sites for many of the transmitters, because the UHF transmitters pattern produced different coverage areas from those of the VHF network. BBC-1, starting on UHF construction five and a half years later, in November 1969, had reached, within only two years, 87% coverage of the population. The advantage that the sites and transmitter accommodation had already been provided for BBC-2 as a pilot network is obvious. The IBA UHF network enjoyed the same advantages. The proposed fourth network, when constructed, will ride on the back of these three. It will proceed at the same kind of pace as the BBC-1 and IBA UHF networks. Again, the asset built up by the pioneering work of BBC-2 is tremendous. The only significant problem – and it is not to be under-rated – could be the provision of Post Office vision links between studios and transmitters.

Transmitter development is only one half of the problem. The unit of broadcast distribution is the transmitter *plus* the receiver. The speed with which a network can become effective depends substantially on receiver distribution. This proceeds at a slower pace, reflecting, as it does, a number of individual decisions in individual homes to buy, or sometimes to postpone the purchase of a new receiver. What sells a new receiver most quickly is the provision of a popular new service, or a highly attractive new facility such as colour. The figures show that by 1954, eight years after the post-war re-opening, and when only BBC transmissions were available on VHF, about 30% of the population had bought receivers. (By 1954 transmitter coverage was in excess of 77% of the population.) In 1955 ITV came on the air and those who wanted to see the service had to buy a converter or a new receiver with the capacity to receive Band III VHF. Between 1955 and 1963 – some eight years – the number of people able to receive both the BBC and ITV services, rose from just under 5% to some 76%. Those movements are really quite long drawn out, when one considers that the inducement to buy a new set was the substantial one of an entirely new service which deliberately set out to have a very popular appeal.

The same sort of pattern demonstrates itself in the field of UHF receiver distribution. The BBC-2 service which started in 1964 required the audience to buy a new receiver with a UHF capacity. By 1968, four years later, about one-third of the audience had equipped themselves to receive the new service.

In 1969, when BBC-2 and ITV began to be available through transmission in colour, the stimulus to buy the new single-standard sets – and much more, the stimulus to industry to make and sell them as a simpler product – resulted in substantial increases in sales, and by the end of 1973, nine years after the start of UHF, it was estimated that some 85% of the audience was equipped to receive all three services on UHF, of whom some 30%, or nearly 5 million homes representing some 16 million viewers, were equipped to receive colour.

The present situation (1978) is that three UHF networks – BBC-1, BBC-2 and ITV – have attained coverage which is substantially national – over 97% in terms of transmission. In terms of reception by viewers, about the same proportion of the population have suitable sets. These are figures which must be regarded as virtually national for planning purposes.

The fourth network remains unallocated[2] and unbuilt, but in every other respect it is ripe for development. The physical structure of the network has been established by the pioneering work done in site finding, frequency distribution and physical building for the first three. The distribution of receivers to the population has been achieved before the network has even started transmission. Those to whom the fourth network is allocated in the end will be in an extraordinarily privileged position.

When I originally discussed this subject in public at the Royal Institution in February 1974, I reviewed the argument put forward by Independent Television that the fourth network should be allocated to them to provide a complementary service to ITV-1. I suggested that if the new network were to be used by them to provide a mass audience service the general effects would be damaging to all the existing programme services. It could hardly be expected that a new channel of this character would have a different effect from that which had initially followed the opening of the commercial channel in 1955. True, there had been a recovery from the

[2] Now to be ITV-2 (1979).

worst effects of competition, but the danger remained. I suggested therefore that the fourth network should be devoted to serving specialist audiences. I expressed considerable doubt as to whether this target would prove commercially viable, and therefore that the network should not be placed in the hands of Independent Television. Essentially, I said, there was no case for a fourth general television network. The BBC believed there was a strong case for the allocation of a fourth network to genuinely minority viewing, or rather to specialist viewing. The specialist viewer had as much right to be treated as a normal human being, he worked and ate and slept and viewed at the same time as most other normal human beings, and would therefore view in those hours which are commonly known as 'peak' hours, because they are the hours when most people are available to view. These were the people who under the dispensation of 1974 were given a relatively raw deal. The main point in any discussion about a new television network is always what happens at peak time. I believe that the specialist audiences should have their chance to share it, for that reason I argued the case for Welsh language speakers to have access to the new network in Wales, and for the Open University to have corresponding access throughout the United Kingdom. I thought at the time that there might be other contenders, and indeed the Annan Committee made additional suggestions as to the occupation of the network.

There is one further aspect to be touched on – that of the availability of equipment among the audience. To be effective, a choice in peak hours in the normal family means the availability of two sets in the home. It is useless to provide programmes in the Welsh language if the household itself is split on whether to watch in English or in Welsh. It is useless to provide programmes for the Open University student if the rest of the family wants to watch Morecambe and Wise. The second set is an essential part of the concept. That is the investment which the minority audience must take if it wishes to enjoy its viewing in 'peak' hours. In 1974 there was already about 2½ million two-set homes out of 17 million in the country. The number was steadily growing, partly as a result of the retention by many homes of a monochrome receiver when they acquired their first colour receiver. By 1978 over 60% of the population were receiving in colour, though a high proportion of these were single-set homes depending on a rented receiver.

The issue still remains to be finally decided. But whatever decision is reached will set the future for television programme policy for decades to come. Frequency allocation decisions are virtually irreversible, partly because the audience becomes habituated to the pattern of the new service to whomsoever it may be allocated, and partly because, having equipped itself to receive a particular service on a given standard, it will be reluctant to abandon its receiving equipment thereafter. That consideration is one which substantially affected the discussion of the establishment of local broadcasting at the end of the 1960s.

Local broadcasting has been a subject of study and discussion in the BBC since the early 1950s. I remember seeing Frank Gillard, the great advocate of local broadcasting, just before he left for a visit to the United States in 1954, where he was to study the operation of small stations directed to local audiences. Some years later Frank Gillard's demonstration tapes of what could be done from local stations in Britain were part of the evidence offered by the BBC to the Pilkington Committee. When the Pilkington Committee finally recommended that the BBC should undertake a local broadcasting system the arguments about implementing the proposal related in large measure to the frequency pattern on which the system should be based. At that time the major audience in the United Kingdom was equipped to receive radio broadcasts on medium and long waves. A VHF system of three networks had been inaugurated in 1955. But some ten years after the start of broadcasting on VHF only 30% of the audience were equipped with VHF receivers, and ten years after that it was doubtful whether the figure had reached more than 40%. Of those 40%

a relatively small proportion, according to BBC surveys, appeared to make extensive use of the VHF facility on their receivers. The whole situation was complicated by the fact the original BBC calculations for the VHF network had assumed an intention of national coverage for each programme service, and the use of an outside aerial with a high efficiency receiver. In fact, the advent of the transistor radio meant that most receivers with a VHF capacity were portable, relying on an extensible rod aerial. This was theoretically insufficient to receive the VHF signals at high quality throughout the country, although in many parts it was possible to receive a perfectly adequate signal.

When the plan for local radio was being worked out, therefore, the question of whether the broadcasts were to be on medium wave or VHF raised some very difficult problems. Evidently, the receiver situation for VHF was not sufficient to encourage high hopes for a new service which was aimed at a local rather than at a national mass audience. But the situation on medium wave was apparently even more difficult. The BBC's approach to the question of further broadcasting in Britain on medium wave was conditioned by the national policy which had developed after the implementation of the Copenhagen Plan on frequency allocation in 1948. It was the same approach as had originally been devised by the BBC's Chief Engineer, Peter Eckersley, before the Second World War in order to carry the BBC's two major services – the one explicitly national, and the other capable of operating regionally. The whole system rested on the assumption of high power transmission from relatively few transmitters, each giving wide area coverage.

When it came to the question of the possible use of medium wave channels for local radio, the BBC's Copenhagen pattern of operation was not encouraging. In 1948 as one of the victorious Allied Powers, Britain had been able to secure at the conference a relatively generous allocation of frequency channels in the medium band. Moreover, most of these

channels were authorized for operation at the highest permitted power of 150 kW. For Britain at any time after Copenhagen to seek to take into use frequencies not allocated to her
under the Plan would have been equivalent to suggesting that
the case which was being made by other less-favoured
countries for revision of the allocations set out in the Plan had
some justification. That would not have been a sensible tactic
for a broadcasting power which considered itself as having
been well treated. Consequently, the British position of not
wishing to seek a revision of the Copenhagen Plan was, at the
same time, an argument against taking into use, even at low
power, frequencies which had been allocated to other countries,
even though, under Article 8 of the Plan or, alternatively,
under Article 9 of the Radio Regulations, provision was made
for such additional low power use. The BBC's position in the
early 1960s was, therefore that since medium wavelengths
were not available, local radio should operate on VHF which,
with its relatively restricted radius of transmission, was, in any
case, held to be more suitable for local coverage. But, as I have
explained, the audience was not ideally equipped to receive
VHF. Local radio would undoubtedly have gained from a
start on medium wave.

As the sixties progressed, the feeling of other countries less
well treated on the Copenhagen Plan than Britain that the Convention should be revised, became constantly more intense,
and by 1968 there was a majority among the European states
who had been signatories to the Convention, or for whom
provision had been made under it, in favour of revision. From
the moment that revision of Copenhagen became inevitable it
became more possible for Britain to consider the use of
medium wave for local broadcasting, because such a change of
front would not in any way alter the political decision already
made – that the agreement should be revised. It could still be
held to weaken the British position at the conference table,
since the more frequencies that were taken up by Britain for
local radio use, the stronger could be the argument which

other countries might advance against the relatively generous provision of channels for high-power use with which Britain had emerged from Copenhagen.

When discussion first started about local radio, the calculation had been made that the so-called 'international common frequencies', of which there were two under the Copenhagen Plan, could provide up to 8 locations in the medium wave band, operating at the maximum low power, of 2 kW, for local station purposes. But this assessment was based on the assumption that the medium wave service would be intended to provide a day and night signal, for up to 24 hours daily, throughout the stipulated coverage area. This view began to weaken as discussion progressed. It began to be argued that daytime auxiliary cover on medium wave would be a considerable asset in recruiting audiences for the intended local stations. The basic coverage could still be provided on VHF, whose coverage changes relatively little between night and day. As television increased its hold on public attention, the available local radio audience was more and more to be found in the daytime hours when television was not operating. If local stations were to be established they were more likely to find their audiences in the mornings, at midday and in the early evening, when medium wave would still be relatively effective, especially during the summer, when the interference resulting from ionospheric reflection was less.

There was a notable change in the situation when the so-called Policy Study Group, set up in 1968 during the second phase of the McKinsey enquiry into the BBC's management of resources, discovered that there were some twenty medium wave low power transmitters already installed in some of the potential local radio locations. These transmitters had been part of the long standing defence plan and had been intended to provide local service in the event of a war emergency. They were still in operating condition, and all that was needed was a frequency plan and some transfers of location in order to put them into effective local station operation. Duncan McEwan, the engineering member of the Policy Study Group, suggested that frequencies could be found by taking the international common frequencies, together with a channel in use principally at the so-called 'filler' stations which provided peripheral supplements to the main coverage of Radio 3 from Daventry. If some of these relay stations could be closed down, their frequency could be made available to local stations each operating independently, provided they were sufficiently far apart from each other for the simultaneous use of the frequency in different parts of the country not to cause mutual interference. This was the beginning of the BBC's move towards a plan for local radio based on VHF, but with a day time medium wave supplement.

The Group's studies produced a plan which showed that, with varying degrees of strain, both in financial resources and installation capacity, some fifteen local radio stations could be put into operation in between two and five years, each of them having a medium frequency. The plan, presented late in 1969 involved removing the Radio 3 'fillers', which operated on 1546 kHz – a frequency which had been allocated to Britain at Copenhagen for use at relatively high power, but had never been taken more widely into service because it was thought to be too near the end of the reception band on most receivers and therefore difficult for listeners to find. Six of the stations were to operate on the frequency of 1340 kHz which was in use as the main frequency for Northern Ireland. Additionally the supplementary West Regional frequency of 1457 kHz, used from Clevedon to support the main Start Point transmitter, would have been used for four stations. One station was to be accommodated on the international common frequency of 1484 kHz and one on the channel used by the External Services directionally towards Europe – 1295 kHz.

A further study, reporting in May 1969, on the general deployment of the BBC's frequencies, showed even more interesting conclusions. The study made the assumption that the Copenhagen revision, which by that time was a clear prospect, was unlikely to end up with the BBC having fewer frequencies than had been allocated at Copenhagen. On this basis proposals were made for medium wave allocations to 47 possible local radio stations, and this, it was argued, could be done at the same time as providing improved coverage for Radio 1 and Radio 4, and an additional frequency for the External Services to be used towards Europe. (This would restore the position of the External Services which had pre-vailed between the end of the Second World War and the surrender to domestic use of 1340 kHz after the closure, for financial reasons, of the Norden relay station in north-west Germany in 1960.) One difficult aspect of the proposals was the suggestion that the medium frequency which gave coverage for Radio 3 over the major part of England and by booster stations in certain parts of Wales and Scotland was to be redeployed. It was a proposal which created a furore in some quarters, and notably among those who listened to music during the day on car radios – many of whom seemed to be driving to and from Westminster.

This more substantial plan for 47 local radio stations, all using medium wave, assumed the use by local radio of the Radio 3 supplementary frequency, with 7 stations operating on the international common frequencies, and 12 on frequencies which would be shared with other Copenhagen Plan users. London would have had a 10 kW station. The plan was ambitious and was eventually adopted as the possible line of development in the period which was expected to follow the approval by Government of a BBC local radio development.

In the Summer of 1969 the Labour Government had given approval in principle to the development of a system of 40 local stations operating on VHF, to be financed by a licence fee increase which was to come into effect in April of 1971 – that is, *after* the last possible date for the next General Election. The medium-wave proposal continued under discussion.

When the Election was finally called and lost by Mr Wilson in June 1970 the new Conservative Government immediately made it clear that it would carry out its declared policy of introducing commercial local radio as an alternative to the BBC service. The new minister, Mr Chataway, was aware that the BBC was interested in medium wave allocations for local radio, and was fully conscious of the commercial importance of this possibility. But he was not at all convinced that the BBC should be operating in local radio at all. The question of frequency allocation rested, in any case, with the Government, and therefore, in practice, with the Minister. Intensive studies were carried out between 1970 and 1972, when the White Paper setting out the Government's proposals was finally endorsed by the House of Commons. The related frequency planning resulted in the transfer from the BBC to commercial local radio of one high-power frequency and a half-share in another. This, together with the hypothetical clearance of frequencies primarily allocated to other countries, provided the theoretical base for a 60-station commercial local radio system. In the discussion, the great issue had been whether the BBC would be left with any local radio at all. In the end Mr Chataway decided that the 20 stations already opened by mid-1970, operating at that time on VHF, should be allowed to continue, and with a medium wave daytime supplement. For the BBC that represented a considerable political success in adverse circumstance, even though the twenty stations constituted only the half-way stage in the original full national plan.

During the discussions about frequency allocation for local radio the BBC had continued to argue that the medium wave channels to be allocated to the local stations should be regarded as a useful daytime supplement rather than as the principal medium for the service. If this case had been fully accepted they could have been operated at relatively low power and the VHF channel would have been regarded as the main service throughout the day and most of all in the periods of darkness. The BBC had always hoped that the re-allocation of medium frequencies which had been envisaged in 'Broadcasting in the Seventies' would leave some room for the improvement of the national services, especially Radio 1, by the re-allocation of the frequencies which had hitherto been deployed on Radio 4. If, however, the view of the ITA about the allocation of frequencies and powers to local commercial radio were to prevail, there would be much less chance for the BBC's improvement proposals to be put into effect. The ITA argued strongly that in order to ensure the commercial success of their new local service medium wave would have to be regarded as the main service vehicle even after dark. This meant that relatively high powers would have to be used and that daytime coverage would therefore be on a quasi-regional scale. The higher powers sought by the ITA – soon to become the IBA – for their stations would mean that in many cases the received signal from the local station would be stronger than that of the BBC national service in the same area. There would, therefore, be an expensive competition for both in seeking to achieve parity of reception strengths. The BBC would certainly have had to augment its signals, especially those of Radio 1, which would be open to the main competition.

In addition the IBA was arguing for a particular allocation of frequencies which could have reduced the BBC's capacity to re-deploy the national frequencies for strengthening the national networks. Of the three frequencies available for possible local radio use that on 1546 kHz could be used at relatively high power. The disadvantages of its location at the end of the tuning scale were disregarded, in the belief that manufacturers would soon produce receivers capable of tuning easily to this frequency. The second frequency to be allocated for local radio use was 1151 kHz, formerly used at high power as the main channel for the North-East Region of the BBC in the Radio 4 network. This was a relatively clear channel, and excellent for wide area coverage both in daytime and at night. The third channel, however, 1457 kHz, although available for relatively high power, was subject to substantial interference from other stations operating on the continent of Europe –

notably from Albania, where a high power station had been installed to broadcast language services to south-eastern Europe. The interference pattern from this station was very considerable, and lessened the value of the use of 1457 kHz in Britain at night. The BBC argued that because of its lower number of potential local radio stations and its relatively higher target of area coverage under the White Paper, it should be allowed to retain 1151 kHz for its own use, either for use by local radio or for supplementary coverage of Radio 4. In the end the Minister decided that the demand for commercial viability for the IBA local stations was the overriding consideration, and this frequency was allocated to their system, with 1457 kHz being allocated to the BBC's local stations. These decisions left BBC local radio with a considerable continuing handicap, principally because of the need to use 1457 kHz, with its known shortcomings, to serve the major conurbations of London, Manchester and Birmingham.

The coverage proposals for commercial local radio introduced in Britain for the first time the idea of using directional aerials in order to enable each allocated frequency to be used in one direction at a particular location, while still giving protection to the primary frequency user elsewhere. The BBC had not favoured the use of directional aerials in its previous plans because the high-power large-area coverage arrangements for the national networks benefited most from omnidirectional aerials. Only one BBC station had made any significant use of the directional aerial – that at Start Point, which used a moderately directional aerial directing the signal principally to the area of Devon and Cornwall north of the transmitter location. But the anxiety of the commercial stations to secure access to the British market meant that they were prepared to spend considerable capital sums which would establish them with a frequency in a given population area. They could do this by putting their capital into aerial hardware. It was, in a sense, a wasteful deployment of capital from a national point of view, but looked at commercially it was obviously justified if it gave the station and its backers a place on the air.

The whole of this frequency discussion, besides providing a medium frequency basis for local radio operation, meant that the old regional radio system operated by the BBC since the 1930s had become impossible. The frequencies which were now available for the BBC for the coverage of England were sufficient only for the provision of a single service to the whole of England, since the same frequencies had to be used synchronously radiating the same programme at different locations in order to secure a total coverage of the country. The five frequencies previously serving England had been reduced to three – 692 kHz, 908 kHz and 1052 kHz. This was partly the result of the transfers to commercial local radio, but also, in part, of the transfer proposed in 'Broadcasting in the Seventies' of one frequency to the External Services for use towards Europe – a promise which could hardly be withdrawn.

What had begun as a BBC idea which would have enabled its own local radio system to be more effective in reaching its audience and establishing itself as a new element in the BBC's total broadcasting service had become the subject of an intense political debate about the viability of commercial radio. There was no question in the commercial advertisers' view that the only way to reach a satisfactory audience on radio was to broadcast on medium wave – hence the force of the arguments they addressed to the Government. But beyond these immediate consequences the whole issue of regional radio – or even area radio – for England had been finally settled in a way which precluded it ever being restored.

It is interesting to recollect that one of the elements in the proposals put forward by the Policy Study Group in 1969 had been a proposal for area broadcasting on medium wave in England which would have been adopted, had the BBC not been allowed to go ahead with its local radio system, and if commercial radio had been authorized by the Conservative government whose election had been predicated for the early

1970s. Whether the BBC would have ever been allowed by the Government to set up such a system of area medium wave broadcasting in England it is impossible to say. But technically the plans had been laid against that possibility.

Once this new frequency pattern had been established, and the resulting programme pattern firmly fixed, it was almost inevitable that the question of greater independence of programme planning for the national regions should arise. If there was to be no local radio operated by the BBC in either Wales, Northern Ireland or in Scotland, then the BBC was certain to be faced with the question of separatist broadcasting sentiment. The Government plan, as devised in 1972, specifically excluded the BBC from local radio operation in any of the three nations, while giving the opportunity to commercial radio. When I was asked, soon after the approval of the Act setting up local commercial radio, what opinion I could give about its likely success, I said that if I were an applicant for a commercial licence, I should look to one of the areas where the BBC was prevented from operating, and for preference I should choose the station in Glasgow, making sure that the transmission could be heard in Edinburgh. In that way I would be absolutely certain that I could compete for the Lowland audience with BBC Radio Scotland and tap a very substantial market without much fear of direct programme competition, since BBC Radio Scotland had to fulfil a multiple series of duties – first to the Glasgow metropolitan audience, then to the Lowlands in general, then to the Borders, then to Buchan, to the Highlands and Islands and to the Orkneys and Shetlands. It was an impossible brief, and it remains so.

In the light of commercial local radio developments the radio systems in the national regions had to be considered as a new and intensifying problem. In Wales there was the question of language; in Northern Ireland there was the acute question of local politics; and in Scotland there was the plain fact of a developing sense of national identity, together with the unsatisfactoriness of the task given to Radio Scotland of seeking to serve multiple audiences within a limited possibility of opting out from the United Kingdom version of Radio 4.

When, therefore, the prospect of re-negotiating frequency allocations became an immediate reality in 1973 I discussed with the then Director of Engineering, James Redmond, how we could better satisfy the national aspirations in each of the three smaller nations of the United Kingdom. The old philosophy had been that the long wave should be used, as in most European countries, for popular entertainment, on the ground that programmes in this category had no local character and therefore should be distributed throughout the country on a single transmission and on a single frequency. I thought that this approach to frequency use was now obsolete so far as Britain was concerned. If we were to have increasing opting-out at the level of the constituent nations of the United Kingdom this could most appropriately be done on medium wave. But if the Radio 4 network, which at that time consisted of a series of medium wave transmitters all linked for most of the day, were to be broken up for longer periods than had been the practice for the last 40 years, then the capacity of the BBC to give a coherent news and information service to the whole of the United Kingdom would be very seriously affected. I thought that the time had now come for the BBC to use its one long wave allocation for the purpose of its basic United Kingdom news and information service. This service would always include a certain amount of middle-of-the-road entertainment, both musical and spoken work, but its central characteristic would continue to be that of giving news and information. If the long wave were used for this purpose then the medium wave channels which had been allocated to Scotland, Wales and Northern Ireland, could be far more extensively used to carry programmes of local origination, since they would no longer have the obligation to carry for great parts of the day the basic Radio 4 service, which up till that time had been the main United Kingdom information and news medium in radio.

The BBC's engineers studied the potential alternative uses of the frequencies which we thought might still be allocated to the United Kingdom after Geneva, and came forward with the plan which provided for the pattern I had suggested. In addition, it seemed possible that as a result of the change from a Radio 4 United Kingdom network made up of a number of medium wave transmissions to a long-wave service we could also re-deploy medium wave channels in order to reinforce the relatively unsatisfactory transmissions of Radio 1, carried since 1967 on one channel throughout the United Kingdom, but not properly audible to all the audiences who should have received it. We could also provide a medium wave network, carried on two channels throughout the United Kingdom, to replace the long wave transmission of middle-of-the-road light entertainment, together with a certain element of news and information – the old Radio 2.

Such a major switch of wavelengths was bound to provoke a great deal of public criticism when it happened. Audiences become deeply habituated to finding their programmes at particular spots on the dial, and they find it extraordinarily difficult to adjust themselves to the idea that they may have to tune in order to find the station. This, indeed, had been one of the major difficulties in introducing radio audiences to the concept of VHF, since these channels depended on a minor amount of searching by the listeners, because the frequency carrying a particular service differs in different parts of the country so that markings on the tuning face of the set are hard to devise. There had always been a difficulty in persuading the audience to look for the transmissions on the VHF band. We were now about to introduce temporary uncertainty to the medium wave band, though there would be stability over the long term. We knew how resistant the audience might be, since we had changed certain programme arrangements at the time of 'Broadcasting in the Seventies' so that programmes which had formerly appeared on medium or long wave were available only on VHF at certain times of the day. In 1967 we had discovered, when we split the medium wave and long wave which had formerly carried the old Light Programme so as to form Radio 1 on medium wave and Radio 2 on long wave and VHF, that some listeners were quite unaware that they had a long wave facility on their receivers. Some of those who did know were unable to use it because they had never tuned to that channel, and the connections within the receivers had become so corroded that they would no longer operate. When we embarked finally on the plan to switch the frequencies on the massive scale which was implied in the proposals I had made, so as to give Scotland, Wales and Northern Ireland greater programming freedom, we knew that we would be in for trouble.

I could have wished, when making these proposals, that the prospects of changes in the programme schedules of the most deeply affected network – Radio 4 – would have been held to a minimum. If people were going to find their old tuning habits changed, they would at least want to have the maximum stability of expectation in the programmes which they expected to find, and would be seeking, on the new wavelengths. Instead, there were wholesale changes in 1977, when I did not feel in a position (because of my impending retirement) to intervene, in the pattern of programmes at those times of the day and when the majority of audiences tended to listen. I cannot help but feel that this will prove, in retrospect, to have been a major disservice to the audience which would have to grapple with the results of the wavelength changes after November 1978 – the date of implementation of the Geneva frequency plan.

The principal advantage of the new disposition of wavelengths was that the basic service of information to all United Kingdom listeners could be maintained on the long-wave channel, in its supplemented form, while the medium-wave channels in Scotland, Wales and Northern Ireland which had hitherto had to carry the dual responsibility of carrying this service for most of the day while seeking to satisfy for much shorter periods of the day the regional interests of listeners in each of the nations, could now concentrate for the whole day on their regional interest, being free from the criticism that their fulfilment of this task was depriving others of access to the programmes available at the same time to other United Kingdom listeners. The benefit in Wales was twofold, in that the English speaking audience in Wales could enjoy its own national service as a fully free choice against that offered to United Kingdom listeners, while the Radio 4 VHF network in Wales could carry Welsh language programmes without depriving English speakers either of programmes of Welsh interest or of the United Kingdom service. Similar considerations applied in Northern Ireland and Scotland, though without the same intensity of interest in the language issue. And to have, as an incidental gain, a formidable improvement in the reception of Radio 1 throughout the United Kingdom by day and by night, was a major bonus.

All these discussions about the allocation of wavelengths, both for local radio and for the redistribution of national channels in 1978, had illustrated very clearly one fact about the habits of the British listening audience – their dedicated resistance to the concept that VHF transmission could be regarded as a main service rather than simply as an auxiliary to the medium and long wave network. I once said that the British audience for broadcasting was the greatest collective connoisseur of the obsolete in the world, and I believe that characteristic constitutes one of our greatest handicaps in maximizing the use of our frequencies in Britain. When the plan had been brought forward in the 1950s for the duplication of the medium wave and long wave networks on VHF, it was thought that the audience would be seduced by the better quality of frequency modulation transmission into buying receivers capable of accepting the new signals, and that they might gradually come to abandon their old amplitude modulation receivers. The facts were quite otherwise. It became quite evident that unless a new service was being provided people would not buy receivers with substantially new characteristics. They would stick to their old ones for far longer than the manufacturers had estimated their useful life.

Furthermore, the plan for VHF duplication had envisaged only three national networks, corresponding to the post-war Haley plan of Home, Light and Third, each having either a long wave or a medium wave channel carrying it in each part of the country. When the challenge of the ship-borne-pop-music commercial 'pirates' in the late 1960s resulted in the Government's request to the BBC to initiate Radio 1 it could be done only on medium wave – and at that unsatisfactorily on one frequency. There was no VHF national network possibility. It would have been a feasible decision at that time to have decided to start Radio 1 on VHF only, separating the channels on one of the networks, and to hope that the young audience, prepared to spend money, would buy VHF receivers to patronize the new service. But this was politically unacceptable. There was the fear that the attraction of the pirates would have continued, since they would have been operating on medium wave to a market already supplied with receivers.

Further evidence of the resistance of the audience to reception on VHF alone came when 'Broadcasting in the Seventies' put forward a proposal that the medium wave channel should be taken away from Radio 3 and listeners should be asked to use VHF only. A considerable argument in favour of this course, was that the quality of listening was much higher, and one might have supposed that for music enthusiasts this would have been a considerable attraction. Further, stereo listening could be provided only on the VHF channels and not on medium wave. That too should have attracted the music lovers. But these arguments were not sufficient to prevent a major protest, largely coming from people who claimed to listen to music on medium wave in their cars. It was a fact that the strength of the national VHF signals and the aerial characteristics of reception in cars could not guarantee continuously good reception on car radios, and there was some force in this argument. Again, when the audience for cricket commentaries was regularly offered the Test Matches on the medium wave channel of Radio 3, there were protests from the music lovers who found themselves limited to VHF reception. They argued that their service was being 'displaced', although it was a fact that for years before the broadcasting of daytime music the medium wave channel on Radio 3 – then Network 3 – had been made available for just these cricket commentaries. The only success in confining reception to VHF transmission was in the service to schools, where, after giving eighteen months' notice in 1970, it proved possible for schools to equip themselves to receive on VHF and school broadcasts on Radio 4 were thereafter confined to those channels, permitting the broadcasting of general interest programmes on the main Radio 4 medium wave channels.

The fact was, however, that the demands of the audience for an increased range of programmes could be satisfied only by the splitting of the VHF and medium wave channels, and in the case of Radio 2, the long wave and the VHF channel. The limiting factor was money to provide the programmes rather than channel space to transmit them. That, at least, was how it appeared from the point of view of the broadcaster. But the audience remained unconvinced, and when parliamentary broadcasting started on a permanent basis in the spring of 1978 there were still people ready to write to *The Times* protesting against being 'compelled' to buy VHF receivers in order to hear *Woman's Hour* and *Afternoon Theatre*. It did not help the broadcasters that receivers imported into the country were very often of Japanese, Taiwanese, or Hong Kong manufacture and did not include a long wave tuning band, because there was no long wave transmission in the Asian broadcasting area or in the Americas, where these receivers were normally distributed. In a sense, therefore, many receivers on ready sale to the public were inadequately equipped for the British frequency situation, which called for the use of long wave, medium wave and VHF receiving capacities. No set which did not have all three could be regarded as adequate for the long term situation in Britain.

The whole problem of the use of long wave, medium wave and VHF channels illustrates ideally the inescapable interconnection between frequency policy, receiver distribution policy and programme potentialities. None can be considered without the other, and this fact of broadcasting life will continue to govern policy decisions even in the long term future.

The next great problem to face broadcasters and makers of public policy will be that of the use of potential satellite broadcasting channels. These were discussed in a comprehensive way at a symposium organized in May 1977 by the European Broadcasting Union and the European Space Agency. A full account of the proceedings is given in the papers published at the time by the European Space Agency. As I saw the outcome of those discussions, the practical potential of satellite broadcasting had been demonstrated. Only the political issues remained to be decided.

In summing up the proceedings of the conference I said that it was clear from what had then been published that the technology of satellite transmission had been fully worked out. The available satellites would be capable of providing a broadcasting service if the policy decision were taken. The nature of the service to provide it had, in effect, been pre-determined by the Geneva frequency agreement of 1974, which had resulted in an allocation of frequency channels for broadcast satellite use which could be accepted by countries throughout the European broadcasting area. The main issue had been that of overspill. Although it had proved technically possible to devise means of transmitting signals from the satellite to areas whose shape on the surface of the earth would range from circular to extended ellipses, it was clearly impossible to design a signal so exact that it would conform precisely to the complicated detailed frontier indentations of the individual countries of Europe. Moreover, some of the countries in Europe were of such small dimensions that any signal from the satellite would be bound to extend over their frontiers into the territory of others. Technically, therefore, overspill in some degree was unavoidable. No satellite broadcasting system could be introduced which could wholly limit transmission to the national territory of the target country. The agreement in Geneva had divided the pattern of frequencies and various orbital positions in such a way as to minimize this unintended overspill, and it appeared at the end of the conference that this minimal overspill would be acceptable to the countries of both Eastern and Western Europe. Once that political question had been resolved in the technical plane there was a limited necessity for some juridical regulation of the kind of programmes which would be acceptable within even this unavoidable overspill area. That, however, was a matter still under discussion in the relevant committee of United Nations.

Nevertheless the transmission question had been answered in its main substance. It appeared, too, in Dublin that the capacity of industry to design and produce receivers which would be of an acceptable size and a reasonable price for the mass audience had also been demonstrated. The problem would not be in the industrial capacity to produce such receivers, or indeed to produce the transmission equipment for the satellite. It would prove once more to be in the issue of how the audience could be persuaded to buy receivers of a totally new kind for a service whose value had not then been demonstrated to them.

The real questions were about the nature of that service. This is the essence of every broadcasting policy question when new transmission modes are proposed. There are no separate, 'technical' issues.

It was demonstrated in Dublin by Mr Carlo Terzani of Italy that the costs of the satellite mode of transmission, compared with those of the terrestrial mode, leaving out of account the cost of writing off capital at present invested in terrestrial transmission systems, would be acceptable. It is true that the amortisation of present capital costs cannot in practice be ignored, but in the long run the fact of financial viability for satellite modes of transmission will assert itself in the planning of future systems. Mr Terzani showed quite clearly that the satellite mode should not be regarded at present as one to be used in substitution of the present terrestrial services. He doubted whether it would be seen in this light even when the question of replacing the existing systems arose as they became obsolescent. One French contributor to the symposium argued that the rate of technological development is always faster than the rate of development of use, and suggested that it might well be that if decisions were not taken to provide an extra variety of services, the replacement rate of receivers, which seems always to be the critical factor in these policy calculations, would be an insufficient economic base to support the mass-production industry which would be needed to respond to the availability of satellite transmission.

Taking the United Kingdom case, the number of receivers in use is at least 18 million. If we assume that receivers are replaced every ten years (and that is a normal British assumption), it means that the annual flow of all replacement sets in Britain would be 1.8 million. We have to think whether that is a sufficient mass of production to enable the receivers to be produced at an acceptable price, taking only the British market, and assuming that all receivers bought in replacement would be of the new type – that is, satellite-capable – which will not necessarily be the case. The figures would be somewhat similar for Germany, Italy and France. We have to look to the United States and Japan, because they may well form the mass market which would justify the production of receivers at all. If they turn out to be the pioneer countries, in transmission and service development, the commercial certainty is that they will supply the rest of the world with its receivers. So the broadcasting policy question becomes a matter of industrial and trade policy.

The European Space Agency experts have shown that

receiver production at low cost is possible, if the demand exists. It is purely a matter of scale. Everything depends, therefore, on decisions about the supply of programmes. The situation may be affected, as time passes, by the development of fibre optics for cable transmission. The use of translucent plastic fibres instead of copper could multiply almost infinitely the channel capacity and distances of transmission over physical paths. Most broadcasters have worked so far on the unspoken assumption that these developments will not be available until some time in the 1990s, and that there will therefore be an interval during which satellite transmission will not have to face the competition of fibre optics. They may be wrong in making that unspoken assumption, and it might need to be re-examined. But all the evidence suggests that the prediction is broadly correct. It is a very important factor in the whole satellite transmission equation.

But programmes are the key. If development depends on mass distribution of receivers (and mass distribution is essential if they are to be made at low cost) there must be a programme which appeals to the mass. It is logically absurd to postulate the sale of receivers in mass to a minority watching minority programmes. That fact poses a very clear question about the nature of the programme service to be provided by satellite. First, it will have to be different. Experience everywhere has shown that the take-up of sets will be faster for a new programme than for a service which is merely a new way of receiving an existing programme. Difference in programmes is costly. Good programmes are not produced cheaply. If the requirement is for good, different programmes, the costs will be high. And there is another philosophical problem. Programmes intended for the mass – which seem to be inherent in the problem – are, in a sense, the enemy of choice. If the argument for satellite transmission is the development of greater diversity of choice, the practicalities may well conflict with the objective.

I do not think I can do better in summing up the difficulties on the programme side than to cite the opinions expressed in Dublin by Mr Stelio Molo (Director-General of Swiss Broadcasting) and by Mr Robin Scott of BBC Television. Mr Molo put his finger very precisely on the issue of cost and quality of programmes when he said: 'The technical restrictions of channels have at least the merit of enforcing a certain measure of selectiveness. Since the technical infrastructure is far from representing the greatest part of the cost of broadcasting, one may wonder if, apart from the overcrowding of the wave bands, it will be finance which will form the sole obstacle to a totally unrestrained supply of programmes, and one may also wonder if that would be fair and sensible if this were the case. Here the challenge is a sociological one at the level of the individual, and a political one at the level of societies as a whole.'

Robin Scott's argument epitomized the hopeful views: 'No single system holds the key, to future communications or entertainment. The way forward may be through the encouragement of local diversity via terrestrial systems whilst creating new national and international satellite services. Thus may we rekindle the sense of wonder which we have partly lost at the sheer miraculous delight of television. Thus may we give fresh opportunity with exciting visual and audio standards to a new generation of creative people, justifying the precious new channels of communication which Man's ingenuity had made available to Man.' I posed one sceptical question, which I still pose. Does diversity necessarily lead in the mass media to greater creativity? I am not sure.

One issue raised by Mr Haas of Swiss Television is central to the problem of adding new modes of transmission. It is that of the personal use of time. He mentioned the figures of viewing in the Federal Republic of Germany, which suggested that the multiplication of channels did not result in longer individual viewing. He could have cited the experience of Britain when BBC 2 was introduced. British advertisers know that the common assumption – that television is now taking up so much of people's time that they are bound to be spending less on, for example, the reading of newspapers – is untrue. The amount of time spent on average by people reading newspapers has been practically invariable over the last ten years. That fact implies something important about how people resist change in their life patterns. There is a degree of displacement, certainly, but it has to be remembered that, if there is to be more television by satellite, people will still probably spend the same total amount of time viewing. All that will happen is that more cost, more resources, will be devoted to keeping people occupied and entertained by television for precisely the same amount of time. The unit of live entertainment enjoyed by each individual simply becomes more costly. This fact cannot be lightly disregarded because in the end, all broadcasters, whatever their revenue base, have to make a case to Governments for more resources. That is true whether they depend on public or on commercial revenue. There is always a public factor in the proportion of resources taken out of the economy for entertainment. If broadcasters are to use satellites for extra services, they will be applying more resources to the same range of entertainment addressed to the same number of people. There is a case for caution.

Despite all these political, technical and financial problems, nothing has been more difficult in the discussion of satellite broadcasting potentialities than the legal issues. Nevertheless, the meeting in Dublin suggested that the questions of private law – that is, the interests of the holders of the rights in written work, music composition and performances – seemed, after some years of discussion, not to be nearly as insoluble as they had at first appeared to be. The question of public law was much more difficult. The international problem of overspill had to a great extent been removed by the frequency agreement which minimized the area of overspill and therefore of conflict. Nevertheless, the argument still persisted. The Soviet Union still argued, in the relevant United Nations committees (the Legal Sub-Committee of the Uses of Outer Space Com-

mittee) that the prior consent of other countries was necessary
to what was contained in broadcasts which could be received
in overspill areas before the system could be initiated. The
Third World representatives still remained fearful of the
erosion of their own cultural identities by those of the Western
World, which could be expected to be more aggressive in the
development of satellite programme services. Indeed, the
extent of their doubts was demonstrated by the fact that no
agreement was reached as to the allocation of satellite frequencies which should be used to cover their areas of the
world.

In one respect the satellite frequency allocations for Europe
will produce a new and potentially disturbing phenomenon
which would raise serious questions about the possibility of
maintaining national control of broadcasting policy in some of
the major countries. Each of the European 'statelets' (Luxem-
bourg, Andorra, Monaco, Liechtenstein and San Marino – as
well as the Vatican) has received an allocation of four frequencies. It is true that the assignment to these channels of
different orbital positions and signal polarisations from those
which apply in the contiguous major states are intended to
place obstacles in the way of easy reception by the general
audience of programme services from these small territories.
But adaptations to receivers would certainly be possible at a
not impossible cost, and the provision of highly competitive
programme services would certainly be commercially practical.
Given the availability of possible cable extensions far into the
major countries such as already exist in parts of Italy, services
of national importance in the major countries could be
originated within these minor states. The phenomenon of the
so-called 'peripheral' radio stations, which has substantially
affected the general programme pattern for listeners in France
could well extend to television viewers in France, Germany,
Italy, Austria, Switzerland, and even Spain. Since each of these
statelets has a sovereign character, national legislation within
the major states would theoretically be powerless to influence

the content of these television programme services. Moreover, since, under present technology, the maximum antenna length which can be accommodated within present launch vehicles is of the order of three metres, it follows, technically, that the minimum radius of the area to be covered at full power would be some 200 kilometres. Given, too, that the area in which a satisfactory signal would be receivable is not represented by a sharp cut-off line, reception would, in practice, extend further than the diameter of 400 kilometres which would be suggested by this practical limitation. Un-intentional overspill would be considerable, even if no cable extension of the service were contemplated. The central question of the capacity of nation states to control the nature of broadcasting within their frontiers would come seriously into question.

The nature of the discussions about potential satellite broadcasting illustrates dramatically the inseparability of frequency problems, political distribution problems, financial questions, and above all of questions about the nature of the programme service to be provided. And in the background there is the formidable weight of the demand from industry that it should always be devising some new consumer product for sale. It is more than possible that a decision about satellite broadcasting will be taken on the ground of the need of industry to develop a new product with a new market, rather than on the need of the audience for a new service. It may well be that the new services, when ultimately devised, and when means of paying for them has also been found, may justify the industrial development thrust. But the more I hear from other countries of their intentions in the matter of satellite broad-casting, the more I suspect that the decision will ultimately be one of production of hardware rather than a production of programmes. Perhaps that has always been the case in broad-casting, and we, as broadcasters, ought to accommodate our-selves to that fact. But it is a matter which tends to thrust into the background the major question of quality of programmes with which all broadcasters ought to be concerned. I am left with a residual suspicion that the great decisions about broadcasting are not, in the last resort likely to be taken for broadcasting reasons.

CHAPTER XII

Structures

IT WAS OFTEN PUT TO ME that the BBC must be very difficult to manage because it was so big. But size is not the problem. I have never thought that scale in itself is a major difficulty in management. The real issue is complexity of the work done. If the business is a large one, the combination of complexity and scale does create problems, especially of communication between the constituent parts and the individual members of the staff of the organisation concerned. The essential difficulty in managing the BBC is that it requires a quality of editorial judgement alongside the normal capacity to handle resources, financial, technical and staff. And the editorial problem is the greater because, as I have explained in previous chapters, the decisions are largely a matter of indicating how delegated authority should be exercised by the head of the production department, and even more by the individual producer. So the problem for the chief executive is to combine in himself a capacity for editorial judgement, along with all the briefing that that implies, while at the same time being able to accept that most of the critical decisions will in practice be made by others within a framework of general guidance. This editorial role has to be combined with the capacity to absorb a range of technical issues, which will be explained by technicians but which will have to be resolved by policy-makers like the Director-General and his supporting staff. Little of this ever moves slowly. Decisions are always required yesterday, and the fact of speed means that the problem of communication with those who are affected by the many decisions taken is even more difficult than the scale of the organization would in any case imply. And since most decisions in broadcasting involve relations with staff either in the programme or in the technical or the administrative side of the business, the Director-General has to be able to operate with speed and delicacy in staff relations, and more especially in Union relations.

It is not surprising, therefore, that the Director-General as the Chief Executive to the Governors calls upon the professional support of substantially autonomous Managing Directors in each of the programme service, and of specialist directors in each of the central supporting functions – Engineering, Personnel and Finance. But nevertheless, he remains the Chief Executive. It has been suggested that one way to operate the BBC under the Board of Governors would be to have three entirely separate Directors-General, each responsible for one of the programme services – Television, Radio and External Services. But if that were to happen, then the Board, and more especially the Chairman, would find themselves carrying the executive role of adjudicating between the claims of each of the programme services when they came into conflict. To take just one practical example, it is quite common for the interests of the External Services and Radio in the matter of regulating overtime payments to staff to be different from that of the Television Service and this can be a major factor in negotiations. Somebody has to reconcile the difference, and it must either be a Chief Executive reporting to the Board, or the Board itself, through the Chairman, which becomes involved in the day-to-day business of the Corporation – and necessarily, because of their amateur status and relative remoteness from the day-to-day business, inefficiently.

The authority of the Managing Directors rests, in practice, on their control of air time within the mode of transmission for which they are responsible. The more I consider the question of management structure in the BBC, the more I am convinced of the crucial importance of control of air time. One could argue that the BBC should be organized functionally –

so that, for instance, there was a department which dealt with all sports programmes in both radio and television, and another which dealt with all drama in both media. And so on. There are areas of the BBC where, as I shall explain later, this functional organization operates, but the fundamental consideration is that the availability of air time dictates the total provision of resources, and the allocation of that air time decides how those total resources should be disposed. And above all those decisions directly reflect the view taken by the BBC of the correct editorial proportions of its programme schedules. Thus, it is the existence of the two networks, and the allocation of time on them, which defines for the Television Service the character of the Service and the nature and volume of the resources to fill those networks. The primary decisions about air time govern all decisions in these other areas. There are, it is true, devolutions of air time, particularly in the National Regions, but the basic principle is that control of air time dictates all other decisions. This is more than theory. It is inescapable practice.

The same statement can be made about the domestic radio services – with one interesting variation. The local radio stations have their own transmission resources, and therefore their own air time. They operate by opting *in* to the network, and not by opting *out*, as do the national regions. They are therefore genuinely free agents. Local radio answers to the Managing Director, Radio. But its independence of action, which was a deliberate policy decision by the BBC, is the reflection of the reality of the control by local stations of their own air time, and therefore of their individual programme flavour.

Similarly, the External Services have their own transmission facilities and so, their own air time. Because they control their own air time, and are therefore in the position to decide what resources should be made available for programmes, the External Services properly constitute one of the BBC's three managing directorates, with its own budget. This is, of course, constitutionally necessary, because the BBC has to account to Parliament, through the Foreign Office, for the estimates and expenditure under the Grant-in-Aid.

But if the three Managing Directors are, in their way, 'little Directors-General' then they too will need to operate by delegation. And indeed they do. In my view the key figure in the operation of the BBC's programme services has always been the Network Controller. This is true whether one looks at the Television, the Radio or the External Services. The origin of the 'Network Controller' concept lies in the Haley re-structuring of 1947 which produced the Home, Light and Third pattern in radio. This was the most publicized aspect of the Haley changes, but internally the BBC recognized the Network Controllers as editors and the production groups as 'supply' departments. That basic concept has prevailed through all subsequent BBC developments. The supply departments offered ideas to the Network Controllers, who then allocated air time and resources to accommodate the programmes proposed and to enable them to be produced. When television developed, the same basic structure emerged for the single BBC channel which operated alone until 1964, and the radio pattern of Network Controllers operating as the central decision-makers in distributing air time and resources – both human and material – emerged in the two-channel situation. Thus, BBC-1 and BBC-2 both drew upon the same programme production departments for their respective programmes. Each network controller was responsible for selecting the programme proposals which he considered most appropriate to his editorial design.

But the significance of the network controller is not simply that he is a resource manager. It is also his responsibility to set the standards of programme content – operating, naturally, under the general guidance of the Managing Director, and, more remotely, of the Director-General and the Board of Governors. The Network Controller is the pivotal point of BBC judgement on programme taste and editorial duty. He is at the centre of the representations which come from within the BBC about what ought to be done, and from the general public. It is for him to judge what will meet the demands of popular taste and what it is necessary to reject if justifiable criticism is not to be incurred. He is the representative within the BBC, *vis-à-vis* the production departments, of public taste when it has to be matched against creative impulse. It is not sufficient for him to appeal to commonsense or to what will be acceptable to the 'ordinary family'. His judgements have to be made on more sophisticated grounds than either of these two simple criteria would suggest. 'Common sense' will unerringly exclude the extraordinary. Some programme material which ought to be shown will never be acceptable to the 'ordinary family'. Some which would be called for by the avant-garde would be so intolerable to the general audience that it should not be accepted at all. The crucial initial decision in any of these respects must rest with the Network Controller, subject always to the necessary safeguard of reference upwards to the Managing Director or to the Director-General. It is for the Network Controller to decide when, and on what grounds that reference should be made. If the 'faceless bureaucrat' resides anywhere in the BBC it is in the office of the Network Controller. And none of them that I have ever known has ever been a faceless man. The bureaucracy may have been theoretical. It was never personal – and bureaucracy with a human face can hardly be a ground for reasonable objection.

It is true that the complexity of the resources which are employed in television production requires the system of Network Controllers to be supported by a 'Controller of Programme Services' or his equivalent. Radio has much less need of this specialized type of resource management, because its logistics are very much less complicated. When the McKinsey study reported on the location of decision-making in the BBC, they found that instead of the 7 or 8 decision-makers which they had expected to find in BBC Television, as in any major organization, there were no fewer than 1500 –

each in charge of a production team to which resources had been allocated for the making of programmes. That multiplicity of decision points reflects the range of resources which have to be applied to television production and which defy central control at any higher level. But it does not diminish the centrality of the Network Controller as the key point of the allocation procedure.

These are the simplicities of the BBC programme management structure. Complexities arise when external editorial considerations require that the exclusive power of the Network Controllers over the allocation of their own air time should be modified. These external considerations arise in the areas of current affairs, regional broadcasting, education, and religion and the structural problems to which they give rise merit treatment in a separate chapter.

Certain specialist functions which affect all three programme services of the BBC call for central professional support for the Director-General in his capacity as Chief Executive. These are Engineering, Personnel and Finance, each of which calls for professional knowledge in the preparation and implementation of plans, and in the management of current operations. I propose only to deal here with those aspects of the central specialist functions which bear on the Director-General's responsibility for the coherent administration of the BBC as a single entity.

The Director of Engineering is responsible for the provision of the transmission network and for its operation; for the design and installation of the production studios, as well as for the training of the staff who operate in those studios; and for the general capital construction requirements of the BBC. This last is given to him because it is in the engineering division that the necessary skills are to be found. At one time the capital planning of the Corporation, especially in its accommodation aspects, was placed under the general guidance of the Director of Administration, but my experience suggested that when this function was transferred to engineering after the

McKinsey Study had reported in 1970 the reconciliation of the problems of construction and operation with those of finance were much better handled than they had been before, when non-technical administrative minds were applied to the business. But none of this delegation of technical matters to the Director of Engineering absolves the Director-General himself from a full understanding of the issues – for example, the frequency problems I have explained in earlier chapters. Nor is he released from a need to understand the full implications of the capital planning programme, including those of technical capacity of the installations once constructed. He has to understand the objectives which the Director of Engineering sets for the Research Department, which is central to the constant process of technical development which has characterized the whole fifty years of the BBC. The Director-General cannot, of course, decide what research should be undertaken. He must understand, however, that funds have to be provided for purposes which, in essence, will be decided by those who know the areas which are most likely to give results.

One perennial structural issue for broadcasters was again brought into prominence by the McKinsey study of 1968/69. The normal sequence of development is for the research engineers, whether within the BBC or elsewhere, to develop some new application of electronics which makes possible a more faithful visual or aural representation of the producer's programme intention; for this to be used experimentally under the supervision of research staff; for the device subsequently to be produced in sufficient numbers for more general operation, but still under the supervision of qualified engineers; and finally, for a version to be brought into service which can be used by non-technical staff, with the engineering staff requirement being reduced to maintenance. The dividing line between the engineers and the operators has always been the studio and its control gallery. By 1970 studio discipline and equipment had been sufficiently developed for the studio operating function to be transferred to programme responsibility. This was also logical in management terms, because the effective decisions on the scale and elaboration of studio facilities were taken by the programme departments when they made their plans for the year's programme schedule. The process of making studio operation non-technical is bound to continue. Videotape editing, for example, which remains an engineering function, will soon be manageable by non-technical staff, because of the development of inexpensive cassette editing which can convey computerized instructions to the full-standard video-recording machine. The whole development reflected the history of radio studio management twenty years earlier, when the 'programme engineering' function was transferred from the Engineering Division to the Radio Directorate. This pattern will recur as technical progress removes from technical operations the element of engineering judgement which is required in the development stages.

The Director of Finance operates in his field in a similar way to the Director of Engineering in his. He is responsible for the working out of longer-term budgetary implications of programme plans as presented by the three services, and for the initial presentation of arguments for the increase of the licence fee – or for the restraint of expenditure in the absence of an increase – whenever that should prove necessary. In general, it is his business to conduct the initial negotiations with the responsible Ministry, now the Home Office. The Director-General comes into the discussion only when the issues have been set out and the possible range of decisions to be taken is clearly indicated. And at that stage, too, the Director-General may advise that the Chairman should be involved in the discussions with the Home Secretary himself. Indeed, the Chairman will usually indicate to the Director-General that he wishes so to be involved, and the matter is then taken to the highest level. But the whole process depends on the basic work carried out by the Director of Finance in his capacity as the chief estimating officer of the Corporation. But he is also the chief accounting officer. He has to provide the operational accounting services which monitor the expenditure of money by the programme and other services, and which make the payments to the people who provide all the services which go to make up programmes. He is also responsible for operating the salary mechanisms of the Corporation, and it is a remarkable tribute to the work done in these areas that there has been no serious breakdown at any time in the history of the BBC. At times, the Director of Finance will become involved also in the discussions of contractual payments into the collecting societies like the Mechanical Copyright Protection Society and the Performing Rights Society. It is for him to present the BBC's case – for example to the Performing Rights' Tribunal supported by the specialist departmental officers who are responsible for the relevant contractual discussions. In all these areas, as well as being an executive officer, he is the principal staff adviser on finance to the Director-General, who must be in a position always to explain to the Board what is being done on his behalf.

The Directors of Engineering and Finance are, of course, essential aides to the Director-General, but they operate in fields which, on the whole, can be described as presenting tangible problems. But in broadcasting the least predictable element in management is the handling of personal relationships, and for that reason, the job of Director of Personnel is perhaps more difficult than either of the others. A Director-General needs strong support here, because he has to run a broadcasting service through the enthusiasm and inspiration of the staff who produce the programmes and who provide the technical and other supporting facilities.

It was in this area that management in broadcasting probably changed more substantially during my period of office than during that of any previous Director-General. There were a number of reasons for this change. To my mind – and I write as an observer of the broadcasting scene for 30 years and not as a professional social scientist – there has been a change in the approach of people in broadcasting to their job.

They are still as proud of their profession as they have ever been – and in some respects I think that their professionalism is greater than it ever was. But where it was once assumed by those concerned with the production of programmes that the job had an overriding claim on the whole of their lives, I doubt if that is true any longer. Any man or woman is free to give everything to the job, according to his own lights. But an employer on a substantial scale, such as the BBC, has to operate according to recognized rules towards the people he employs if petty and arbitrary local tyrannies are to be avoided. Moreover, a man or woman employed in a large organization, no matter how splendid its purpose, has the right to be regarded as a member of a family at home as well as a member of a family at work. There is a tyranny of obligation which comes from a high sense of purpose, and which can oppress the individual if the organisation to which he belongs is not scrupulous in its regard for his personal liberties and commitments. There has been a change in the BBC from the assumption that all could be expected and demanded, to a condition in which much is still expected – and given – but a life of personal freedom is left to the individual. There are changes required in the temper of management when this change in attitudes occurs.

The second change was perhaps more predictable. When any operation starts and develops, as has the Television Service since the war, pioneer experiments will be undertaken and will fructify; things will be attempted on sketchy resources which are clearly not sufficient to maintain the operation beyond the pioneer period. But there is a temptation for those who took part in the pioneering exploits to assume that the original manner of their execution can continue. It does not. The pioneer generation moves on. When that time comes the stresses which the pioneers accepted as normal have to be moderated to meet the reasonable expectations of their successors. More staff and more equipment are needed to do what was done on a shoestring, and sometimes on a prayer. In establishing a permanent base for what had been a pioneering experiment there come questions of personnel management. There are virtues in pioneering. There are also virtues in treating work as a rational routine. Management has to recognize both – and try always to cherish pioneers when they turn up.

The third factor which affected the personnel situation, certainly in the seventies, was the increasingly effective unionisation of people who would formerly have considered themselves professional staff not overly occupied with union organisation. I am not opposed to unionisation. Indeed I very strongly support it. The individual members of the staff of any large organisation ought to be able to communicate through management channels, but very frequently human nature makes it difficult for them to do so. In those conditions a union channel of communication is essential, both to management and to staff. There will be disagreements between unions and management. That is inevitable when two people look at a problem from different points of view. But the process of exchange of views is positively useful and helpful in running by consent a large society which cannot run except by consent. The making of programmes is, beyond any doubt, a consensual activity.

Disagreements can lead, in the extreme situation, to strikes – as happened twice during my period as Director-General. I do not like the use of the strike weapon because I believe it reflects a failure of reason in one quarter or another. But I believe that the unions equally dislike the use of the strike weapon and would wish to avoid it. I prefer infinitely a resort to arbitration. After all, one has to recognize that all arguments can potentially end in deadlock. Managers faced by a strike have to keep their heads and try to deal with the reasons for it, identifying reasonable grievances while resisting unreasonable solutions. Fundamentally, the reason why the BBC had its last prolonged strike in my time – of production assistants in 1974 – was not that the BBC did not recognize a reasonable grievance, but that it did not accept the solution proposed from the union side. From time to time that is bound to happen. Management must be able to cope with such situations. That will include maintaining the service at times of dispute, because that is the BBC's obligation to the public.

At the right hand of the Director-General in handling these situations the Director of Personnel will always have a central role. He is responsible for the whole area of staff administration – for example, the running of the appointment and selection procedures, the negotiations with the unions about pay and conditions of service, the administration of a necessarily complex grading system assessing the relative responsibilities of different categories of staff so that their rewards may be proportionately calculated. And, perhaps most important, he is responsible for assessing the relative merits of the arguments put forward by individual Managing Directorates when conflict arises between them – when one service thinks that its interest demands special treatment for its own staff, even though that treatment may bring problems for other parts of the BBC. It is for the Director of Personnel not only to make a judgement about where fairness and advantage lies, but also to persuade the Managing Directors of the wisdom of his case, without, if possible, drawing in the Director-General, though in the last resort that may be inevitable. The extent to which a Director-General can know that the calls on his attention in this respect will be minimized by his Director of Personnel is an important reflection of the quality of the Director-General himself.

The question of assessing the fairness of rewards throughout a Corporation whose activities call on the services of an enormous range of professions and crafts has always presented a difficult problem for the BBC. In the days of sound broadcasting and the monoploy there were very few comparisons which could easily be made with outside employers, and from the time of the Ullswater Report until Beveridge (that is, from 1935 until 1950) the BBC consciously aligned its rates with comparable levels in the Civil Service, even though the establishment of what was comparable presented difficulties. Beveridge suggested that, especially in the programme area, this alignment prevented the establishment of adequate rewards for creativity and recommended that the criterion should be abandoned. But even when the BBC cut adrift from the direct Civil Service comparisons it still stood in need of some form of internal assessment of fair rates for comparable responsibility, and of some corresponding external comparison. In the immediate postwar years the Central Establishment Office, as it was then called, subsequently to become the Grading Department, was busy working out 'principles of grading', which became embodied in the so-called 'Grading Document', which was presented to many arbitration tribunals as union challenges to BBC assessments began to be made. The intention of the document was to draw out the different factors of responsibility, which could then become the basis of comparative gradings for widely disparate jobs. These gradings could then form the structure to which rates of pay could be attached on the basis of information about rates paid outside the BBC where job content and responsibilities could be reasonably compared. That, at least, was the ideal theory, the whole process was under the aegis of the Director of Personnel, who was responsible for union negotiations about rates of pay.

As one of the senior members of the administrative team in the External Services in 1960 I was asked to speak to the members of the Central Establishment Office about the difficulties which they were having in convincing the Departments they serviced of the logic and the wisdom of the grading processes they were trying to apply. The invitation reflected the tensions which naturally arose between the executives who were having to operate the broadcasting service, and the analysts who were trying to derive some logic from the operational structure which the executives were managing. It was all too easy for the executive departments to claim an upgrading (almost never a downgrading) for some job which they were finding particularly difficult to fill, and to seek to subvert the theories of the graders, who were interested, quite properly, in establishing consistency in the studies which they were carrying out in all parts of the Corporation. I think that I typified the attitude of many of my fellow executives towards grading when I said that I was 'as mystified as most other people by the metaphysical terms of the Grading Document' when I tried to work out how it should be applied in a particular case.

I identified certain irrational factors which made for conflict, some operating externally on the BBC, and some the result of internal difficulties. It was very evident that the assessments of responsibility which arose from the grading process did not always produce salaries which corresponded to outside relativities, and this became even more true as television developed. The economic assessments of responsibility which were made by the market outside the Corporation, operated to the disadvantage of the rationality sought by the graders within it. Moreover, the unions representing the staff never formally accepted the validity of the Grading Document, and consequently there were not infrequent disputes about whether the gradings which resulted from the efforts of the graders could, in fact, be rationally justified, as the graders themselves maintained. Moreover, recruitment from outside the BBC, resulting from advertisements which reflected the grading judgements and the salaries related to them, frequently did not produce satisfactory candidates, especially in the expansionist phase through which television was going. The grading system quite frequently had to take second place to the needs of the Service, either through the application of special salaries on a more general basis than could possibly be justified under any legitimate principle of rewarding exceptional talent, or by attempts to 'fix' the grades themselves which served as the basis for the advertisements. At one time the BBC found it virtually impossible to recruit architects in the planning boom of the early 1960s, and the Unions were well aware that such recruiting difficulties represented their best ground for an adjustment of grades. And in the last resort there were always the unique hazards of arbitration. The consequence of 'splitting the difference' could not possibly be reconciled with the logic of the grading case which had to be presented to the various arbitration tribunals at different times.

Added to these external irrational processes operating against the successful operation of the grading system there was the simple failure of BBC middle management staff to understand the purposes and operation of the grading system, combined with the desire of the thrusting local manager to claim for himself the maximum degree of flexibility, which could often only be granted at the expense of the coherence of the grading system itself. There was the view which held that a man who deals with important people will claim to have that importance recognized in his own status and pay, even though what he does for those important people may in itself be relatively unimportant. This confusion of status and responsibility is fatal to any system of logical rewards, but it seems to be built into human nature.

The Director of Personnel is at the centre of all these arguments about grading, which will continue within the BBC, for the simple reason that the range of jobs will continue to be very large, and the need for fair internal and external comparisons cannot be ignored. In carrying this function, a Director of Personnel will be suffering for the Director-General one of the penalties of a unity from which so many other benefits spring.

The basic structure of the BBC, therefore, is that of the three Managing Directorates reflecting each of the three major Services, each controlling its own air time, supported by the professional departments which provide the resources which are commonly required by all, and in which coherence of policy makes good sense. The whole system is designed to ensure that programmes operate with maximum independence within a unity which gives strength, order and consistency.

CHAPTER XIII

Structures: Special Problems

LOOKED AT PURELY AS an internal exercise in organisation, the evolution of a management structure for the BBC would not be impossibly difficult. But programmes have a direct impact on opinion in society, and some points of impact are much more sensitive than others. Current affairs programmes, educational services, religious broadcasting, and regional services in my experience represent the most sensitive points, and the structure of the BBC has reflected this sensitivity. Logically, all these categories of programme could simply be treated as part of the management responsibility of each individual Service, so that Television Current Affairs would be exclusively the concern of the Managing Director, Television, and so on. But in each of the categories of programme I have mentioned, external representations to the BBC will come inevitably to the Director-General and to the Board. The response that each individual Service answers for its own programmes in each of these areas, without any central responsibility attaching to the Director-General or to the Board, would simply not be believable. Consequently, some means has to be found of reflecting, within the BBC's structure, the fact that these categories of programme will attract special responses, and will require a special focus of accountability within the Corporation.

Current Affairs programmes have always been a point of extreme sensitivity. Every Director-General since the foundation of the BBC has had to concern himself very directly with programmes of news and current affairs. Lord Reith exercised authority in the smaller scale of broadcasting in his day and in the circumstances of a far more restricted treatment of current affairs than is possible today. But his authority was direct, as was his accountability and his acceptance of it. Sir William Haley, having under his control three sound networks, of which only one was engaged in a major sense in news, and the Television Service, which engaged only in a very limited sense in news and current affairs, went so far as to let it be known that no change whatever in the arrangements for the broadcasting of news should be made without his direct approval and instruction. Furthermore, he held that no suggested change in the arrangements should be argued purely on the basis of audience research information, no matter how seemingly convincing. This kind of control was practicable when the services were as restricted and as little complicated as they were in his day.

Some specific references illustrate this analysis very clearly. During the General Strike of 1926 the BBC, for the first time, broadcast bulletins during the day. Earlier news reporting had been confined to agency messages compiled into bulletins in the evening only, because of Press opposition to anything more. Sir John Reith personally supervised the contents of the bulletins during the Strike and indeed, read some of them. It was only after the General Strike the BBC introduced a newsroom to handle the collection and treatment of news. Even then the prohibition of controversial broadcasting of any kind, renewed by the then Postmaster-General, was not removed until 1928 and then only as an 'experiment', in which condition things remained until 1939. Indeed, it was not until Haley's post-war innovations in radio that there was any unscripted discussion on radio, though there were long scripted talks. I myself produced, in 1947, regular fifteen-minute talks and scripted discussions on matters of highly topical interest. I produced, as an experiment (not very successful), a five-minute post-news topical talk in the Home Service – in July 1949 on the impending docks strike. The first unscripted political discussion was *Editorial Opinion*, introduced on Friday evenings as a forty-five minute experiment during the fuel crisis which stopped publication of the weekly periodicals. This later became *Friday Forum*, and was the real beginning of genuine political discussion on the air. The election campaign of 1950 (February) was the first in which there was any reporting of the poll in the BBC current affairs programme (I produced myself the round-up of the day at the polling booths from 8–9 pm – but with no suggestion that the results would be given in any form other than that of factual summary in the following day's bulletins). And until 1957 the 'Fourteen-day Rule' precluded discussion on the air of any subject due for Parliamentary discussion within the next two weeks.

I recount this history in order to illustrate both how close has been the preoccupation of outside authorities, and therefore necessarily of the Board and Director-General with political broadcasting by the BBC, and how very rapid has been the post-war growth of current affairs broadcasting, in radio and television. By the mid-1950s Sir Ian Jacob, having to face the extension of controversial current affairs broadcasting encouraged by Haley, both in radio and in television and with a Television Service which was developing very rapidly in the face of aggressive competition, felt it necessary to appoint a Director of News and Current Affairs to assist him, but the ambiguity of the functions of this post was such that when Hugh Greene became Director-General he insisted on merging the duties of the Director, News and Current Affairs, with the duties of the Director-General. He held consistently thereafter that it was impossible for the Director-General to divest himself of the general responsibilities which have to be exercised in this field. Indeed, when McKinseys suggested the devolution to the Managing Director, Radio, and the Managing Director, Television, of responsibility, both managerial and editorial, for news and current affairs operations, Sir Hugh argued strongly against their view and suggested that in order to achieve the declared target of greater managerial efficiency, what was needed was a strengthening within the news field of the budgetary authority of the Editor (News). This post, which had long been responsible for the editorial and operational management of the News Division, incorporating the news staffs working in Radio and Television, had continued in existence during the brief 'DNCA' interlude. When Hugh Greene abolished the post of Director, News and Current Affairs, he added to the duties of the Editor (News) the function of advising the Director-General on the whole range of radio and television current affairs programmes, and gave its holder the new title of Editor, News and Current Affairs. All that was now needed, he argued, was to reaffirm this advisory function and the title. In presenting this case he made the reservation that the Managing Directors of Radio and Television would have preferred not to strengthen, at their expense, the budgetary responsibilities of the Editor, News and Current Affairs, in the news field. The Managing Directors saw this concentration of managerial authority in the post as a serious derogation from their own authority, and they would certainly not have agreed to the excision from their Managing Directorates of the current affairs programme departments. Indeed, to have removed these departments from Radio would have left the Managing Directorate in a severely truncated state – with virtually only entertainment and music as its major preoccupations. McKinseys themselves said that to remove anything more than the news budgetary functions from the Managing Directorates would be substantially to undermine the whole Managing Director concept, which sought to place executive authority over resource provision and application at the point where practical editorial authority normally resides. By the time Sir Hugh Greene left the BBC therefore, the practice and tradition of personal responsibility by the Director-General for news and current affairs editorial matters was well established and the limits of logistic centralization had been thoroughly argued and further centralization rejected. I believe that this point of managerial stabilization was the correct one.

A vigorous argument has been conducted in recent years about the justification for the editorial separation of news and current affairs material. The case has been advanced that what journalists regard as the basic 'facts' of news are neither comprehensible nor really true if left to stand by themselves. They need a context before they can be properly understood, and it is argued that they should not be isolated in programmes or schedules from those contexts. The editorial argument is strong, but before considering the extent to which those arguments for unification are valid it is necessary to look at the organizational issues first. It is my contention that the nature and availability of the material which constitutes a broadcasting news service is such that the service can only effectively be organized if a separation is maintained between 'news' and those treatments of public information which are generally referred to in British broadcasting as 'current affairs' programmes.

The first fact is that of insistent and rapid change in the technical possibilities. Even in Radio the use of telephone circuits for the passing of voiced despatches was very slow to develop, and until very recently there was considerable resistance, on grounds of inadequate technical quality, to the incorporation of such voiced despatches in news bulletins and programmes. That was true even for domestic reporting. In intercontinental communication the first trans-Atlantic cable did not come into service until November 1956, and until that time short wave communications links were all that was available. They were used, but the quality was undeniably variable, and sometimes very difficult to listen to. The domestic listener does not have the strong motivations of those who listen internationally to short wave broadcasting, and is less ready to tolerate departures from the standards of quality which he expects from his domestic Radio service. It was not until the intercontinental telephone cable system developed after 1956, and, in parallel, methods were evolved of bringing domestic telephone line recordings to acceptable broadcast quality, that even radio developed the full flexibility of place which is really necessary for a full news reporting service.

Similarly, the development of television news reporting has depended on the evolution of versatile cameras and fast film stock capable of handling substantial variations in light conditions. Now there is the even greater flexibility of electronic news gathering which involves the use in the field of portable electronic cameras and recording gear, in place of film cameras with stock which has to be processed before use in programmes. So the reporting of even domestic material in pictures, and then of intercontinental reporting, had to wait for these improvements and for the availability of satellite picture transmission in the late 1960s before it could claim parity of speed and ubiquity with radio. But once these had been developed, the working methods of Radio and Television News Departments displayed the same organizational characteristics.

In any newsroom there is a constant supply of up-to-date news and the operation has to be organized as a daily routine, working on a shift pattern, with the normal intake, copy-tasting and presentation routines which govern any news editorial operation, whether it be in broadcasting or in the Press. Organizationally, the system has to be designed to cope with this constant flow. The time patterns of Current Affairs programmes are quite different, even when the programmes are daily in their rate of strike. They are best run as separate teams of staff, each with its own accommodation and facilities, working to deadlines which depend essentially on the programme schedule and on the editor's choice of subjects for each edition, rather than on the flow of events. So I start by saying that the nature of the flow of news material – constant, relentless, with inbuilt editorial imperatives – dictates the organization of separate units for news, and for current affairs. That is a practical matter. It is not a philosophy. It is common sense.

The second consideration, which derives directly from

that which I have just described, is the schedule. If there is a daily flow of material – and though my emphasis has been on foreign news, similar considerations apply to domestic news – there has to be a regular daily pattern of programme spaces into which the news will fit. There is no point in building up an enormous overhead of daily reporting and then to find oneself without sufficient outlets either to justify the original outlay or to satisfy the people who are doing the reporting. A reporter without an outlet is a demoralized citizen and soon becomes a bad reporter. So there has to be a predictable pattern of news bulletins in the television schedule, and it is a daily pattern with more than one opportunity during the evening to display and update the available wares.

This daily and repetitive pattern is quite different from that which has to be devised to accommodate the amplification material which seems to me to be proper for the current affairs programme. There is not the same dictation of routine in current affairs, because the current affairs editor can choose what subjects he wishes to cover – which subjects does he think important or interesting or capable of being covered. He is not bound to report what happens on the day. He can wait, if he wishes. It can be as relevant to report an argument or a perspective on Monday as to report it on Friday, because it is still interesting for its own sake and not simply for the fact of being conducted on a given day. This relative inflexibility of news schedules and relative flexibility of current affairs scheduling once more suggests a separate organization for each type of output with people working to different sets of deadlines.

Scheduling is a different matter. News material and Current Affairs material can certainly be juxtaposed in the schedule, and with advantage to the audience. The question which really arises is how much information about the current scene the audience really wants, and how long it is prepared to stay with such programmes. I believe there is a strict limit to the length of time for which the interest of an audience can be held for a News or Current Affairs programme. One of the interesting features about the one-day strike of broadcasting journalists in December 1975 was the audible sigh of relief which went up from articulate members of the audience at not having to see and hear so many news bulletins full of repeated gloom. The psychology was significant for those who offer news and current affairs material.

There are no absolute rules about the association of news and current affairs material in the schedule, either for or against, but I think there is wisdom in remembering the tolerance of the audience. It should not be stretched too far. And in the last resort, the nature of the flow of news material dictates a separate departmental organization from that of current affairs. That is a practical consideration, and too much theory has been devoted to disputes about whether the two elements should be combined organizationally. In my view combined departments simply would not work.

The real issues are those of the proper relationships between broadcasting and the world of public affairs. In the early 1970s the Board of Governors became greatly preoccupied with the problems which were arising for the BBC as a result of the changing character of current affairs broadcasting, the more so because of the high sensitivity of senior British politicians to any treatment of public issues by radio and television. Moreover, the bitter hostilities in Northern Ireland presented, with a special severity, the question of the obligations of free journalists working within a responsible free broadcasting authority. I was pressed more than once to consider changes in the structure of control for News and Current Affairs broadcasting. I have already explained how Hugh Greene resisted in 1968 the McKinsey suggestion that editorial and management responsibility for News should be devolved to the Television and Radio Services. The suggestion was now made that the answer was greater centralization under a 'Managing Director, News and Current Affairs'. I argued strongly that the basic organizational assumption in the BBC was that Radio should be treated as a single set of services and resources and Television as another. The philosophy was that the basic resource management unit was the network, and that the superior management unit, from the point of view of major structure of the Corporation, was the collection of networks of the same character. Thus, four Radio networks went together and incorporated every kind of programme under the single management of the Managing Director, Radio. The two Television networks went together, operating under the single management of the Managing Director, Television. The allocation of resources within each of these Services was effected by the planning machinery within each Managing Directorate. It was very difficult to see how Current Affairs could be hived off from each Managing Directorate, to be combined with News into a separate managerial unit, having its own Radio and Television resources, which would have to include its own specified and permanently reserved times on the air. Such a unit would need to establish its own planning machinery, which would be in parallel with, and in substantial duplication of, the existing machineries of the Radio and Television Directorates. The resultant overlapping would lead to confusion and dispute, in which the Director-General would ultimately have to arbitrate, and would have to do so either without adequate information of his own, or with the aid of an additional planning unit designed to provide him with the material which would enable him to resolve conflicts between the others. That would once again duplicate, complicate and confuse. My argument that a Managing Directorate of News and Current Affairs would be an un-reality was eventually accepted, though not without some contention.

A basic problem was rooted in the natural process of broadcasting development. A characteristic feature of the later 1950s in television had been the production of a new vein of television current affairs programmes – most notably *Panorama* – alongside a steadily improving news service. The growth of the ITV services in these areas was a marked stimulus – and especially Granada's coverage of the 1958 Rochdale by-election. The 1959 election campaign was the first to be substantially covered in television – and indeed, the first to be reported at all seriously in broadcasting. There was a variety of Editors (News) in television over these years, but all shared an innovatory spirit. In current affairs the key figure was Mrs Wyndham Goldie, who reconciled in herself two complementary functions – that of stimulating creative innovation by her producers (mostly young men), and maintaining an iron control over the editorial concepts which were deployed. Her presence in Television Current Affairs concealed for a long time the need for a more formal structure of editorial management – at least, that is how it looks in retrospect. The development of BBC-2 after 1964 made available considerable resources, both production and air time, for a substantial expansion of current affairs output. In the 1960s *Tonight*, as an early evening magazine, gave way to *24 Hours*, as a daily BBC-1 late evening magazine. *The Money Programme* was introduced on BBC-2. In addition, film documentary became increasingly significant in the factual area – *Man Alive* on BBC-2. On BBC-1 *That Was The Week That Was* – the first attempt at satirical treatment of current issues and its successors absorbed much energy from the Current Affairs Group and created special hazards. By 1968 Television Current Affairs output was a wholly different entity from that which had existed at the beginning of the decade – whether looked at in terms of air time available, production techniques, innovation in ideas, or freedom of editorial range.

Mrs Goldie retired in 1965 and it proved difficult to devise some structural mechanism which would replace her peculiar strengths. A very considerable burden fell on the slenderly constructed central machinery of Broadcasting House. Sir Hugh Greene took a very strong personal interest, as a former journalist, and used the full authority of the Director-General to determine policy and to exert discipline. He relied on a

Chief Assistant (in succession, Harman Grisewood and Oliver Whitley) to maintain liaison with outside interests, especially with the political parties. The personalities were important in themselves. In parallel, the Editor, News & Current Affairs was responsible for the day-to-day operations of the News Division and for canalizing the flow of consultative exchanges between the Current Affairs departments and the Director-General.

There were certain difficulties. One was that the liberty of current affairs programmes to deal with new and difficult subjects was constantly being extended and was, equally constantly, attracting criticism from outside. The second was that current affairs were increasingly being treated in documentary and feature programmes based on film, using different techniques and subjects to different limitations from those which had been recognized in the studio and in straight film reporting. Radio had always had some kind of managerial provision for straddling the two areas of talks and features – sometimes a Controller, Talks, or a Controller, Programmes, or an Assistant Director. Television had not had such machinery, and it was clearly going to be needed. Finally, there was the difficulty of people. Appointments had to be made, and occasionally they did not work out as well as was hoped. But they were the best that could be made at a time of headlong development.

Meanwhile, Radio had been developing rapidly in its handling of current affairs. *The World at One* – a combined news bulletin and magazine sequence – inaugurated a new type of news coverage and comment. *Today*, in the early morning, began to follow the same track, as did *The World Tonight* after 1970. All were characterized by a sharper presentation of opinion alongside the straight bulletin reporting of news. These developments paralleled the corresponding spirit of innovation in Television, and produced new problems from an audience which was unaccustomed to the new mix, and tended to resent what looked like a blurring of the traditional frontiers between 'news' and 'comment'.

In the end the discussion in the Board in my time returned to the original question of how to maintain a reasonable central editorial check. For me the question could have been resolved by the strengthening of the powers of the Editor, News and Current Affairs, in the editorial field, so that he could operate with greater authority in deciding programme issues within the Television and Radio Services. To that end his voice needed to be heard in the debate about the allocation of resources in those Services. And the problem was how to establish a channel for his representations to the Managing Directors. Like my predecessor, I took the view that the need for homogeneity in editorial approach in News, applying the basic principles of impartiality, was overriding, and I believed that the News Service should operate as a single managerial unit. As to Current Affairs, it was equally important that there should be a homogeneous editorial view, seeking to avoid inconsistencies of principle between News and Current Affairs, as two aspects of the same kind of operation, and between Radio and Television, as two divisions of the same institution. But central managerial direction of Current Affairs programmes was not practical. Whether the supervising post was called 'Editor, News and Current Affairs' or 'Director, News & Current Affairs' was of very little significance. What mattered was that the holder of the post should be seen to have the full backing of the Director-General and of the Board in carrying through his editorial instructions. I believed throughout that my Editor, News and Current Affairs, should be a member of my Board of Management and regretted that the Board of Governors did not always accept my view because of an error in assessing individual human quality. John Crawley was acceptable to them. Desmond Taylor, his successor, was not. I believe that the Governors were profoundly mistaken in their assessment of him.

News and Current Affairs organization is not unique in highlighting the structural problems which arise from the basic BBC pattern of parallel Television and Radio Services. The same need to respond to legitimate external interests dictates similar solutions in educational and in religious broadcasting. They were different, in that the external interests were special and institutionalized in the educational and religious worlds. There was also one substantial programme difference, in that neither educational nor religious broadcasting incorporated the element of a constant externally dictated flow of material which had to be accommodated in regularly scheduled programme spaces throughout each day. There is no educational or religious broadcasting equivalent of the news bulletin. Furthermore, the times of schools broadcasts are fortunately dictated by the hours at which the schools operate, and these happen to coincide with the times at which major general audiences are not available, or can be avoided by the sensible use of alternative network planning. In religious broadcasting, longstanding convention, such as that which established the Daily Service in the very first years of broadcasting, or accidental semi-official prescription, such as the establishment on television of the 'closed period' in the early part of Sunday evening, virtually resolved for many years the air time planning problem.

The answers to the questions 'how much?' and 'at what time?' which pose some difficult questions of public responsibilities for the schedule planner when he considers Current Affairs programmes have been substantially removed from the area of dispute in educational and religious broadcasting by these solutions. Further education has been a more difficult matter because the target audiences are simply members of the general audience expressing a different interest, and having to be considered, usually, as minorities within the general scheduling problem. The value judgements in placing further education programmes, especially in Television, but also in Radio, resemble very closely those which arise when the planner is considering current affairs questions. The issues were further complicated after the Pilkington Committee, when the Government of the day produced a formula under which extra television hours could be broadcast to accommodate further education programmes whose content conformed to a particular definition.

From the very beginning the BBC recognized that broadcasting to schools could be successful only if the active co-operation of the teachers were enlisted. That could be done only if they were involved in a formal consultative machinery. From the very early days representatives of the professional teaching bodies were incorporated in the School Broadcasting Council, whose terms of reference were reaffirmed in 1947 when the BBC was returning to full-scale new style broadcasting. The remit of the School Broadcasting Council was then described as being to 'stand sponsor' with the educational world for programme services offered by the BBC to schools. That formula has worked successfully because the teachers and their representatives, together with representatives of the Inspectorate, were involved not merely in formal consultations, but in active discussion, in three Programme Committees, of the preparation of each year's series of programme offerings. These Committees were not involved in production itself, which was recognized to be the professional business of the staff of the BBC. They were, however, invited to suggest the treatment of the various subjects proposed and to comment on pilot productions and scripts. This deliberate and constructive involvement of the external interests with the professional staff concerned within the BBC meant that the BBC was rarely seen, in its schools broadcasting, as an object of criticism by those to whose area of professional interest the broadcasts were directed, even when such delicate areas as sex education were explored. Such criticism as tended to develop usually came from the audiences outside the schools who happened to see or hear programmes which were intended to be used in schools under the direction of teachers. Thus, some of the more recent broadcasts discussing social and ethical problems provoked comment among the general audience who happened to tune into them and who were not aware of the discussion documents with which the teachers had been provided, or of the deliberate objective of these programmes to provoke discussion of matters about which there could be more than one point of view. Such audiences, unintended but unavoidable, greatly resented being described as 'eaves-droppers', a word used almost in a technical sense by the educational broadcasters in the BBC, but perhaps not best designed to soothe the external critic who was less than completely informed about the intentions of the broad-casters.

Similar consultative processes were followed when the BBC returned to further education broadcasting after the war. The Further Education Advisory Council was set up in 1964, in the post-Pilkington expansion of television, and although it did not have the same formal power to require that all further education programmes should be specifically submitted to its sponsorship, in practice the BBC always sought its endorse-ment for the series which it intended to provide for further education audiences. The problems became more difficult when the Open University came into operation in 1970 because it was clear from the first that its programmes could well develop in a competitive way to cover areas of interest which were already partly occupied by the activities of BBC further education programmes. There was an inevitable tension between the Further Education Advisory Committee, which, however greatly respected by the BBC, was never-theless consultative in status, and the Open University, which had its own specific allocation of air time, completely handed over by the BBC, together with its own financial resources, provided by grant-in-aid, and its own academic government on characteristically independent university lines. True, the process of programme production, carried out by the BBC staff for the Open University, was described as a full partner-ship, and real value was attached to this description both by the BBC and the Open University participants. But the relation-ship was of one independent body dealing with another on the basis of a formal legal agreement, and it called for considerable delicacy and tact.

In all these three areas – Schools, Further Education and the Open University – it was necessary for the BBC to have a central point of reference, from which it could speak with a single voice, answering for both Television and Radio. The post of Controller, Educational Broadcasting, set up in the postwar years, remained central in the structure of the BBC, responsible for the operational conduct of the Radio and Television production departments in all three sectors, and answering to the Director-General through the Director, Public Affairs (or through the equivalent earlier post of Chief Assistant to the Director-General). But it was important that the Controller, Educational Broadcasting, always had the right of access to the Director-General, for he was required to speak for the BBC in its relationships with the educational world, and he could do so with authority only if he knew that he could speak for the Director-General, and for that reason, with the ultimate authority of the Board, in which at least one Governor – often the Vice-Chairman – had a specific commitment to the world of education.

A similar position, but on a smaller scale, existed traditionally in Religious Broadcasting. The first of the BBC's Advisory Committees to be set up was the Central Religious Advisory Committee. It came into being, as the 'Sunday Committee' as a result of exchanges between Reith and the Archbishop of Canterbury in 1924. The Archbishop had initially been unconvinced about the potential virtues of religious broadcasts, but his discussions with Reith led him to the view that religion must be represented within the range of broadcast programmes. From that time onwards the official representatives of the Churches were in formal contact with the BBC about the character and content of BBC religious programmes. Over the years the brief of Religious Broadcasting was described in the BBC Handbook as being to 'present the worship, thought and action of the churches, to explore the contemporary relevance of the Christian faith for listeners and viewers, be they church members or not, and to reflect fresh religious insights'. From 1928 onwards the Daily Service was broadcast every day in the principal radio network, and religious services were regularly relayed from churches and chapels of the different denominations. The question of denominational proportions was settled by reference to the Central Religious Advisory Committee when necessary. There was rarely major dispute in this aspect of religious broadcasting. But in presenting the relevance of the Christian standard to the present day world there was clearly room for increasing tensions as the practice of religion, and the attitudes of the general public towards it, began to change with increasing speed and to find greater public expression. And the exploration of 'fresh religious insights' was unexplored and dangerous territory, likely to provoke considerable public response, both hostile and approving, to which the BBC had to respond as an institution. In this respect religious programmes could not be regarded as simply another kind of programme, liable to provoke personal reactions but not involving the BBC in any public institutional tensions. Religion, for the most part, was embodied in public institutions which would find it natural to make their representations to the BBC when they felt that programmes were affecting their position or the beliefs and sensitivities of their adherents. It is this characteristic of institutional representation to the BBC which creates a special need for the representation in the central machinery of the Corporation of Current Affairs, Educational and Religious programme responsibilities. The Director-General needs support, as does the Board, of a voice from within the Corporation which can establish a consistent response to the representative institutions which face the BBC when matters of difference arise between them and broadcasting.

When I was asked, in 1974, to speak to the staff of the Religious Broadcasting Department in the BBC I made this direct comparison. I argued that in certain particular respects the BBC required that the ratings be subordinated to its duties to the public, and had chosen in these three areas certain particular ways of seeing that this was done – in some cases by organizational separation, in others by the creation of expectations that particular times would be set aside for these types of programme. Programmes which would not of themselves have automatic mass appeal were nevertheless given placings which created the potential of larger audiences than might otherwise have been expected for the subject matter, or of a greater guarantee of certainty for the audience of finding these programmes at reasonable times than could be offered if ratings were the only consideration. This philosophy represented the exercise of the BBC's normal function of balancing its output so as to ensure that material which deserved serious consideration by the audience was guaranteed a reasonable place in the schedules.

When I was faced with the claim that the BBC had certain moral responsibilities to encourage particular views I denied it. I did say, however, that the BBC had a moral responsibility to ensure that every view that deserved a serious hearing had a chance to find an outlet on the air. The decision about what constitutes a claim to a serious hearing is, of course, very difficult, but it ought to be liberally taken. Nothing appears more clear to me than that religion has a claim to be taken seriously in a country which has a Christian history and a Christian tradition. It is for that reason that religion has its place in the BBC's schedules and it is because the BBC recognizes that argument that I felt able to say to those who accused the BBC of moral negativism that we respected and presented those opinions about life which presupposed a moral content in it. It was not necessary for the BBC to commit itself to those views, but it was necessary for us to commit ourselves to their exposure.

Many among those who would wish to support religious broadcasting will seek to add a dimension of special moral justification, a basis of primacy for the claims of religious broadcasting, which for them will seem to be entirely natural.

I suggested that it was dangerous for the Religious Broadcasting Department within the BBC to accept that kind of support too uncritically, because their stronger claims were those which rested on a homogeneous view of the BBC's philosophies – a view which would be closer to that of the preponderance of their colleagues, and which rested on the concept of a general obligation to secure a fair hearing for material which, in the pure programme sense, were not of guaranteed majority interest.

My view was that religious broadcasting was moving out of the status of a category of programmes which was specially protected because of its content and was becoming simply one of those areas in which, because the BBC had to meet an external institutionalized response, it had to have some centrally answerable group within itself to make the necessary self-consistent responses for the institution as a whole.

Current Affairs, Educational Broadcasting and Religious Broadcasting are the areas which call for this kind of central focus of answerability within the BBC because of the content of the programmes and the nature of the external responses which they may provoke. The structural problems thrown up by regional broadcasting similarly cut across the functional division of Television, Radio and External Services which form the basic organizational pillars of the BBC, but the reason is one of social geography, not of programme content. As I have explained, the national network is the basic planning and editorial unit on which the BBC's structure rests. But if the BBC is to respond, as it should, to the sense of regional identity – and, more particularly in recent years, of national identity in Scotland, Wales and Northern Ireland – the transmitters which constitute the national networks have to be used at certain times of the day to carry programmes of special interest to their own geographical areas. On the old Home Service, and on Radio 4 until November 1978, certain times of the day were set aside to carry regional programmes, produced in the regional centres. In the Haley postwar scheme these regional centres included three of major importance in England as well as the national regional centres in Scotland, Wales and Northern Ireland, but after the changes introduced under the 'Broadcasting in the Seventies' policy regional programmes on radio in England ceased, with the exception of a very small proportion of area news bulletins carried on VHF.

In television, BBC-1 had been designed almost from the beginning as a VHF network which could be split into its regional components, although the capacity to produce programmes in centres outside London was very severely constricted until the late 1960s by technical and financial factors. The plan put forward in 'Broadcasting in the Seventies' envisaged a substantial further expansion of production capacity in Scotland and Wales, and the establishment of three major production centres in England (in Manchester, Birmingham, Bristol, as well as eight specifically regional production studios – three of them incorporated in the network centres in Manchester, Birmingham and Bristol). These regional centres were to have access to the so-called 'opt-out' times within BBC-1, and the amount of these opt-out programmes was to increase, as resources permitted, to some four hours a week for each.

The structural problem was how these regional activities, embracing both Radio and Television, were to be managed at the network and regional production centres outside London, and yet still be accommodated within a BBC structure which rested on the assumption that air time and resource allocations were carried out by Network Controllers in London. But clearly, regional sensitivies, and especially the national sensitivities in Scotland and Wales, were unlikely easily to accept the thought of dictation from London. And yet there was no logical escape from the fact that the final control of resources must rest with the Network Controllers who were planning the schedule within which regional programmes were to appear. This was true even in Radio, where the intention of 'Broadcasting in the Seventies' was that regional production should be increased rather than diminished, but should be accommodated within the national network structure rather than as opt-outs from it. The suggestion was sometimes made that there should be a Director of Regions with a seat on the Board of Management, and I have no doubt that this idea will be resurrected from time to time because it appears to have a certain logic. But the logic is that of public relations, not of management. Nothing can remove the basic fact that Television resources must be planned and allocated by a central television programme planning unity, if a sensible schedule is to be produced, and if there is to be maximum economy in the development of the resources necessary to sustain a network. The same is true in Radio, though the financial penalties of error are less. A Director of Regions would be no more than another voice at the conference table – not a genuine manager of resources.

My conclusion, whenever I considered this problem was always that there must be a senior BBC manager in charge of each of the major production centres (and in England, in charge of the series of regional studio operations in each area) in order to see that the total BBC unit was operating efficiently and that its requirements for successful operation were made known to London. Naturally, such a manager would have a public relations function in his area. But the essence of his job was to secure the delegation of resources which would enable him to fulfil a network programme commitment decided in London, but whose proportions were subject to argument from the regional manager, with the knowledge that his case was always supported by very strong political considerations which London could ignore only at cost of peril to the whole standing of the BBC throughout the United Kingdom. I believed that the organizational difficulty reflected a real difficulty on the ground. Current needs might change the particular shape of the mechanism from time to time, but in the end the system had to be made to work by the quality of the men who were put to work in it.

The problems in Radio will have been significantly eased by the changes in wavelengths of November 1978, because, for the first time, they put into the hands of the Controllers in each of the National Regions complete power over the air time of their own transmitters. Each National Region will have its own wavelength, which will not be required to carry the United Kingdom service of Radio 4. That is the principal effect of transferring Radio 4 to the single long wave channel with coverage of the audience. Once the Controllers have their own power to schedule their national wavelengths the problem of balancing the conflicting demands of those who feel deprived of the United Kingdom service when the relevant 'national' programmes are being broadcast, and those who feel restricted in their access to their own national material because of the requirement to carry UK programmes for substantial parts of the day, will disappear. The longstanding argument that the audience in the National Regions for the so-called 'national character' programme is really a minority will be tested against the reality of total separation, and the parallel availability throughout the day of the UK service. There is natural anxiety among the Controllers about the financial and technical resources which will be available to them for the production of an adequate programme service, and the difficulty that long term resources have to be allocated in London will still remain. But the view which I took, when it seemed certain that some adjustment would have to be made to the wavelength pattern in the UK after the outcome of the Geneva Conference was known, was that the tide of national sentiment in the three nations was certain to become more significant as the years passed and that attempts to patch up compromises between the individual national requirements and the UK need were doomed to friction and failure. My argument was not that the provision of Radio 4 on a single UK basis was necessary for political reasons – of holding on to unity in the political sense – but rather that there were two conflicting demands in the audience which could only be satisfied by the separation of both, if it could be reasonably achieved. The one area which remains a problem for the future is England, and for the time being the development of local radio, which, for the BBC, has so far been limited to England, will have to attempt to satisfy local sentiments. There is no other solution in sight within the wavelength provision which can be made. And in Television the existing national networks do not allow for any other solution than that based on the concept of the 'opt-out' programme. It may be that when the fourth network eventually comes into operation, particularly if it is operated by an Open Broadcasting Authority, or something following a similar philosophy, arrangements might be made for the transmission of 'national' television programmes within the National Regions in the air time available on the new network. That would relieve the strain of opting out which at present has to be borne by the national networks, whether of the BBC or of the IBA.

There is a regional problem for the BBC just as there is a regional problem for the United Kingdom. It will not be abolished by constitutional or structural mechanisms. The difficulties can be eased by commonsense and good relationships. I am sure that that is the approach which has to be followed by the BBC. The main risk is the classical insensitivity of the English to the sensitivities of those who are not English. It is a central function of the Director-General to remind his English colleagues that they are likely, by the accident of birth, to be insensitive brutes. Only by the practice of decent anti-chauvinism will the necessary management structure of the BBC be made to work in its regional contacts.

Nothing in the special problems of Current Affairs, Education, Religion and the Regions has ever convinced me that it would be right to change the structure which rests on the reality of the distinction between the BBC's three principal operations. They must remain the bedrock of its organization. The variants must be made to work as well as possible, and with as much understanding as men of good conscience can command.

CHAPTER XIV

Changing the Pattern

I HAVE DESCRIBED the structure of the BBC as I knew it in the 1970s. With the exception of the violent political rupture establishing competitive television in the 1950s, the whole history of BBC broadcasting had been one of organic growth, with almost no changes of direction in services already established. The original local radio stations set up in the days of the Company were, it is true, amalgamated into a national service, and that represented a substantial change of character which set the pattern of broadcasting in the country for a generation and more. But whenever further development was contemplated it was always as a result of an official enquiry – the Ullswater Committee in the 1930s, a Government enquiry after the war, and Beveridge and Pilkington at approximate ten-year intervals thereafter. But it could not be assumed that every change of direction in the BBC would happily coincide with the setting up of an official enquiry, and in the late 1960s, in the absence of the early prospect of the usual Committee, it seemed right to look again at the structure of the radio service, now that substantial audiences had moved over to television in the evenings, and local radio was beginning to develop. The BBC therefore embarked on its own enquiry, under the stimulus both of natural questions asked by the Radio programme managers and of others raised by the McKinsey study groups. The result was the publication of the document 'Broadcasting in the Seventies', which was an attempt to place the outcome of a professional enquiry and its recommendations before the public in order to secure consent for the plans proposed. This process exposed the dilemma which must face any professional public servant when seeking to change the nature of his service in the absence of legislative action.

The technocrat's dilemma can be quite simply stated. In planning resources it is very difficult to state a general proposition without providing a great deal of detailed information. In order to assemble that detailed information the planner has to make certain calculations which rule out certain possible courses, and the process of preparing the plan itself, including alternatives within it, leads to certain conclusions which appear to be inescapable. The planner has to go a very long way towards a series of alternative final solutions before he can present his ideas to the public. And so he lays himself open to the accusation of having had everything cut and dried before the general idea ever reaches the public for discussion in principle. That is the nature of the dilemma. Does one secure public consent by offering the general principles without the supporting detail, or does one also present the detail with the conclusions which emerge inevitably from it, as the basis for public discussion? Whatever one does will be wrong. In the first case, the planner will be accused of presenting half-baked ideas unready for public discussion. In the second, he will be accused of leaving no real possibility of choice to the public, and therefore no reality in the discussion. In this chapter I try to set out the history of the development and presentation of the proposals of 'Broadcasting in the Seventies' and the public reception which was accorded to them.

The problem begins with the inflexibility of the basic resource – wavelengths – and proceeds to the technical complexity of the management of programme production resources. The wavelength question is further complicated by the fact that the BBC, as a user, enjoys its tenure only by Government allocation, made on grounds of use stated at the time when the original service is proposed. It cannot be assumed that a wavelength allocation will automatically be continued by the Government if the BBC states a wish to change the content of the service in a substantial way. It is improbable that a wavelength would be taken away unless there was substantial public upheaval, but it is wise not to tempt the fates too far when proposing change.

As to the technical complexity of the production processes, to professionals involved in the business of production and transmission, contracts and copyrights, balance in current affairs and of musical tastes over centuries, the mass of information relevant to broadcasting decisions may perhaps be daunting, but it is manageable. I suspect that it is not so to the general public, and a very special effort is needed before these technical complexities can be even explained, let alone made the subject of popular discussion. And yet they cannot but be the subject of popular discussion.

'Broadcasting in the Seventies' was an attempt by a public corporation to propose changes in a service of high interest to the public, and to do so in a way which presented the various arguments in an understandable form and permitted public discussion on those matters where it appeared that there were real choices. The rub lies in that last phrase – 'where it appeared there were real choices'. Of course, it appeared to the *professionals* that there *were* real choices. It is very difficult to know who else could have judged whether that was so. And as to the range of these real choices, that again was a matter of judgement and many felt disposed to dispute the judgements that had been made, and to detect professional double-talk.

The 'Broadcasting in the Seventies' proposals emerged from the decision by the BBC's Board of Governors, considering advice from the then Director-General Sir Hugh Greene, to call in the American-based firm of management consultants, McKinsey Incorporated, in order to study the financial and operational efficiency of the BBC. That decision was related to the political need to demonstrate managerial efficiency as a preliminary to an argument about the level of the licence fee. But out of their first survey, in which

McKinseys generally endorsed the operational efficiency of the BBC, there came also a decision by the BBC to review in particular the future roles of radio, and of the regions, and the possibilities of reducing the cost of music programmes. The task of carrying out those studies was given to what became known as the policy study group – a combined team of senior BBC executives and McKinsey advisers. It began work in November 1968. It presented its report to the Board of Governors in May 1969. Its conclusions were broadly endorsed by the Board and published as a pamphlet in July 1969. There was then a period of public discussion until October, when it was announced that the plan would be put into effect, and in January 1970 the new schedules were published for Radio and they came into effect in April.

The first decision which had to be taken in November 1968 was about the way in which the Policy Study Group should work. Should it immediately take into consultation all those who might conceivably be affected by any change in the pattern of Radio or of the regions or of BBC music? The BBC knew from ordinary organization and method studies how voluminous discussion of even the smallest change could become. On practical grounds, therefore, there was a strong argument for keeping the discussion within a relatively small group with a mission to ask all the awkward questions. Further, it was clear that the mere asking of awkward questions might be sufficient to provoke uncertainties in quarters which, in the end, would almost certainly be unaffected by the conclusions which might emerge from such a study. On the principle of limiting the field of unnecessary anxiety, it was decided that the workings of the Policy Study Group should be kept confidential to the most senior management staff and to those directly involved. This clearly imposed certain security requirements on the extent of the enquiries and the distribution of the papers and the amount of consultation at the operational level. But none of this seemed to be an impossible handicap. The senior people working on the study were very conversant themselves with the operational requirements which they were examining, and they were by no means of an uncritical turn of mind. If they had been, they would have had to answer the awkward questions put by McKinsey's who were members of the Group.

The decision the Governors and management took, therefore, was to conduct a confidential study, the results of which, of course, would have to be the subject of much wider discussion within the BBC at professional levels; with the advisory bodies, who would clearly be deeply interested in any proposals having potentially such a broad effect on our services; and finally, with the public – so far as that discussion could be encouraged by the BBC.

All previous enquiries of this scope into broadcasting in this country had been instituted by public decision. They had been carried out by committees of enquiry appointed by Ministers to report to Parliament. They had occurred at moments when the constitutional instruments were due for renewal, and they therefore rested on necessity rather than on choice. It goes without question that Parliament must, from time to time, institute enquiries into the activities of public bodies like the BBC, and seek recommendations as to their future operation. It is much more open to question whether such public bodies themselves can institute a process of self-enquiry on such a scale as was attempted by the BBC in 'Broadcasting in the Seventies'. One might ask, by what constitutional authority was this done? But it seems to me that, when the State has set up a corporation responsible for managing its own affairs, it is very difficult to require it not to change itself if the reason for change seems to have presented itself. Constitutional powers are not straitjackets. When I consider the question, therefore, of whether it is right for a public organization like the BBC to institute wide-ranging enquiries into its own work, I answer in the affirmative. There is, indeed, a direct injunction in the Charter for the BBC to do so. The Governors ought not to be restrained simply by the argument that Parliament has not specifically authorized an enquiry of that kind. One cannot assume that change will be required at the precise intervals which represent the duration of Charters and Acts of Parliament.

The object of publishing the 'Broadcasting in the Seventies' proposals was to secure the participation of the public in the proceedings. The public discussion of 'Broadcasting in the Seventies' took place in three phases. The first was the phase of rumour during planning. The second was the formal phase of public discussion – including a Commons Debate – between publication of the plans in July 1969 and the decision date in October. And the third was a period of harassing criticism from mid-September 1969 until the plans were finally put into effect in April 1970. That last period included debates in the House of Commons and the House of Lords.

During the first period of public comment – that of rumour as the study proceeded – the number of people who were aware of the general drift of the enquiry was steadily increasing. It became very clear at this stage that contacts were being established between senior BBC staff and the Press. These contacts must have been with senior BBC staff because only very few people knew as much as was being revealed. But the stories were incomplete, partial in their presentation, and, to a substantial degree, inaccurate. It was quite clear at one point that a document written for one of our regional advisory councils – and possibly more than one copy – had reached two leading newspapers. I did not believe that any member of those councils released that document, though I recognized the very considerable strain on the loyalties of advisers who knew of what was being discussed, who might feel strongly about it, and who had to consider whether their loyalty to their confidential relationship with the BBC ought to be stronger than their public responsibility for protecting, as they saw it, the service which was being given by the BBC.

The total period during which the proceedings and findings of the Study Group were regarded as confidential lasted from mid-November until early July – some seven months in all. The Board of Governors saw and approved the plan in May. It was then presented to the General Advisory Council, convened in a special meeting to include regional representation, in June 1969. Every extension of the area of information, as in all such operations, increased the risk of some public disclosure, even by accident. The BBC was fortunate in its advisers, in that they gave a very wide assent to a request that the whole plan be published as a single statement in early July.

The nature of the decisions which had to be taken in the first decision phase on what alternatives were to be presented in the published document explains the reasons for confidentiality. First, and overwhelmingly, there were the financial calculations. In a broad sense, anybody can calculate what the BBC's net income from licences is likely to be over a given period. What they cannot do so easily is to calculate what assumptions have been made about the agreements likely to be negotiated both with the staff and performers on the rates of payment. This is understandably a critical factor in any budget drawn up during an inflationary period, and it would be the height of folly for any negotiator to disclose his hand in public. As a rough guide, at least 50% of the BBC's expenditure is on staff and a further 30% is on contributors' fees. (The detailed figures vary from Service to Service, and I go into them more fully in a later chapter.) The inflationary provision in the budget therefore applies in full to at least 80% of the BBC's operational expenditure and is a major factor. That alone argued for confidentiality on the budgetary side.

Secondly, some of the proposals which were studied as possibilities involved reductions in staff or in categories of programme provision. There would have been no point in telling those who might have been affected before it was certain that we wished to make such proposals. There was a good deal of argument within the BBC, including the Board of Governors, before it was decided, for example, precisely which orchestras to disband. The BBC knew how explosive this issue might be. Indeed, I have an original *Punch* cartoon which shows me looking out of a window at Broadcasting House at a busload of musicians coming in at the front entrance with their violin cases, with Lord Hill saying to me: 'When the fatal announcement's made, Curran, I want them all frisked for weapons'. It was only a slight exaggeration. In the end only one small group was disbanded and the remainder survived. There were other uncertainties which it would have been unwise and unnecessary to propagate before they became certainties. And even then they were certainties only in the sense of being accepted possibilities, not approved decisions.

These were the major considerations arguing for confidentiality. By the spring of 1969 BBC management was operating in an atmosphere of rumour, some of it wild to an astonishing degree. There was even one which suggested that Radio Licence revenue was going to be diverted to finance development of Colour Television. Ridiculous though it was, on purely financial grounds, it was taken so seriously that Sir Hugh Greene found it necessary to issue a formal denial.

In July 1969, by which time I had succeeded Sir Hugh Greene, the BBC published 'Broadcasting in the Seventies'. It seemed a straightforward planning statement, including possible choices. It was introduced at the best-attended news conference ever held by the BBC. I appeared with some of my Directors on Television that evening to explain points in the plan. As a preliminary move I had addressed some 250 of my senior staff to explain what was coming. The pamphlet itself was distributed to all members of the staff, all members of the advisory councils and committees and to the Press. Copies were sent to MPs and to many members of the House of Lords, as well as to many organizations and individual leaders of thought and opinion. The BBC sent out many others in response to written and telephone requests. The total print order in the end amounted to over 60,000, most of which were distributed. *The Times*, *The Daily Telegraph* and *The Guardian* published the document virtually in full. There was editorial comment in all but one of the national dailies and many provincials. Subsequently I took part with Mr Mansell, Chairman of the Policy Study Group, in a Third Programme discussion of the proposals. This was, in turn, reprinted in *The Listener*. Special presentations were made to the Sunday newspapers, especially *The Times*, *The Guardian* and *The Sunday Times*, reflecting the discussions very fully and included contributions from senior BBC executives.

On 22 July there was a Commons Debate on the future of broadcasting which took account of 'Broadcasting in the Seventies'. On 24 July I addressed the Parliamentary Press Gallery on the way in which the proposals had been devised and put forward, and then, early in August, Lord Hill and I were asked to see the then Prime Minister to discuss certain aspects of the proposals. They were, respectively, our proposals for local radio on a national scale, the higher licence fee (necessary whatever the outcome of the proposals), and the suggestions about the reduction of the BBC's orchestral resources. The conclusion of that discussion was that a proposal for an increase in the licence fee was adopted by the Government, as were our proposals for local radio on a national scale. We, for our part, undertook not to reduce our orchestral resources in any substantial way. In effect, the Government decision on 'Broadcasting in the Seventies' had been made. We all went off on holiday thinking that the argument was virtually over.

I returned from holiday in mid-September to find that the whole issue had been reopened by an organization which called itself 'The Campaign for Better Broadcasting'. They were suggesting that the plans represented a demolition of high culture in broadcasting. There followed a controversy which became more heated than anything which had gone before.

At the end of September, Frank Gillard, the Director of Radio, contributed a long letter explaining the radio proposals to *The Times*, rebutting the accusation that the proposals would debase radio standards. Lord Hill spoke in Leeds and I was interviewed at length by *The Times* and by *The Daily Telegraph*. (These, incidentally, were the only two requests to me for interview. I responded to both.) There was other detailed argument on the nature of the proposed adjustments to the spoken word output on radio, which had been a particular target of the Campaign for Better Broadcasting.

By this time the continued controversy in the Press and the absence of any firm statement of the BBC's intention either to abandon or to pursue the proposals was having such an effect on staff morale that I recommended to the Board that an immediate announcement should be made that they would be implemented, discussion having gone as far as it constructively could, I announced this decision on 16 October. In effect, what I was saying was that the proposals having been properly published and discussed, with Government having announced certain decisions on the proposals made, and with the growing state of uncertainty beginning to hamper the management of broadcasting in the BBC, a decision had become inescapable. This point is bound to come in any process of public consultation. I think it just possible that the BBC may have delayed it too long in our desire to see the fullest discussion by the public of the proposals we had made, although I certainly would have liked to have more consultation with the Unions. This was frustrated by the considerations I have mentioned.

It was clear that the BBC had to explain in detail to its own staff what was actually proposed. They were afraid for their own future; they were afraid for the standards of broadcasting. Fear in such situations is always likely. It is not enough simply to denounce it. The reasons for exaggerated fear have to be shown not to exist, or to be reduced to realistic proportions. I therefore addressed successive private meetings of staff in Bristol, Birmingham and Manchester. Once again, Press rumour was rife about what I had said. Some of the misconceptions were serious and damaging. The tensions were not eased by the BBC's simultaneous dispute with the Association of Broadcasting Staff about the then current salary negotiation, over which the BBC had, in fact, been subjected for the first time to industrial action by them and taken to a Court of Enquiry. The atmosphere was not good, because the suspicion was prevalent that the only reason for the BBC proposals was to make economies – which was very far from the truth.

We carried forward our plans for the restructuring of radio and regional broadcasting and I issued further statements explaining to staff how this was to be done. These statements were, of course, published and available to the Press. The Minister of Posts announced that he had given permission for twelve new BBC Local Radio stations, which was a first step towards implementing the decisions of the summer. We issued a special edition of our house magazine *Ariel* to reply to staff criticisms of 'Broadcasting in the Seventies'. This, too, was given broad press coverage. I myself took part, at the end of November, in a televized discussion in *Daytime*. There was a further House of Commons Debate early in December and just after Christmas we met the Association of Broadcasting Staff to discuss how the proposals for the regions should be carried out, they having taken the view that, although they were critical of the proposals in general, they wished to be involved in the discussion of their implementation. This was one of the few gleams of light which came through at this time. It was accompanied by a settlement of the pay dispute on the basis of the Court of Enquiry Report.

But although the formal discussions with our staff on how the new proposals might be implemented seemed to be on the right track at this stage, we were in for more trouble – some of it more bitter than enything we had so far encountered. The BBC published the new schedules for Radios 3 and 4 on 13 January. They were given very close attention by the Press and they were published in very full form in *The Listener*. Nobody should have been able to say that they did not know what the BBC's intentions were in the only terms which mattered – programmes which were going to be heard by the listeners.

It was the start of a stream of letters to *The Times*, few of which seemed to take any account of what had actually been said. The phrase 'the Third's demise' became a standard heading in the correspondence columns of that newspaper. 'Debasements of quality' became a standard phrase of denunciation. Some of the longest letters from BBC executives ever published by *The Times* explained very fully the true facts. They produced brief letters in reply whose substance was often exceeded by the number of signatures appended. Printers' ink, to judge by the uses to which it was put, had become vitriol when critics discussed the BBC's intentions. George Camacho, a former senior much-respected member of staff of long experience, wrote to say that while he could not endorse all the 'Broadcasting in the Seventies' proposals he would ask that 'any criticism be based on knowledge of the facts and some understanding of the dilemmas of the public service broadcaster rather than on emotive reaction and bald assertion'.

The climax of the campaign seemed to have been attained when, on 14 February, 134 BBC staff wrote to express their collective protest in *The Times* at the implementation of the proposals, denying that the intentions stated by their seniors could be achieved. This produced what, to my mind, was the only appropriate response – from Sir Hugh Greene. What was being improbably alleged, he said, was that BBC management, including himself, were 'a lot of bloody liars'.

A leader in *The Times* alleged that programme producers had 'not had a fair opportunity of influencing the minds of administrators' and spoke of 'accumulating evidence that the BBC authorities are less concerned than they were with their traditional role as the sponsors and protectors of quality broadcasting'. The evidence for that proposition came, of course, from tainted sources, and the charge itself was nonsense. I replied on 23 February in what was certainly the longest letter I ever expect to have published in that news-paper, once more pointing out that rumour and mere assertion were not a sufficient basis for the criticism of public policy, declared and published. My letter ended with words with which I think any Minister or Permanent Under-Secretary would agree: 'Here is the essence of the case. There has been endless discussion since October. None of it has convinced us of the case presented by our critics. There is disagreement. When that happens, those who are in charge must make the decisions.'

The whole affair was wound up by the House of Lords Debate at the end of February in which a great deal of common-sense was spoken, including a compelling remark by Lord Goodman. The BBC, he said, was 'entitled to be judged by the results. We have not seen the results. What we have seen is the most unholy clamour before anyone has felt the slightest prick'.

In March the Press began to accept – as did others – that the new plans would go through. The barrage of hostile criticism and inaccurate information began to subside. There was a late run by the newly formed '76 Group', which was more concerned with the genuine question of whether change in a public service ought to be introduced by the initiative of the responsible public corporation rather than as a result of formally constituted public enquiry. It is a proper question to ask, and it applied to Independent Television, and in particular to London Weekend Television, as well as to ourselves. The two Commons debates, in July and December 1969, were, of course, an opportunity to consider the whole range of the BBC proposals as they had emerged from the phase of public dis-cussion earlier in the year. The substantive question remains. Is the BBC free to reform itself? That is a permanent issue. Despite the BBC's experience over 'Broadcasting in the Seventies' I maintain my belief in the distribution of informa-tion and the attempt to secure consent by discussion on controversial matters of this kind.

I think that there were certain special circumstances about our experience. First, broadcasting is a subject of intense interest among those who use it. It is general in its impact. Television is a peculiarly personal possession. It is the face in the corner of one's own living room. Anybody who plays about with it is liable to attack. Radio is even more so – a valued friend, something to be defended against change at all costs. On these grounds alone the BBC should have expected trouble.

In the second place, I believe that there were certain ephemeral circumstances about the situation of broadcasting at the time which led to unwarranted suspicions. First, there was the awareness in the public mind of Lord Hill. He had been an active politician, with a reputation for acting vigorously elsewhere. And furthermore, he had given evidence of this capacity during his Chairmanship of the Independent Television Authority. And the fact that that was where he came from did not lessen the suspicions of those who felt that BBC broadcasting should stay in the image which they had formed for themselves. Furthermore, I was new and unknown as Director-General, and appointed under his regime. There was ready-made suspicion in people's minds, however unfair it may have been for both of us. Finally, there was the presence of McKinseys, the American managements consultants. Besides the original sin of being American, they had committed particular sins in previous investigations, such as their criticism of regional operations in British Rail and their radical approach to the management objectives of the Post Office. What might they do to a revered institution like the BBC? It was quite clear to the suspicious that all the objectives of the Third Programme would fall under their knife; that regional broadcasting would be jettisoned, and that financial criteria would be the only ones applied in future to programme judgements. Couple all this with the growing pressure for public participation in public decision and the cumulative effect was bound to be a difficult passage for any new proposals which might be put forward by an established institution – indeed, an institution of the Establishment – like the BBC.

But the basic problem was that the BBC was trying to proceed knowing that although we might have wished for one, there would be no public enquiry, but that there was a need for change. The BBC laid itself open to public question and public debate. I now doubt whether this kind of self exposure is an adequate substitute for formal public enquiry.

When I was invited to discuss the problems we encountered in a lecture to the Royal Town Planning Institute, I drew attention to the close parallels between our experiences and that of planning authorities advancing new proposals. The Skeffington Committee rightly pointed out that there are limitations to the concept of participation. Of these, one is that 'responsibility for preparing a plan is and must remain that of the planning authority'. They added another: 'The completion of plans is a task demanding the highest professional standards of skill and must be undertaken by the professional staff of the planning authority.' Those two limitations on participation are precisely where the difficulties occur. Those who dislike the basic decision will seek to continue the debate indefinitely, and they will also cast doubt on the integrity of the professionals who must be charged with the formulation of precise planning details. 'Bureaucratic double-talk' is the sort of phrase which recurs in these situations.

Publicity for proposals is easy but effective participation is much more difficult. The effort to take proposals far along the road towards practicability before publication produces a strong disinclination to alter them once published. And from the public's point of view, the process creates an appearance of the denial of the opportunity to comment. There is the central dilemma.

One of the innovatory features of the 'Broadcasting in the Seventies' debate was that the BBC laid itself open for discussion on its own air, both radio and television. It was not an easy experience for those of us who had to appear, and when people say to me that it is no part of the functions of, for example, a businessman to appear on the air, I can understand the implied reluctance to undergo the experience. But I am more convinced than ever before that it is an inescapable part of the public responsibility of running any major institution for the senior executives to be prepared to face public discussion and questioning, and, above all, broadcast public discussion and questioning. The BBC is under a particular constraint in this respect because it must not seem to be using its own medium to its own advantage. Nevertheless, I think that the general balance of all our appearances on the air was one of advantage, both to the public and to ourselves.

Looking back, I do not see even now what we could have done so very differently. The technical parameters would have had to be worked out, and by the professionals. The options would have had to be reduced to those which were realistic and not allowed to include those which amounted to no more than pie in the sky. It would have been very difficult to embark earlier on the public debate without being accused of putting forward half-baked plans not worth the consideration of the public and indicating only our managerial incompetence. It would have been quite wrong to have excluded the advisory councils from the discussions at the time when we invited their comments. It would have been equally wrong to extend imprecise discussion to them and to the staff before we knew exactly what the BBC wanted to offer. And in the final phase it was certainly right to have published the plans. What we did not foresee was the rolling wave of protest which followed the phase of formal public discussion. I believe this was attributable to quite other elements in the situation than the straightforward proposal to change BBC radio broadcasting plans.

Despite this experience, I remain unrepentant in my view that consent is the paramount requirement in the establishment of public policy on any scale. I remain constant in my view that those who propose cannot put forward half formulated plans. Those who defend and uphold the principle of consent as the basis for the management of society must be prepared to face the risk of seeking it. But the defence of the principle of consent in the face of the inevitably uncomfortable accompaniments of the attempts to secure it, requires more courage than the alternative course – that of deciding to impose, by arbitrary decision, proposals which may seem professionally justified but which have never been submitted to the test of public acceptability. The role of the technocrat in this situation is to explain fully what he means, having worked it out as well as he knows how, and to be prepared then to accept criticism, to take account of it if necessary, and thereafter to face the prospect of decision on the basis of all the factors in the debate, not merely on some, with the certain knowledge that to decide on change is even more unpopular than to propose it.

CHAPTER XV

Destroying the Model

AS A BROADCASTING ORGANIZATION the BBC is exercising power – and in some cases very considerable power – yet it is using that power, in principle, solely to satisfy the individual expectations which listeners and viewers have of the broadcasting system. The fact of this power has from time to time attracted a certain amount of speculative dissection of the BBC as an institution, with the underlying idea that that dissection might become actual rather than speculative whenever the constitutional instruments are due to be renewed. Criticism of the BBC's programmes, which has always been more vocal than would be thought justified from any examination of the size and enthusiasm of the audiences, has seemed to some to be an indication of the BBC's failure to meet the expectations of the society it was set up to serve. Those criticisms have come most prominently from politicians who feel that at certain moments the BBC has given them less than fair treatment, and from moralistic groups who either dislike what they see by way of moral precept on BBC programmes, or believe that the BBC should commit itself to the advocacy and propagation of a particular moral view of life. This varies according to the group which is making the criticism at any particular moment.

A favourite right-wing political solution, which has also come occasionally in other forms from the left, is that the BBC, which is seen as being too big, should solve its problems by being broken up and ceasing to exist as a unity. One such proposal – from the right some years ago – suggested that because of the 'mounting torrent of complaint and criticism' it was no longer 'practical' for the BBC to continue in its present form, and that it should be split up into separate parts, 'each developing its own style and character'. This would enable the consumer of broadcasting to make his own choice, as readers do with newspapers. This move, according to the proposer, would not necessarily stop charges of bias being made against the surviving parts but the accusations would be no more acrimonious than those now levelled against the daily newspapers.

The hyperbole can safely be discounted. It is a provable fact that the level of criticism reaching the BBC is fairly constant. The double barrel of the accusation which precedes the prescription is that the BBC is 'too powerful and too dictatorial', and at the same time 'too undisciplined' and 'too incapable of responsible control by the Governors'. Either the BBC is too powerful or the BBC is too weak, but hardly both at the same time. So, dismissing the hyperbole contained in these analyses – and the one from which I quote is only an example – we are left with two lines of attack.

One is that the BBC is too big to be capable of successful management on a purely practical basis. The other is that the splitting up of the BBC would disperse a centralized source of controlled opinion, and would bring into existence a number of separate sources of divergent opinions – and this is the particular virtue which is sought by the reorganization. Broadcasting would become more efficient because organized in smaller units, and more diverse in its coverage of opinion because each unit would be free to develop such opinions, as the BBC is now not free to do.

I take first the question of diversity. I assume that public finance would continue to be available for the successor organizations to the BBC. As a practical matter, there is no other source of revenue which would be adequate to sustain them. Advertising might provide a part of the necessary funds, but it would not provide the whole, quite apart from the serious questions which would arise, as Annan noted, from mixing advertising revenue with public finance, and the effects of such a change on the printed media. Are we then to contemplate small organizations with committed opinions, each financed from the public purse and each equally free to disregard the opinions which might be expressed about its programmes by those who were providing the finance? I find that a very difficult concept. There would no doubt be one organization committed to the official Government point of view, and one to the Opposition point of view. Would there be others to reflect the different strands of opinion within the official Opposition, and similarly would there have been, for example, on particular issues such as the Common Market, an organization which took an official Labour or Conservative line and which was paralleled by yet another which took a Labour or Conservative, but anti-Common Market point of view? And would all these be equally happily financed from a public licence fee? I do not find this a convincing picture, nor do I believe that the range of opinions which would then be presented would be wider or more effective than that which is offered under the present dispensation. Indeed, I believe that the range would be narrower.

And in order to achieve even this limited diversity of opinions, it would be necessary to split up BBC-1 and BBC-2 in television, and the four radio networks, each to a separate, known commitment. The first consequence would be that the public would lose the present possibility, which is properly exploited, of complementary planning between BBC-1 and BBC-2, which was the argument for the establishment of BBC-2, and has since been used as an argument for a proposed ITV2. The complementarity between the two channels would be in the nature of the opinions which they favoured, and not in the general character of their entertainment programmes. In that respect they would be competing directly with one another at the same time, since it would clearly be in the interests of the strands of opinion which they represented to secure as audiences for those opinions the maximum numbers which could be recruited. It is a problem which has already faced the Dutch system. The Dutch have come to the conclusion that programme planning in television has to take much the same shape in Holland as it does here and in every other country, and that the political or religious commitment of each operating society has to take second place to these considerations, since life has to be lived for much of the time in the real world of popular taste and not in the world of political allegiance. The same has proved to be the case in Italy within a single organization divided on political lines.

As to radio, the four networks would no doubt be divided so as to reflect various shades of political commitment, the first consequence being that the programme distinction between Radio 3, Radio 4 and Radios 1 and 2 would go. Radio 3 would certainly disappear. Would the sponsors of this break-up proposition really wish that to happen, and if so would they dare to argue so publicly? I doubt it. However one looks at these proposals to break up the BBC into its constituent network components in order to permit each of the new units to develop an opinion colour of its own, one finds very quickly that the idea is not sustainable even on a political level, and it pays no regard whatever to the needs of the audience. One is driven to the conclusion that the objective of those who seek to split the BBC is to make it weak – and therefore presumably to make it more pliable. That, as a motive for breaking up the BBC, would be universally condemned. I do not believe that in general the political parties would wish to see the inevitable weakening of broadcasting which would result – though I can believe that the party in government might often wish it.

It is instructive to look at what happens in Independent Television, where, although there is not the pattern of national division which is proposed by the critics of the BBC whose ideas I have been discussing, there is a fragmentation of power according to geographical areas of coverage. Thus, Thames and London Weekend cover London and the South-East, while Granada covers the North-West. If the critics of the BBC are right, then this division of ownership ought to produce a genuinely different political colour in Granada from that which is produced by London Weekend. Some might say that this in fact happens, and that the effects are seen on the national network when a Granada programme is shown. But my concept of the function of the IBA was that it existed precisely to secure that the proper political balance was maintained despite the existence of a federalized system. Indeed this duty of political balance is specifically laid upon the IBA in the Television Act. It does not seem to me that diversity of ownership or organization leads to diversity of opinion unless there is a positive political wish to have organizations which are committed to such different opinions, and I do not believe that any Parliament will set up a system which deliberately seeks to foster quasi-monopolies – because that is what all broadcasting must be – with specific political commitments. Indeed, the great criticism of those in all political camps who dislike the BBC is that they feel that it is politically committed. It is not, in fact, the political commitment which concerns them. It is the fact that it is always on the other side.

As one who has tried to run the BBC under two kinds of government, I can confirm what all my predecessors have said: that the attitudes do change in a very interesting way when parties come into and go out of government. The un-popularity of broadcasters has nothing to do with the kind of opinions they are said to express. It has everything to do with the fact that they are not expressing the opinions of the party in power. This is a crude formulation, and there are many in both parties who understand perfectly well that they cannot enlist the broadcasters as political allies, but in moments of discontent there will always be some in every party who will find the broadcasters unreasonable because they refuse to accept the Government line as the only rational one.

If we consider the question of whether the size of the BBC

prevents it from being efficient, purely as a managerial consideration, one can look at the other schemes which have been
put forward from time to time for dividing it up. It is sensible
to argue that it is not wise to break up an existing institution
until one can prove that the alternative suggested will be
better. I can see no point in break-up propositions which are
likely to produce less efficient operations. Many years ago, at
the time of the Beveridge Committee, there was a view in
several quarters that the BBC might be broken up into its
three principal components – a Television Corporation, a
Radio Corporation and an Overseas Corporation. This
proposition would certainly leave each of the constituent parts
with an obligation to comprehend in their programmes a
diversity of views. They would still be arbiters, holding the
ring for the disputants. Managerially and technically, they
would be divided, and from a philosophical point of view this
proposition is not open to the same objections as the earlier
one which I described. Nevertheless, it would have certain
damaging consequences.

I have no doubt that at home it would still be seen as a
political move to weaken one of the media – and the one
which, is, at the moment, the most respected. The effect
outside the country would be devastating. In the European
Broadcasting Union, the Commonwealth Broadcasting Association and in every broadcasting body which I know, the BBC
is held in the deepest respect, and for any government to break
it up would be seen by broadcasters overseas as a betrayal of
the principle of independence which has led them, for fifty
years, to regard this country as having achieved the most
successful solution to the broadcasting problem which faces
every country. Internationally the break-up of the BBC would
be regarded as a broadcasting disaster – and the reason would
be that the evidence of what we have broadcast is so powerful
that nobody overseas would believe that there could be
sufficient reason for destroying the instrument which has been
responsible.

There is another reason which relates to opinion overseas. It generally goes without dispute that the BBC's External Services broadcasting to Europe and overseas are of the highest quality. They are the most reliable source of news and opinion about this country – and indeed about international affairs in general – which many communities overseas can hope to find. Much of the independence of the External Services derives from their connection with a powerful domestic institution which all Governments have found it difficult to influence. If the domestic parent is relatively immune from Government influence, it is also and equally true that the overseas subsidiary – the External Services – is also immune, sharing the immunity of the parent.

The practical objections are equally powerful. It would hardly seem sensible at a moment when the Government is proposing to confirm and extend the system of commercial broadcasting under the aegis of the IBA, for the parallel publicly-financed institution to be split up. The Government of 1970/74, in its White Paper on 'An Alternative Service of Broadcasting', said: 'In general it is desirable to avoid adding unnecessarily to the number of public authorities.' I agreed with that as a general statement. I believe that public authorities ought to be strong, independent and few. They need the first two qualities to operate successfully and they need the third so that Parliament can effectively see what they are doing. A multitude of authorities makes for an impossibility of supervision.

And what do those who want to break up the BBC propose to do about the splitting of the licence fee?

I am assuming, that a substantial element of public finance is included in their calculations, and that the licence fee would continue to be collected, because it is difficult to see the Treasury relinquishing it, especially if the source of public finance for broadcasting became a direct grant. The radio licence fee was abolished as a separate entity because it was becoming too expensive to collect in relation to the yield. The fee is still there, as a proportion of the television licence fee. Would there be some sort of a controlling board to divide up the proceeds of the collection ? And if so, would it not have to have some considerable knowledge of the arguments for a particular proportion of division? Would it not be involved in assessing the validity of the broadcasters' plans, so as to judge the rightness of the proposed allocations? And would not that bring in the BBC again – or its equivalent – by a back door and in a very inefficient form? It makes no sense.

When people speak of the practical difficulties of managing an organization which is the size of the BBC they forget to make comparisons. There are many larger organizations with similar problems. The real question when size is the objection raised against the BBC, is whether it is efficiently organized. But that is a very different argument. The organization of large bodies is a question of effective devolution, and I believe that BBC organization is now effectively devolved, and that those elements in its operation which are critical to the centre of power are in fact controlled by the centre of power – that is, by the Director-General and the Board. Those crucial areas are frequencies, finance, senior appointments, recruitment policies, labour relations, and, most important of all, the general editorial content of news and current affairs programmes. There is a myth that programme editors in the BBC can do exactly what they want. Very often they do, because it happens to coincide with that they know the Director-General wants. But there are times when they do not. The decisions which have then to be made are not matters of prejudice. They follow well-known basic principles of BBC policy – such as impartiality, fairness, accuracy. These principles have to be applied in particular cases, and they are so applied by an editorial machine which communicates, for the most part, very effectively indeed. Any organization will make mistakes. I believe that the BBC makes very few, and those few spring more from individual failure than from organizational weakness. If anybody can tell me how to make men perfect then I will show him how to run an organization without mistakes. I shall have to wait a long time for that day.

I would add a practical argument to this general statement of the case about the unity of the BBC. There are the economies and the potentialities of scale – and how much less prejudicial it is to use the word 'scale' than to talk of 'size'! There are many examples of the way in which scale has its advantages in the BBC. I take only two, though there are many more which could be cited.

The first is the Engineering Research Department. For a public corporation with an annual income now approaching £300 million a year it is an entirely feasible matter to set aside something like £2 million a year for a technical research department. It is an operational and a financial necessity. Thus, to take only one example from my time, when the plan was approved for the conversion of the UK television transmission system from 405 lines to 625 lines for the sake of European compatibility, the BBC was faced either with the need to re-equip all its studios for the generation of a 625-line signal and to arrange for the conversion of that signal to 405 lines for radiation by the existing transmitters, or with the need to maintain, over a period of years, a dual system of studio origination in which both 405-line and 625-line signals would be generated with separate transmission systems continuing in existence to transmit the separate signals. This second course would have been very expensive indeed. The existence of properly financed Research and Design Departments made it possible for us to produce successive models of signal-converter which in turn enabled the BBC to achieve a very rapid change-over in the studios from 405 to 625-line generation and for conversion of those signals to 405 lines for transmission by the existing distribution system. Without the converter, television in this country would have been faced with highly uneconomic and complex production and distribution problems. It seems highly improbable that the converter would have been produced by any other agency than the BBC's own Research Department.

Further, the same Research Department proved itself capable of working out highly sophisticated plans for the most intensive use of the UHF channels available for all three British television networks now in operation (BBC-1, BBC-2 and ITV): this represents a total national economy. In fact, the BBC's Research Department is responsible for the whole frequency planning of the three networks, and for making possible the concept of a fourth UHF network – just as it was responsible for the working out of feasibility studies for the use of frequencies for BBC and commercial local radio.

My second example is of the potentiality of size – the BBC's role as a patron of live musical performance in this country. There is no question, as was made very clear in the studies undertaken at the time of 'Broadcasting in the Seventies', that there could be more economical ways of producing broadcast music than to run the various orchestras which have been sustained directly by the BBC. But only an institution of national scale and finance which could sustain this kind of burden once the decision has been reached that this should be a function of broadcasting. There is no recent evidence – and likely to be none in the future – that a similar role could be performed by smaller or by differently motivated broadcasting bodies.

One final consideration. In a body as big as the BBC, and concerned with the expression or presentation of opinions, the very size of the organization itself compels pressure towards neutrality. The BBC is, because of its size, a very obvious target for outside criticism. The BBC itself is a body politic within which opinion can be generated and argument flourish. It does flourish, and if any particular part of the BBC, given the knowledge that it is publicly committed to impartiality, were to begin to develop a propagandist intention, in some particular political direction, the criticism which would arise from within the BBC and outside would in the end be sufficient to block the further development of such propagandist units. Everybody in an organization like the BBC, with its public commitment to impartiality, is concerned about the survival of the institution, and about its adherence to its stated principles. When they see colleagues endangering that survival and those principles their criticism is far from muted. The BBC is hardly in a continuous state of what the Communists call auto-criticism, but it has always been clear to me that no marked aberration could long survive within the BBC without expecting to be heavily criticized from within, as well as from without. And usually the internal criticism is generated first. This is not a statement of complacency, of mere confidence in automatic checks and balances. There is a very considerable responsibility on senior BBC management to try to forestall developments of this kind, and senior management is very much aware of the currents of professionally critical opinion within the BBC about its own programmes. There is a systematic communications of such opinion to the very highest levels.

I cannot see that the break-up of the BBC in order to create small units, each having its own slant of opinion, would be at all workable. Nor do I believe that it would be of any benefit to the audience: certainly of no greater benefit than the present system and its diverse opinion offerings. I see a very considerable weakness in any scheme to break up the BBC according to its technically divisible parts. I do not accept the argument that the BBC's size makes it unmanageable for I see other institutions which are bigger and which are certainly manageable, and because I know that the present system does effectively manage the BBC and has been recognized many times as being unusually efficient. I do not accept that size is a bar to good management. I believe that the real questions relate to the devolution of managerial responsibility. I believe that large organizations, provided they are efficiently managed, produce economies of scale which, in the case of broadcasting, are in the public interest. And I believe that the very size and conspicuousness of the BBC as a national institution committed to impartiality is in itself a long-term guarantee that that will remain its character. A BBC which allowed itself to be committed to a political point of view would be a BBC which was bent on suicide.

The arguments for the break-up of the BBC were once again rehearsed in the deliberations of the Annan Committee, and rejected by a majority of that Committee. The Government proposals which followed the publication of the White Paper of July 1978 appeared to be an attempt to embody the proposals for breaking up the BBC within a revised Charter which purported to maintain unity. The denunciation of these new proposals by one of the authors of the proposals for division within the Annan Committee, Mr Phillip Whitehead, was an appropriate comment on the line taken by the Government.

The proposals for the establishment of three new 'service management boards' within the BBC for Television, Radio and External Services were justified, by implication, as being an appropriate response to the Annan Committee's comments on the need to ensure better control and to lessen bureaucracy. Before considering whether the proposed measures could be effective it is necessary to examine the propositions that 'bureaucracy' exists and that 'control' has not been effective enough. Only after that examination is it sensible to consider whether the structures proposed would be desirable.

The charge of bureaucracy, half-adumbrated in the Annan Report, was based, in my experience, on three arguments. The first, reflected in the Annan comments, represented a criticism of the apparently complex internal organization of the Television Service. The second was derived from the complicated personnel management rules on appointments procedures and conditions of service, especially in relation to grading and premium payments. The third, and probably the most sensitive, because it involved MPs among others, represented the effect on external correspondents of the responses they received from the BBC in reply to complaints and criticisms.

The central organizational problem of the Television Service, and of the other Services to a lesser degree, is the need to incorporate the basic unit of the individual programme production team within the large management unit which is required to provide and regulate the complex and extensive range of facilities used in large-scale production. A similar reconciliation of apparent opposites is required to maintain the editorial rein which protects the broad principles expected of the BBC by the public, while allowing effective independence to the producer. The mass of resources which makes possible the range and sophistication of production also requires a hierarchical structure to allocate those resources efficiently. So Heads of Department, Heads of Group and Network Controllers – or their equivalents – become necessary elements in the whole production management process. They may sometimes be seen by producers and those who hear their grievances as hindrances. That is in the nature of any control mechanism when seen from the point of view of the controlled. The Annan Committee's puzzlement in understanding the phenomenon reflects no more than the inadequacy of the time they gave to its study. Hierarchical systems will always produce incidental unintended rigidities, which it is the business of good management to remove. But their occurrence is not a reason for doing without the system. And the financial restraints of the last decade have intensified the need for the hierarchy to have at its command the financial control structures which I describe in a later chapter. Naturally, every creative programme-maker regards these restraints as bureaucratic. But their existence as a guarantee of economy and efficiency is hardly a ground for Ministerial criticism of the BBC.

As to the second argument for the existence of BBC 'bureaucracy' – the rules governing the various personnel procedures – those affecting appointments are a direct reflection of the need to give public assurance of the probity of the system and date back to the suggestions of nepotism and favouritism which formed part of the background of evidence to the Ullswater Committee of 1935. They also reflect the need to give proper assurance to the staff of the BBC, especially as represented by the Unions, on the same issues. The Unions have also been an important element in the elaboration of special conditions which, not surprisingly, accompanied the growth and development of the BBC's operations into something resembling in scale a more or less typical industrial enterprise. The whole structure of special payments and the mysteries of the job grading system were, moreover, considerably affected by the pressures of successive incomes policies in the post-war years, which diverted claims for increases in basic rates of pay into the excessive exploitation of grievances about 'unsocial' hours and the pursuit of fringe changes in relativities between jobs. Thus pay structures and job evaluations which had once been regarded as basically fair were forced into patterns which were both difficult to understand and to administer. But this problem could hardly be said to be unique to the BBC, and I have never seen it as justifying the charge of bureaucracy as a natural product of the BBC management system in particular.

The effect on external critics of their dealings with the BBC is perhaps more understandable, but hardly more relevant to the charge of bureaucracy. I remember Sir Robert Cockburn, when Chairman of the Television Advisory Committee, once saying to me that he recognized in the BBC's submissions to the Committee – the orderliness and completeness of factual evidence and the depth of argument – the characteristic attributes of a self-confident organization relying on high professional competence and extensive practical experience which he had so often found in other Governmental and quasi-Governmental organizations of high reputation. The effect was logically convincing but psychologically provoking, leading to an almost compulsive response to question the conclusions advanced. That must often have been the effect on critics of BBC replies, however right they may have been, and I suspect that the effect was heightened when the matter under discussion was opinion about programmes, in which personal views are strongly held and not very responsive to logic. But to accept, as the White Paper appeared to do (paragraph 10) by repeating the Annan Committee comment that 'the greatest volume of criticism about the present structure had come . . . from those who believed that the broadcasters had been insensitive *in the past ten years* (my italics) to the views expressed by large sections of the public', that the phenomenon of BBC non-responsiveness was recent and therefore called for some new mechanism, was to ignore the substantial facts of Lord Hill and Sir Michael Swann as successive Chairmen, both of whom insisted on – and practised – understanding responses to public comment. I say nothing of my own corresponding role in that time in convincing my professional colleagues of the rightness of this approach and in practising it myself.

I saw, in the criticisms which reached the Annan Committee, as they had previously reached the BBC, no more than a predictable reflection of the difficulties of running a large creative organization operating in a field – Television – which affected, with unprecedented force, the whole life-style of British society. It was not to be expected that management would be without problems or that public response would be uniformly comprehending. But the problems and the response were as normal an accompaniment to a new development as growing-pains are to growing up. They did not necessarily call for new top structures.

But even if the grounds for imposing new structures were small, how could those proposed in the White Paper be expected to work? They were intended, so it was said, to bring 'a measure of decentralization' while preserving 'the essential unity of the BBC', and to 'encourage greater creativity and diversity of approach in programme-making, including the presentation of news and current affairs on the domestic services'. (The White Paper noted that the BBC's External Services were 'a proven success' and 'a national asset which we should be careful to preserve'. That seemed to dispose of the argument for a news structure affecting that area.) But the management problem of the BBC – and indeed the editorial problem – has not been to secure decentralization. It has been to ensure reasonable co-ordination between the three major services without excessively limiting their programme independence. Indeed, it was my view that the McKinsey changes had probably gone too far in establishing managerial decentralization and that the Director-General's power of co-ordination to meet the reasonable requirements of the Board had been excessively diminished. I tried marginally to reverse that process, and I was helped by my two Chairmen – with more enthusiasm from them than I really wanted. It was better for the Director-General to be seen to be pursuing his own course by his own determination if he was to convince his staff of his own independence. He had to have his own authority. The case for a new supervisory structure for the sake of decentralization simply did not stand up to examination in the light of history.

As for creativity and diversity I make two points. The first is that creativity comes from individual producers operating in freedom. That is the experience of fifty years of broadcasting. It does not come by direction from management committees, however distinguished. And, secondly, it never comes from amateurs. New ideas for programmes are suggested with immense fertility by those who know nothing about the practicalities of programme-making. But it is precisely those practicalities which decide whether the ideas are good. Hence good programme ideas come, as I say, from the professionals. What they need from their supervising bodies are the guarantee that resources will be provided, and that adventures will be tolerated, or even encouraged, against the background of public scepticism and even hostility, which is always likely to greet new projects, especially in the creative field.

Nothing in broadcasting experience suggests that the addition of lay managers to the Television Service management would lead to any of the results implied in the White Paper. Indeed, it was much more likely that the new lay members would be more cautious than the professionals, and tend to inhibit adventure. They would certainly need to be extensively briefed before being able to take part at all in professional discussion on management issues. (Since their role was to participate in 'Service *Management* Boards' I assumed that they were not there simply to be general supervisors or assessors.) That alone would call for the establishment of an additional Secretariat mechanism in order to provide the inevitable papers which, because the present Service management committees are professional, are neither frequent nor extensive. It was simply not true to say, as the White Paper did, that such changes 'should not in themselves increase the numbers employed by the BBC'.

But quite apart from the internal irrelevance of the lay members of the 'Service Management Boards' there was the question of their relationship with the Board of Governors, retaining their 'overall responsibilities', particularly that of 'guardians of the public interest'. The new members of each Service Board would presumably take a Service view on policy issues, and this might well not coincide with the Corporation view taken by the Board. If they did not take a Service view they would be in immediate conflict with their own Service, which would hardly be the best basis for continuing confidence among their professional colleagues with whom they would jointly form a single Service Board. In particular, the Chairman of each Service Board, himself a Governor member of the Corporation Board, might find himself obliged to desert his Service Board's colleagues or to be reduced to a minority voice among the Governors. Conflict would seem to be guaranteed at the maxim number of points, and especially in those matters, such as News, Engineering, Personnel and Finance, where these conflicts have already proved to be most difficult and where the Board of Governors would retain the final authority. The relationship between the Governor Chairman of the Service Board and the Managing Director of the Service would seem to be particularly fraught with problems. The Managing Director (and before him the Director, in pre-McKinsey days) has always been the Chairman of his own management committee, and his authority within the Service would undoubtedly be diminished, both by his replacement as Service Chairman and by the presence, forming half the management committee, of the lay members, over whom his professional writ would not run. What the Television Service in particular has always needed has been a firm voice of authority at the top. The last thing to be introduced at that level should be professional uncertainty. On the purely operational plane the nomination by the Home Secretary of 'half' of each Board seemed to fix its total size. But since, in each of the Services, there have been several changes in the composition and numbers of the present management committees, this external constraint on numbers would seem to be wholly undesirable.

Interesting questions arose as to the precise relationship of authority between the Board of Governors and the Service Board members proposed. The Governors – and this would have applied to the proposed Chairman of the Service Boards – have been Crown appointments. The other proposed Service Board members would be the Home Secretary's nominations. In the public mind – and rightly, in my view – more respect and authority would attach to the standing of the Governors, as individuals and as a body. Would it be possible to find Service Board members content to accept this lower status? The Home Secretary, speaking soon after the publication of the White Paper, rejected the suggestion that political interference with the BBC was in issue, because, he argued, 'the Government' had been making appointments to the Board of the BBC without criticisms of political manipulation having arisen. Quite apart from the question of the literal truth of this defence – in general supportable, but in detail open to marginal question – the Home Secretary seemed peculiarly insensitive to the distinction between 'the Government' as the source of appointment and 'the Queen-in-Council' – in other words, the Queen as advised by Ministers. In the case of Ministerial appointments (that is, Government appointments proper) politically motivated selection to broadcasting bodies would represent an error of political tactics, and probably a substantial error. For 'Queen-in-Council' appointments the same error would be much more – in fact, a constitutional outrage, because it would involve the Crown in politics. The BBC, and especially its Board, have always been acutely and justifiably conscious of the distinction, and it has a direct relevance in considering the relative status of members of the Board of Governors and of the proposed Service Boards.

The final practical considerations provoked by the proposals related to the position of the Chairman and Director-General under the new regime. Nobody denies that the role of Director-General is exceptionally demanding. His assets, besides his own talents, reside uniquely in his access to the Governors, and to the Chairman at all times, and in the fact that he is their choice as Chief Executive. To ask him, against his complex and very time-consuming requirements, to attend all meetings of the Service Boards as a member of each, would be quite unreasonable in terms of human energy. The reason for the suggestion was clear – to keep him equally abreast with his colleagues and the Governors involved of all major Service developments, and to avoid the possibility of his being outflanked. But this risk arose only because of the dual composition of the proposed Boards. The traditional executive management committees in each Service are fully under his command in the executive chain. The change would have confused this chain by introducing a deliberative element of an external character. It would be better avoided.

The position of the Chairman was potentially even worse under the proposed arrangements, for he was not a member of the Service Boards, and was therefore faced with members of his Board – the three Service Governors – more informed in detail, and more committed than he could allow himself to be. He was open to the danger of being outflanked in practical matters in exactly the same way as the Director-General might be. Yet it would clearly be inappropriate for him to be a member of the Service Boards – except as Chairman of each, which, as in the case of the Director-General, would be excessively demanding. Further, there is no doubt that the rest of the Board regard the Television Service, with its dominant position in public awareness, as their central task as Governors. They would not readily accept that this responsibility should be concentrated in one of their colleagues, and no doubt would feel similarly about the special responsibilities of the Radio and External Services Governors. This was precisely the reaction of other Governors to the Finance and Personnel Committees which were established by Lord Hill in 1969. They fell into desuetude because these members of the Board who were not included in their proceedings felt deprived of the fullest opportunity to carry out their duties. The position of the National Governors who were created in 1952 is quite different, in that they are concerned with the special activities in their areas, which do not in any way dominate the affairs of the Corporation, of all the programme Services. The issues which concern these Governors in their capacity as Board members are really those of proportionate claims on central resources of all kinds, including Television and Radio programme resources. The duties of the proposed Service Governors were in no way comparable.

The central point of any such argument, however, must remain the proper execution of the task of the Board of Governors – to act as trustees of the national interest in broadcasting. The White Paper claimed to help the Governors to concentrate on this duty by relieving them of the need to think about the management of the BBC. The claim was that 'this dual role (had) over recent years become a source of some confusion', and particularly that the supervision of the public interest in the domestic services had 'sometimes been subordinated to the Governors' managerial role'. The White Paper noted that the Annan Committee thought the Governors 'should not identify themselves too closely with the day-to-day decision-taking in the Corporation or they would never be able to call for a change of policy in the public interest'. The object of the Government's proposals described as being 'to distance the Governors from detailed involvement in management'. Leaving aside the practical undesirability and the theoretical irrelevance of the proposals as structural remedies for decentralization and the improvement of creativity, the Governors had a quite simple remedy in their own hands.

It may have been necessary, in the early 1970s, to re-assert in public the fact of the authority of the Governors, following the undoubtedly strong personal impact of Sir Hugh Greene and his policies of widening editorial freedom and encouraging creative adventure, but to continue that course too far and too long was to risk mistaking the legitimate need to change the public impression with the non-existent need to change the reality of authority in the BBC. From first-hand observation I knew of the respect which Sir Hugh Greene had both for the persons and the authority of his three first Chairmen – Sir Arthur Fforde, Sir James Duff and Lord Normanbrook. (There were special personal factors in the relationship with Lord Hill which were bound to be quickly resolved by Sir Hugh's departure. The chemistry of the two men simply did not mix.) The public thought, however, that Sir Hugh, a bold editor and a great publicist, was the dominant force. That was not the reality. The Chairmen were in charge on the major issues.

All that was needed to reaffirm the Governors' primary concern with their public trusteeship duties was a decision of the Board that this should happen. In recent years they have rightly been more fully informed about the current thinking of the Television and Radio Services' managements on programme matters, including day-to-day comment on individual programmes. It is easy, when provided with detailed information, to be tempted to discuss it in a detailed way, and it is understandable that the Board should, from time to time, have engaged in such discussion, seeing it as an apparently logical internal expression of the public reaffirmation of their authority. But to be led along this tempting path of allowing information to be the basis for detailed discussion rather than of general briefing is, in the long run, liable to obscure the concept that the duties of the Board are general rather than particular. I believe that Sir Michael Swann understood this. His problem was to convince his Governors that their main danger was that of being over-conscientious in detail. Their protection in such matters lies in reinforcing the authority of the Director-General as the sole channel through which they exercise their powers. Their pressure on him, if they accord to him this exclusive authority in practice, is immense, and they should not hesitate to use it. The Chairman's function is to see that the Board concentrates on the general matters which arise from the detailed information which is put before them.

The White Paper proposals would have undermined the authority of the Governors and of the Director-General by establishing alternative centres of power, and by doing so through an intervention in what was a proper matter for the Governors alone, acting through the Director-General. The proposals had a filial resemblance to those made by the Liberal Study Group and the Fabian Society, to the Beveridge Committee, suggesting three separate Corporations (Sound, Television and Overseas). The latest proposals carried all the disadvantages of this triple disunity, while retaining a facade of unity whose successful maintenance was nevertheless made immensely more difficult. (Even thirty years ago the critics of the BBC, when its strength, at just under 12,000 staff, was rather less than half what it is now, and before any of the major achievement of television had come about, were already talking about excessive size and bureaucracy. The criticism is one which explains something about the critics rather than about the BBC, which seems to be immune from the results which ought to follow if the criticism is true.) To all these counter-arguments must be added the suspicions of political interference which were inevitably provoked, and which rested on appearances whose interpretation could not be changed even by the most rational refutations. Independence is a matter of reputation as much as of reality. It should not be risked for the sake of the confusions of the White Paper.

Almost as a pendant to the proposals the White Paper rejected suggestions that there should be fewer Governors, and even raised the prospect of a larger Board. Much experienced opinion has argued for a smaller Board, as I have myself, for the sake of greater coherence. Even those who support the larger Board of twelve do so as a counter-proposition to the smaller Board, and not with any idea of a further enlargement, which I am sure they would resist. In my experience, dating from 1963, the smaller Board worked rather better, in that collective opinion was more quickly and firmly established, and the larger Board has in practice worked better than it might otherwise have done because of repeated failures by successive Governments speedily to propose new Governors for appointment when vacancies arose, and because attendance by the twelve has been slightly, but noticeably, less regular than it was amongst the nine. Human nature will usually display a certain tendency to 'leave it to the next man' if given encouragement by circumstances.

The White Paper case for the possibility of more Governors rested on the increase in specialized functions of the members of the Board. The Chairman and the Vice Chairman, the three National Governors, and the proposed three Service Governors would take up eight out of the twelve places. The Governor qualified in financial affairs would presumably have to maintain his neutrality between the three Services, as would the 'Trade Union' member, whose concern could well be with the tensions between the industrial relations requirements of each. The Governor drawn in recent years from retired members of the Diplomatic Service has reasonably been expected to show a special interest in the External Services, but, for obvious reasons of suspicion overseas as to his possible role, he could hardly serve as Chairman of the External Services Management

Board. A further three places are therefore accounted for, leaving only one Governor without a special interest, and presumably free to concentrate on Engineering, premises (including catering – a notoriously difficult problem), and, in the programme area, Education, Religion, the English Regions and audience studies.

The enlargement of the Board which might follow would be yet a further argument against the whole scheme, for it would turn the Governors from a moderately manageable committee of twelve into a kind of public meeting, able to conduct a logical discussion towards a decision only with great difficulty, but usually capable only of general debate of an inconclusive kind, and no doubt subject to the log-rolling which becomes a feature of such assemblies.

On all counts the proposals would have brought substantial disadvantage without achieving the ends proposed, and indeed, by their particular form, almost a guarantee to frustrate them. The proposals could carry one possible advantage. Their rejection could be followed by a new conviction among the more rebellious characters of the Television Service, after feeling the hot breath of external supervision so close to home, that the benefits of the more remote and familiar attentions of the Board of Governors may, after all, be worthy of proper respect.

Since the proposals could be shown to have no relevance to the stated requirements and to be totally unworkable, it becomes impossible to assume that they were put forward for the reasons stated in the White Paper. That leaves only one explanation – that they were, in fact, a deliberate cloak for the creation of a means of direct Governmental intervention in the running of the BBC, and especially in its programme management. That objective was certainly not shared by all Ministers. And that certainty draws down upon those who did entertain it the criticisms of ill intention, bad judgement and conspiracy against the decent men of politics, who seemed to have been temporarily hoodwinked.

CHAPTER XVI

Operational Finance and The Licence Fee

ANY CONSIDERATION OF the financial policy of a broadcasting organization must begin by looking at the nature of the service to be provided. There is a great difference between a service which is provided as a requirement of public policy and that which is provided by private enterprise under a commercial system. In the public service – that is, one which is provided at the behest of Government on the basis of public finance – the first requirement is to define the nature of the service itself, and then to derive from the specification of the service the amount of income necessary to provide that service. In the commercial case, the logic is that the technical possibility of a service is the starting point for working out a profit target. In order to secure that profit a given volume of turnover has to be related to the amount of advertising which can be attracted to a particular kind of programme service. The programme service itself is defined by the need to attract advertising revenue. The financial question for the public, officially provided service, is a derivative of the requirement of the service itself. In the case of the commercial service the financial question is the source of the programme problem, rather than one which emerges after the programme solution is proposed. The strategies which will be adopted by either service will, therefore, be different because they start from different points in the argument.

Whichever method of providing a service is adopted in

any particular country the solutions to financial problems, whether of income or of the disposition of revenue, will arise from decisions about how air time is to be used. How much air time is to be made available? Will the service be available at all hours of the day and night? Will it be available on one network or on two parallel networks, or perhaps on more? (That, in itself, is a function of the technical question of how many networks can be constructed from the available frequencies.) Once the question of duration and number of services is fixed, there comes the matter of how they are to be filled. Are there to be many news programmes? Are there to be many programmes of talk produced in studios? Are there to be many drama, or light entertainment productions, or alternatively, programmes of sport? How are the revenues to be divided, for example, between television and radio, and between the different categories of programmes in either television or radio.

Are the resources to be provided from the broadcasting organization's own structure, or are they to be from outside? That is a question which very often can be answered only by considering what is already available in a given country by way of resources for producing films, for example. These obviously could be used for supplying the needs of a television service. But if there is no substantial film industry in a country then television will have to provide most of its own resources, and the availability of hired material does not arise.

There will always be certain basic costs which every broadcasting organization has to provide. I found it a useful guide to remember, from my External Services analysis of 1959/60, that the cost of paying the permanent staff amounted to roughly 50% of total costs. The money needed to pay artists and holders of copyrights amounted to roughly 30% of the total costs. And the balance of some 20% went to meet the miscellaneous operational needs of the service, including the distribution and transmission chain itself. The figures will vary according to the circumstances of the particular service under consideration.

Thus, for instance, the BBC External Services, after continuous cuts, now rely very extensively on the contributions of the permanent staff to the programme output. In 1976/77 permanent staff costs absorbed roughly 66% of their income. Only 8% was devoted to paying fees and copyrights. Some 7% went to the rent of buildings and of transmitters hired from other organizations. Over 8% – an unusually high figure – paid for power, which is related to the number of high power short wave transmitters which are used. Thus, over 90% of the costs were devoted to the basic elements in the service, and of this, only 8% went to pay people outside the service.

About 85% of the total television operating expenditures of almost £150 million went directly into programme making. Of that total, £127 million, or 85%, went into national network operation and £17 million into regional production (11%). The balance (£5 million, or 4%) paid for distribution and transmission. These figures give some idea of the shape of the organization which has to be considered before any financial policy can be worked out. The staff numbers depend on the nature, as well as the extent of the programmes to be provided, and the facilities which are necessary in order to produce them. Some of the resources clearly involve the provision of major amounts of capital equipment, and that, too, has to be a part of the continuing budget. Future financial planning has to protect the provision of capital equipment. Thus, the purchase of a five camera outside broadcast mobile unit at a cost of some £800,000 means that provision has to be made in between seven and nine years' time for its replacement, probably not in exactly the same form, but certainly at a higher cost. That requirement has to be taken into account in calculating the disposition of future income. Similarly, studios have to be re-designed, re-equipped, and sometimes rebuilt. I used to reckon the average life of a building would be some forty years. But the equipment inside it would have to be

263

replaced at least every ten years, and probably more frequently if the invention of new devices suggested earlier
changes.

All these are background considerations within the general
decision which has to be taken about sharing out the Licence
income of the BBC between radio and television. The prior
need is, of course, to ensure that the licence fee is revised
upwards sufficiently frequently, to a sufficient amount to
cover both the development of the service as it has been
indicated by Government policy decisions and by BBC
recommendations, and to cover the continuous inflation
which has affected broadcasting for many years, and much
more acutely in recent years.

The first step in each year's budgeting procedure was for
the question of division of funds between television and
radio to be brought to me by the Director of Finance. We
knew, of course, the amount of income which was likely to be
available to us – at any rate, in years when the licence fee was
not likely to be adjusted. We knew what the cost of the
previous year's operation had been, or very nearly so. We
knew what the inflationary element was likely to be, and we
would have had warning about possible developments, both
technical and programme, for which provision might have to
be made in the coming year's estimate. Every budget begins,
of course, from last year's budget, and in the BBC each new
budget represents the first year of a five-year projection into
the future. We would look at the previous year's costs and the
five-year forecast, estimate what savings were likely to be
made – we always included an element in our plans for the
generation of savings within the Service – and we would then
add the development and inflationary factors which we knew
we were likely to have to provide. With this in mind we would
adjust the figures in what had been the second year of the
previous five-year projection, and then issue to the Television
and Radio Services, after having secured the approval of the
Board of Governors, a statement of the amount which they

might expect to deploy within the coming year, and a forecast for the next four years. That, in turn, became the basis of their internal budgeting procedure. Of course, any five-year period in modern conditions has to assume at least one licence fee increase, and hypothetical income projections have to be made to match the foreseeable expenditure commitments.

Within the amount provided for the first year of the plan, the programme services would not begin with a money question, but with an editorial discussion – that is, the consideration of the programme intentions which they wished to pursue within the year. Many of them would already have existed as ideas in earlier discussions, but the first phase of the budgetary discussion would bring down to earth the many ideas which had been floating in the air. Editorial discussion would then be followed by specific proposals which would be priced in resource terms and in cash. It is important to have both. These proposals, now made specific, would be the result of planning of the individual editorial intentions which the network planners had earlier put forward. The editorial ideas which were not accepted by the management of the Service would have been put aside, and thought would have been concentrated on the chosen projects. It would be the responsibility of the Head of Group or the Head of Department to generate specific planning statements about each programme idea for incorporation within the budget of the Service. At that stage, of course, there would arise the need for considerable compression, because the total of demands would always exceed the available total of cash and resources. Furthermore, the timing through the year of the various demands being made by the different programme intentions would always include peaks which would be unacceptable to the servicing departments, in that they would exceed the resources available at any given moment. The process would then follow, now largely computerized, of smoothing out the peaks of load on facilities so as to make it possible for the programme intentions to be carried out in practice. Some of the smoothing out process might be carried out by hiring resources from outside the BBC, but that would be possible only if outside sources of hired material existed in particular fields.

The final plan which emerged from all these discussions would have to fit in with the total plan of the Corporation, as I had defined it in the budgetary target approved by the Board of Governors. There was one escape from total constriction if resources at the end of the process still failed to match demand. When I became Director-General all funds were dispersed, in the process of annual division which I have described, to the Managing Directors of Television and Radio. The Director-General did not have his own budget. It was assumed that he had sufficient power to be able to insist on the implementation of any programme idea which he might have in mind. But in practice that was a self-deception, because no Director-General would ever have been likely to over-rule his Managing Director in a complex matter like the planning of Television resources. He would be acting in such ignorance as to be likely to make very big mistakes. What I instituted was a minor financial reserve of some £500,000 approximately, which did not carry forward from year to year. This would enable me, at the end of the planning stage, or, indeed, half-way through the year itself, to inject additional money into particular plans which would otherwise be frustrated by marginal lack of money. It would be quite wrong for the Director-General, having given general guidance to his Managing Directors as to how they should plan, then to over-ride them in major ways. But it seemed to me right and proper that he should have the capacity marginally to influence key decisions by the application of small amounts of money held back from the principal budget. That is what could happen at the end of the planning stage.

The process of compiling the plan which I have described – a matter which took place annually, starting in May with editorial discussion, continuing in October with offers from the programme heads and being completed in January or

February for the next fiscal year – did call for the availability of very considerable costs and resources information. This is available in the BBC, but only as the result of some twenty years of continuous work in evaluating costs and in tabulating resource use. The Cost and Management Accountants have been busy on this task ever since the end of the war, and their work was what made possible the conclusions which emerged from the study of McKinseys, the outside management consultants, who looked at the BBC in 1968 and 1969. They themselves said that they could not have made their recommendations without the prior work which had been done by the BBC's finance staff. They were surprised, they said, by the fact that, whereas in most management organizations they would expect to find some seven or eight major points of decision, in the BBC's Television Service they could not reduce the points of effective decision to less than some 1400–1500.

This reflects the cellular nature of production organization in any broadcasting system. The unit is the programme or the programme strand within the year. That is the basic fact which has to be taken into account in the whole offers procedure which I have described. The problem in managing programme production is to bring together these 1,400 little teams into some sort of structure which will enable a single budget to be produced by a single responsible official – in the case of BBC Television, the Managing Director, operating through the Controllers of the two networks. They are the key men when it comes to editorial decisions. But it is the Controller of Planning and Resource Management who is key when it comes to the availability of resources and their organization to meet particular programme targets. Broadly speaking, McKinseys endorsed this system of working and they commented that they did not know of any more efficient way of running a broadcasting system, nor any other system which equalled the BBC's in effectiveness.

Some recent figures will illustrate the working of the system. The BBC's total expenditures in the year ended

267

31 March 1977 – the last complete financial year of my period of office – amounted to some £230 million. Of this, television operations absorbed some £150 million. Radio operations took some £60 million. Capital took nearly £20 million, of which £14 million was for television and £5 million for radio. In addition, there were minor sources of income in the profit from publications and from Television Enterprises – the department which sells television programmes outside the United Kingdom. This amounted, in net terms, to just under £2 million in all.

Radio costs are less complicated than in television. In the year ended 31 March 1977, staff took 55% of the total expenditures on Radio. Fees to artists and payments for copyright and so on cost 22% of the radio budget. But there was a special feature, in that the orchestras which are maintained by the BBC as part of its staff, cost a further 6%, making 28% in payments to artists of various kinds. A total of the figures for staff fees and orchestras comes to some 83% of the budget. Rent of buildings was the principal other item, coming to some 5%.

If one examines the figures in a different way, Radio 1, which was the popular network, attracting most of the listeners, cost some 9% of the total. Radio 2, which was the next most popular and came close to Radio 1 in its appeal to listeners, cost some 18% of radio's outgoings. Radio 3, perhaps the most prestigious of the networks, cost some 20%, and Radio 4, the information and service network of the BBC – the traditional old Home Service – some 24%. Regions cost 13% and local radio 11%. These two have been growing steadily in the past few years and will grow more in the future. Transmission cost some 5%.

But radio costs are generated very much more simply than those of television. They do not call for the same detailed control of resources as television. That would be pointless bureaucracy. The system used is to calculate an average cost per hour of certain types of programme produced by particular departments, and then to allocate to a Head of Department a budget and require him simply to keep within the average cost per hour. Most of the expenditures, apart from staff, are fixed costs of using the installations of the BBC. There is no great apparatus of scenery, costume design, film, outside broadcast units of complicated character, and so on, which require a quite different technique in television.

I have explained that the financial policy of a broadcasting organization will be determined, among other things, by the way in which it is decided to fill the programme hours available for broadcasting. Looking at the BBC's television programme output, and taking account only of the production of network programmes, without allowing for second and further showings – in other words, considering only original contributions to the networks – a very interesting pattern emerged. Out of nearly 4,000 programmes produced by the London programme departments of the Television Service in 1976/77 some 800 were described as children's programmes. A little less – some 780 – were categorized as current affairs. Some 300 were described as light entertainment variety, and about 150 as light entertainment comedy – that is, the situation comedy with which we are all familiar. 340 programmes were devoted to outside broadcasts of sport, and drama, in total, produced some 350 programmes, of which 70 were single plays, 130 plays in series involving the same characters, and 150 were serials. Those figures can be taken a little further in order to show the range of costs involved. The conclusions are quite remarkable.

In the two numerically largest categories – children's programmes and current affairs – out of over 800 programmes for children over 85% cost less than £10,000, and only three cost more than £40,000. In current affairs some 200 of the 780 programmes cost £5,000 or less, but the main bulk of this output – 500 programmes – cost between £10,000 and £15,000 each to make – a relatively low figure. Just under 50 current affairs programmes cost between £20,000 and £40,000, and eight major programmes cost more than £50,000.

In Light Entertainment, contributing a total of some 460 programmes, the 300 or so Variety programmes had budgets spread across the whole range from under £5,000 to over £50,000, but with nearly 100 costing between £10,000 and £15,000, and another 100 or more between £20,000 and £40,000. Out of the Light Entertainment (Comedy) programmes (that is, situation comedies), some 20 cost between £30,000 and £40,000; four notable programmes cost over £50,000. But no fewer than 100 cost between £20,000 and £30,000. Outside broadcast sports programmes, for which, of course, the BBC has a special reputation, included among its 340 programmes during the year 90 which cost between £20,000 and £30,000, 60 which cost between £40,000 and £50,000, and 20 which cost over £50,000. In Drama, the single plays included, out of 70, some 50 which all cost over £50,000; the 130 series plays included 75 which cost between £40,000 and £50,000; the 150 episodes of serials included 85 which cost between £30,000 and £40,000. Only 7 drama programmes cost less than £20,000, and only 24 cost less than £30,000. Opera production, whether from the studio or the opera house, is exceptional.

On this analysis, therefore, the main money went into Light Entertainment, both Variety and Comedy, Outside Broadcast Sport, and all forms of Drama. As a footnote to these figures, I might add that out of some 450 Schools and Further Education programmes *none* cost more than £30,000 and only two cost more than £20,000. Over half had budgets of between £5,000 and £10,000.

How tight is the control over the spending estimates? It would seem quite easy, with a budget of £60,000, to be very extravagant. But the test of extravagance is whether more money is spent than was intended to be spent. Out of all programmes departments, 47% of programmes fell within budget and 33% were within 5% excess of the budget. That is an outstandingly good record to my mind, and should adequately answer the enquiries of BBC 'extravagance'. In fact, in 1967/77 television programmes budgets as a whole were 0.1% underspent, which is a phenomenal degree of control.

Another way of looking at the programme make-up, which has to be considered by the planners before they decide on the financial outlay for the year, is to analyse the contribution made to the total output by the various categories of programme, and the demands which they make on the available resources and their cost per hour. Out of the 91% of programme hours which is contributed by the London production facility to the BBC's networks, the distribution as between the principal categories is as shown in the table below:

	Cost per hour £	Cost as % of programme budget	Percentage of output hours
Light Entertainment (Comedy)	49,000	5	2
Light Entertainment (Variety)	31,000	8	4
Drama – Plays	58,000	6	2
Series	52,000	7	2
Serials	57,000	7	2
Total Drama	56,000	20	6
Outside Broadcasts	8,000	12	24

These figures give a more balanced view of the distribution of costs in the programme budgets than do the figures for the cost of these programmes as compared with other categories. Outside Broadcasts, which produced some very expensive programmes from time to time, nevertheless showed an average cost working out as low as £8,000 an hour – an astonishing bargain, justifying the very heavy capital investment and the occasional well-publicized high fee for rights paid to promoters. Outside Broadcast of sport, in fact, represented, in terms of share of the output hours, the biggest contributor of all. The next biggest share was taken by what we call Purchased Programmes – that is, American series and films. These occupied some 16% of the total network hours taking account only of first showings of all programmes – a figure which is reduced to under 13% if all second and further showings are included in the calculation. But these programmes absorbed only 5% of the programme costs as an average cost of £5,000 an hour. It might be asked why, at the low average cost, there is such a relatively small proportion of these programmes in the total output hours. The reason is that it is programme policy to limit the amount of this material to appear on the air. Financially, the arguments would suggest the contrary course. Editorially, it would be simply impossible for the BBC to show any more purchased programmes, and I believe that BBC editorial judgements will continue to resist any such development. The contrary impression derives entirely from a concentration of much of this material in peak hours – which is, in turn, a reflection of financial restraints on the production of equivalent indigenous material – a point which I have illustrated already.

The other point which ought to be made about the composition of the output is that Regional programmes for the network absorbed some 8% of the total programme hours, requiring some 8% of the total costs, and showed an average cost of £9,000 an hour from Birmingham, the principal centre; £21,000 an hour from Bistol, which produces a great deal of nature material; and £20,000 from Manchester. (The Birmingham average cost conceals, however, a wide disparity of productions undertaken at the network centre, ranging from major network drama to the daily magazine *Pebble Mill At One*.)

Yet another way of looking at the financial and resources problem is to analyse the various categories of programme in

terms of use of resources. Thus, Light Entertainment programmes took up 20% of the available studio resources; 20%
of the design effort (that is, the design of scenery, of costumes,
provision of make-up and so on); and 25% of the scenic
servicing effort (the effort which is required to provide the
scenery which is designed for these programmes). Drama
programmes occupied the largest share of studio time, that is,
30%; similarly, it absorbed the largest share of design effort –
45% – and by far the largest share of scenic servicing effort –
some 50%. The significant element in Drama, and it has
increased in recent years, is the amount of video recording
now in use. Drama occupied some 20% of the recording effort
available. Nor surprisingly again, Outside Broadcast programmes took up some 75% of the Outside Broadcast unit
time available. The rest was taken up substantially by Drama
and Light Entertainment working on outside locations.
Outside broadcasting also took up some 20% or more of the
video recording effort available. *Match of the Day* and *Rugby
Special* are examples.

One further category of information is worth noting. It
concerns the origin of resources available to the production
departments in the BBC. By far the greater proportions of
resources come from the BBC's own staff and facilities. The
general tendency is for the union pressures now being exerted
on the BBC to compel it more and more to employ its own
resources, and indeed, that is not unhealthy. Outside effort
ought to be employed, in principle, only to meet periods of
peak demand. It is much more economical to use the BBC's
staff and resources to meet a constant level of demand. And
the effect of planning, both of programmes and of logistics,
should be to ensure an even flow of work through the minimum provision of capital, facilities and personnel to man them.
That is why the BBC had developed extensive computer
programmes in order to even out the peaks which result from
the discussion of the annual plan as it is being formulated.
In one area outside hire is essential – namely, the provision of

scenery. Over 40% of the scenery used in BBC programmes is hired or constructed outside the BBC's own workshops. It is a major consideration in the planning process, because the availability of a film and theatre industry outside the television industry removes a constraint which would otherwise apply. Although it is desirable for the BBC to use to the maximum its own servicing resources, the non-availability of such resources in the open market can be a total constraint on freedom to plan for additional programmes. If there is no resource other than that in the Television Service, when that resource is exhausted nothing more can be contemplated.

None of these calculations, however refined, and however carefully controlled, can detract from the importance of the basic principle that decisions about the extent and allocation of air time are the principal foundation of any financial policy. Editorial decisions about the way in which air time should be used will depend on the provision of given resources, and an intention to proceed in a given editorial direction will dictate the eventual provision of the necessary facilities. That will establish a base for calculation for the income required to sustain those facilities and, therefore, the amount of air time. Another basic requirement is a knowledge of the productive capacity of the resources which have been made available as a result of previous decisions and those which are to be made available as a result of planning foresight. The central point is that the 'mix' of programmes proposed – that is of each category of programme output included in the final schedule – is the critical cost and resources factor.

All this may appear to be a very complex process – and indeed, it is, because massive and diverse resources come under the command of the producer of any programme, and he has to be a logistics manager as well as an editor. But the remorseless study of all these complexities will produce, in the end, an analysis which can be simplified so as to reflect only those matters which are of critical importance to the planning process.

A good financial policy in television will seek to locate in the organizational structure those points where editorial resource and financial decision come together. We believed that in the BBC we had substantially resolved this problem by placing the total responsibility of the management of finance and programmes in the hands of a Managing Director and by giving to him two Channel Controllers whose responsibility it is to make editorial decisions about the composition of their schedules. Those decisions have to rest on a secure base of knowledge about the available money, the available staff, and the available physical resources, and how their plans can be dovetailed together to make the maximum use of the resources available to the BBC's Television Service without over-stretching them at particular moments. There is, in other words, no financial plan without a logistic plan, and there is no logistic plan without great editorial foresight in order to decide what kind of programmes shall be made and at what moments resources will need to be provided in order to make them possible. Editorial decision, resource planning and financial planning – all three go together. That is the secret of management of any television service.

The effectiveness of the system has been partly the result of the financial stringencies arising from delays in decisions about the level of the licence fee, and the inadequacy of the levels when finally fixed. But the increasingly dilatory and inadequate provisions made by successive Governments have made even the most efficient system of financial control very difficult to operate by making it impossible, in the absence of certainty about future income, to plan ahead with the requisite lead times. Miserly financing militates against economy in the not very long run.

The undermining of the licence fee system began in 1962, after the Conservative Government's endorsement of the Pilkington recommendation that the BBC should undertake the construction and operation of a second television network. Remembering the history of the aftermath of the Beveridge

Report, when the Government then in office had approved the maintenance of the monopoly, but had not survived long enough to give effect to that decision, the BBC was naturally anxious on this occasion to go ahead as quickly as possible with a plan which it had so strongly advocated in its evidence to the Committee. But the question of money had to be resolved. In the end the BBC went ahead on the basis of an assurance from the then Government that the necessary funds would be forthcoming, even if an immediate increase in the licence fee could not be authorized. The most that could be done, so it was argued, with an election in the offing, was to give the BBC the full proceeds of the £4.00 which the public was then paying for the combined Television and Radio Licence. This meant that the BBC enjoyed the benefit of the £1.00 excise duty which had been charged on the licence since 1957. It was known not to be enough to meet the BBC's needs for any significant length of time, and the Government was told so. It was particularly scandalous that the Postmaster-General who had assured the BBC that it would be adequately financed should have boasted in his election campaign of having held down the licence fee. (That he subsequently lost his seat seemed a just, if unintended retribution.)

The election of a Labour Government with a narrow majority meant a further delay, and when the decision came, after intensive scrutiny of the BBC's finances by an Inter-Departmental Committee, the amount of the increase was only £1.00 on the combined Television and Radio Licence. (An additional 5s od. was allowed on the Radio Licence, still then in existence.) Once again, the BBC had made it clear to the Government that this would be inadequate for the plans which it had been asked to put into effect. Further argument continued, and at the beginning of 1968 the Supplementary Colour Television Licence was introduced, at the level of £5.00 per licence. Although the BBC was reluctant to see extra charges applying to particular areas of its service, the Supplementary Colour Licence proved to be the salvation of BBC finances over the next ten years, since the growth of numbers of colour receivers was far greater than anybody had anticipated, and always greater than the forecasts which were included in the licence fee calculations, whether by the BBC or by the Government. The Labour Government was finally persuaded to increase the combined licence fee to £6.00 at the beginning of 1969 – once again, too little and too late, as the Government well knew. The BBC made it clear beyond any doubt that this level of licence fee would last only for a short time, and would lead the BBC, for the first time in its history, into significant use of its borrowing powers. But the overwhelming consideration that the election was in prospect, both in 1966 and in 1970, appeared to mean that satisfactory licence fee decisions could not be expected in the immediately preceding months. Indeed, in the summer of 1969, when Lord Hill and I were negotiating with Mr Wilson personally about the level of the licence fee, the introduction of Local Radio, and the extent of the BBC's employment of musicians, the decision that the level of the licence fee should again be increased included the provision that the date of the increase should be April 1971 – well after the last legally permissible date for the election which was then expected. As it happened, the election, called in June 1970, earlier than most predictions, meant that the Wilson decision was never implemented, and it fell to the Heath Government, in July 1971, to increase the combined Television and Radio Licence to £7.00, and at the same time to abolish the Radio-only licence, as the Wilson Government had already announced. Once again, we demonstrated that, on the BBC's known commitments, and the existing state of its indebtedness, the new licence fee would be below the level demanded by the situation, even on the depressed figures for inflation which the BBC was being compelled to adopt in its forecasts in response to Treasury requirements. It was at this point that the expansion of colour Television saved the BBC from financial disaster. The elections of March and October 1974 made it inconceivable – at least politically – for any further increase in the licence fee to be contemplated, although the financial situation was rapidly worsening. The increases in the combined licence fee for monochrome viewers to £8.00, and in the colour licence to £10.00, finally came in April 1975, with the stipulation that they were expected to last for 'at least two years'. They barely achieved that target, despite the repeated buoyancy of the colour Television revenue. And finally, in my time, there came the increases, in July 1977, of the Television and colour supplementary licences to £9.00 and £12.00 respectively, which the Government admitted were likely to last for only one year, bringing the licence fee system virtually to the level of an annual grant-in-aid procedure. The second successive one-year-only increase to £25.00 for colour and £10.00 for monochrome, announced in November 1978, followed after an interval of 16 months – well over the forecast one-year period – and took full advantage, as had the previous one-year increase, of the BBC's efforts to manage its affairs with maximum economy, even at some expense to the quality of the service. Moreover, the Government knew full well, in making its calculations, that they rested on the assumption that the staff of the BBC would continue to be paid at rates which had been substantially disadvantageous to them in comparison with their colleagues in Commercial Television ever since the introduction of the Government's pay policy in July 1975. At that time the staff of Commercial Television had already negotiated pay increases of the order of 20%, and the BBC had been on the point of concluding a similar agreement to take effect on the customary date, 1 October. The Government's introduction of the pay policy from the beginning of August deprived BBC staff of a comparable increase, and maintained the resulting disparity throughout the period of the new policy, with the sole modification that as the BBC dates for applying the pay policy limits came round they gave marginally higher figures to the BBC than to Commercial Television staff because BBC staff had reached a later phase in the operation of the policy earlier than had their Commercial

Television peers. The licence fee decision at the end of 1978 assumed that this disparity could be perpetuated, and allowed only sufficient cash in the BBC's income to pay the depressed rates. Consequently, when the BBC was pressed by the Government in December 1978 to have the levels of pay considered by the Central Arbitration Committee, following representations by the Corporation and by the unions that a 'special case' existed, the award given by the Committee of an additional $12\frac{1}{2}\%$ on basic rates, with 4% to correct anomalies, made it absolutely certain that the so-called 'one-year licence' would be inadequate.

The crowning disgrace was the subsequent Government decision that the BBC's borrowing powers should be increased from £30 million to £100 million in order to meet the bills which would present themselves. The BBC has always argued that borrowing is an unsuitable way for its current activities to be financed. This was true even when the object of the borrowing was to finance capital investment, because it is almost never the case that additional investment will bring a significantly greater yield of income to the Corporation. The case against BBC borrowing could hardly ever have been better demonstrated than in this misuse by the Government of its power to relax the borrowing limits. All that was achieved was to postpone a decision about a further increase in the licence fees until after an impending election, and to ensure that the ensuing increase would be higher than it need have been in order to pay off the accumulated debts. Both 'one-year' increases were scandalously inadequate and politically craven. The repetition of the process on a second occasion might have been enough to sink the licence fee system for ever. But the universal criticism which greeted the increase in the borrowing limits, and the declarations in favour of the licence fee system which followed, may perhaps have been sufficient to preserve it, and also its corollary – BBC independence.

CHAPTER XVII

Capital—Development and Replacement Costs

THE BBC'S CAPITAL PROBLEMS are concerned fundamentally with the development of the distribution system – that is to say, the transmitter network; the development of television studio production capacity; and also, the replacement of existing facilities which are becoming obsolete – a factor which applies with especial force to radio.

The BBC is now completing two UHF Television networks with the intention of being able to serve most communities with populations of 1,000 or more by 1982. That will cover some 96% of the population. By the time the work is finished it will have cost something near £57 million at 1978 prices. By 1971 the BBC was serving, with two incomplete UHF networks, some 80% of the population. That had cost £14 million. A further £26 million was then the estimate of what was needed to serve the next 16%. There were then no figures for the cost of covering the last 4%. Adding in the cost of covering all communities of more than 500 people – the latest target – and the effects of inflation as seen in 1978, the total actual and foreseen cost of the full programme amounted to £68 millions.

As to television studios, the BBC, in 1971, was completing its colourization programme in London and plans were afoot to bring proper colour facilities to the regions. In some cases that meant moving for the first time into accommodation specially designed for broadcasting. It was necessary to equip and replace facilities at eight main studio locations in England for television and at a further six in Northern Ireland, Scotland and Wales. Some of this work had already been done by 1971, especially in the national regions, and Birmingham was operating in colour in the new headquarters. There was the separate need to stay abreast of current technological developments by phasing out old-fashioned facilities and bringing in modern, or even prototype equipment.

In radio there was a general need for re-equipment, because on the whole the facilities were older, and, in some cases, literally historic. The particular need was to complete the development of the first twenty local radio stations and to develop stereo radio on two networks so far as that was possible within reasonable financial limits.

By the time I left the post of Director-General in 1977 the programme of colorizing the various regional centres was approaching completion, though the final stages of the plan in some locations – for instance, in Belfast, Aberdeen and Newcastle – had still to be authorized. As for replacement, a full programme of re-quipment of eight major studios in London was well under way, and the fleet of Colour Mobile Control Rooms was steadily being replaced. The order of costs was substantial, with the re-equipment of a main television studio calling for capital expenditure of the order of £500,000 and a Colour Mobile Control Room for £800,000. In Radio, replacement programmes for the studios were still badly delayed, and some, particularly those used for educational broadcasting, were professionally unacceptable when measured against the requirements of modern broadcasting network. But the transmitters and distribution networks were at last being properly re-equipped. The wavelength adjustments under the Geneva revision of the Copenhagen Plan had made it possible to settle on a firm pattern for the future of the MF and LF systems, and the new pattern of network distribution meant that the installation at least of a new generation of transmitters, most of them substantially automated, to replace some of the original 40 year old equipment, was at last under way. Stereo distribution had been made economically possible by the development of the Pulse Code Modulation system, and by the negotiation of special rates with the Post Office. The three VHF networks were therefore all close to complete stereo capability. Local Radio had been established on the twenty station basis represented by the half-way stage of the original plan approved by the Wilson Government in the summer of 1969, and awaited completion to a nation-wide scale with the publication of the Government's White Paper on the recommendations made by the Annan Committee. Decisions on the level of the licence fee, the availability of frequencies, the relationship of the BBC with the Post Office communications monopoly, and the allocation of responsibility for local broadcasting had conditioned each of these capital investment programmes.

Every investment programme is governed quite fundamentally by a major political consideration. As a public service it is the BBC's duty to offer fair shares to all the potential audience. This applies in two ways. First, each of the services must be distributed nationally so far as is practicable. That dictates the scope of the transmitter networks. Special considerations apply to local radio, where the local service clearly cannot be national, but where the ultimate target should be a national availability of local radio, and preferably BBC as well as commercial local radio. The second 'fair shares' consideration is that so far as programme content is concerned BBC programmes ought to include a reasonable representation of the tastes of the nation as a whole. The fund of public money ought not to be concentrated on the provision of an élitist service. That statement has considerable implications for the extent and complexity of provision of studio facilities.

The BBC's balance sheet shows capital assets at a cost value – that is, at historic cost – of about £140 million. Roughly half of this is equipment. Its replacement cost will necessarily be very much higher than the historic cost and there is absolutely no doubt that all of it will have to be replaced at some time in the future. Some of the capital equipment has a relatively short operating life. Thus, colour cameras can be expected to be in service for about 7 or 8 years, whereas transmitters may be operational for anything between 20 and 40 years. Buildings, of course, are the most difficult problem of all.

If they are designed to meet specific operational needs they can be of an industrial or comparable type with a reasonably short life expectancy. Moreover, they can be demolished without much trouble. But studios, with a considerable acoustic insulation and structural reinforcement in order to carry heavy loads, or with requirements imposed by their siting and the need to provide something aesthetically acceptable, present a much more difficult proposition. As a building Broadcasting House has for long been obsolescent. It is certainly extremely difficult to do anything with it. The construction is so massive and rigid that any alteration is a major task. Every studio technician knows about 'knocking chits' and the restrictions on knocking which can infiltrate on programmes whenever the studios are in use. That can at times mean a restriction through most of the 24 hours. And yet if the BBC were to suggest demolishing Broadcasting House, or even moving away from it, I can imagine the chorus of screaming protest that would rise from all quarters. Broadcasting House illustrates very precisely the problem of intractable obsolescence.

A capital asset schedule of £140 million calls for a planned replacement programme. One course is to try to ensure that the need for replacement will coincide with some technical development which would, in any case, justify the purchase of new equipment. This approach may still leave a need for substantial replacement expenditure if BBC staff are to have the right kind of buildings and equipment for them to produce good and satisfying programmes.

Alongside this question of replacement of equipment, preferably at a moment of technical development, there are questions of productivity. Broadcasting is a labour-intensive operation. I have noted elsewhere that at least 80% of the BBC's running costs represent payments for services rendered by people in one way or another. There is a limit to the substitution of the mechanical for the live – and in artistic performance, which is the essence of broadcasting, that limit is very soon encountered. The BBC must therefore always be looking at its technical operations to find what savings can be made in the deployment of labour. Only about 10% of BBC staff have programme or editorial responsibility. Most of the remainder work in support of these 10% either directly or indirectly. There is ample scope therefore to take advantage of those technological developments to economize in the use of support staff without reducing the editorial quality of the output. But more and more such proposals encounter union resistance in an age of rising unemployment and compressed salary levels.

One of my most urgent tasks when I became Director-General in 1969 was to review the capital plans. As a first step I looked back at the installation programme of 1963–65. This was one of the peak periods, because during these two years BBC capital investment, expressed as a proportion of current income, was running at a level of about 20%. That compared with a more normal figure of something like 10%. It seemed difficult to strike an average because the pattern is essentially one of peaks and troughs, but these proportions indicate the nature of the peak in these years. The reasons were fairly clear. The BBC was embarking on BBC-2, which called for very considerable additional studio investment and the devising of a complete new production system based on the 625-line system, and was also constructing the first UHF transmission network, at very high speed indeed. (A minor point – the balance sheet reflects the fact that the Radio capital programme was substantially distorted in 1964–65 by the acquisition of the freehold of the Broadcasting House Extension, but this does not significantly affect the picture of the BBC's capital investment as a whole.)

Looking at the detail of that two-year installation programme one thing emerged very quickly. Nearly £5 million worth of equipment was of a kind which would have to be replaced in 1970/71. In other words, about a quarter of the investment programme over the two years in question was going to produce an early replacement problem. About another £5 million represented building, which constituted a replacement problem for the last decade of the century. It could perhaps come a little later, but it was certainly not immediate. Some £3 million represented freehold purchase of sites which ought never to become a replacement problem and indeed, were likely to bring relief by way of future avoidance of the need for investment. A further £3½ million went into the transmission system, principally into the construction of the BBC-2 UHF network, with a 20 to 30 year life. The rest, just over £3½ million – was made up of relatively minor items of which the details are not significant enough to affect this analysis, but where replacement was essentially short term. Were the BBC to be faced with replacing exactly what was installed in those years the need would have been for 625-line monochrome equipment, but the advent of colour in 1968 meant that the replacement problem became a development investment, and virtually all the equipment which would have had to be renewed was being replaced, from 1970 onwards by colour-capable systems. There were some problems of timing to make sure that the development timetable fitted into what would have been the replacement timetable, and some of the original monochrome equipment was re-deployed, for example, into regional studios which would otherwise have had to wait much longer for expansion. True, that expansion was in monochrome, but it was clear that the regions too would benefit from the ultimate need to carry out development in colour instead of replacement in monochrome, while having enjoyed in the meantime the benefit of earlier expansion. What emerged was a bigger problem financially, with a rather different time scale, but it was a sensible adaptation to changed circumstances.

But having converted one kind of problem into another the BBC still had left itself with a further replacement problem over the colour equipment which it was then installing. The effect would be felt in the middle of the 1970s with the need to start replacing the original colour equipment in the studios. So there was an expectation of another peak between 1975 and 1980. The peak could, of course, last longer, and in the end, that has proved to be the case.

I could see, in 1970, that by the period 1975–80 the BBC would be running into the quite different problems arising from its acquisition since about 1955 of successive high cost leasehold office property in central London. It would make obvious sense to build freehold in replacement and avoid thereby the very heavy costs arising from rent reviews. But that is an enormous question. First there is the problem of sites – which could hardly be in central London. Second, there is the problem of managing the capital sums required so that the buildings can be put up at the most economic moment to meet the rent review needs. Third, there is the personal problem of moving staff in very considerable numbers from one London location to another. And fourth, there could be very difficult problems of decanting – of finding places for staff to work while the movement was taking place. The problems have not yet been resolved, but they will substantially affect either the BBC's capital programme or the level of its continuing operating costs at the end of this decade.

Discussion of the need to replace studio equipment at relatively short intervals raises the question of judging the right point at which to standardize. When colour was being brought in there were very difficult decisions to be made about the exact type of equipment to be bought. The art was still in rapid development and if the BBC picked one particular type of equipment it could be expected to become obsolete within a very short time. Nevertheless, because of the quantities needed and the rapidity of the installation programme the BBC could not afford to be constantly changing its specifications. And so it had to plump for certain types of equipment, and having chosen its models it had to stick with them.

The effect lasts longer than might be supposed, and for good economic reasons. Thus, for instance, when the BBC was looking at purchasing needs in 1971, nearly ten years after the original decisions, and some considerable time before the total replacement programme became due, it has to decide whether to mix newer equipment with its older standardized systems, or whether to take up offers of available older equipment even though it might be going out of production. Two such problems arose in that year – in buying colour cameras and videotape machines. The manufacturers, in preparing to introduce new and technically advanced designs, were very ready to clear their shelves of older equipment still in stock in order to open the market for the newer material. At such times very advantageous prices became available. The BBC had to decide in both these cases whether to continue to buy off the shelf at the end of the production run cameras and videotape equipment of the same specifications as were already extensively in use in its studios, or whether to test out newer equipment. When one finds that the offering prices of the older equipment could give ten for the price of five, it is easy to understand why the BBC chose to be just a little old-fashioned for the time being. There is here a direct relationship between capital programmes and innovation. The fact of an existing capital investment which has still to be fully exploited in economic terms can be a positive barrier to innovation.

Returning to the general character of the BBC's capital programme, I propose to examine the pattern of investment in relation to income between the start of competition and 1970/71, and to look at the problem I had to consider in my first five years. The period of my total review was 20 years – a significant timespan. Over the years from 1957 to 1971 BBC income rose from roughly £25 million a year to just under £100 million a year. The level of investment in relation to income at the beginning of the period was about 20%. This dropped at the turn of the decade to something like 10%. It rose in the years 1963–65 to something like 20%. It dropped sharply to below 10% in the succeeding two years. It peaked again briefly in 1967–69 to about 14%. It ran during the succeeding two years at something much nearer to 10%, and dropped steadily until in 1975 its planned level was only 7%.

There are a number of good reasons for this erratic pattern. Any period of innovation and extension is bound to produce a peak. Thus the early high level of expenditure in 1957 was attributable to the major development of the Television Centre and the completion of the VHF Television network. The drop around 1960–61 was attributable to the tapering off of that major period of investment and to the period of suspense before the report of the Pilkington Committee. The peak in the years 1963–65 was mainly attributable to the acceptance by the then Government of the Pilkington recommendations, and the decline thereafter reflects the falling away of that initial impetus. But it also reflects in a very considerable way the severe financial stringency which was overtaking the BBC as a result of political hesitation about the adjustment of the level of the licence fee necessary to support the investment programme implicit in the Pilkington decisions. Similarly, the short peak in 1967–69 reflected the easing of those restraints as the licence fee went up.

The steady fall ever since, to some 8% achieved in 1967/77 reflects the BBC's pessimistic estimates of the availability of money to finance the reduced programme of investment. One of the consequences of that reduced programme was to delay development of television facilities in the regions, and especially in England. I believe that a capital investment rate of 7–8% is not only insufficient to support development in studio facilities in the regions; it is also insufficient to develop as fast as should be done the transmission system in the remoter areas of the country as a whole, and it is certainly not enough to provide an adequate replacement rate. Things will fall into decay; but the BBC is piling up replacement problems for the future – quite slowly but decisively. The Corporation may be floated out of this difficulty by an unexpectedly buoyant colour purchase pattern by the public. In practice, public purchases of colour receivers have consistently been at a higher rate than the BBC's forecasts have suggested, but the curve must flatten out soon. It is true that 7% of an annual £130 millions income in 1975 or 8% of an income of £220 millions in 1977 is very much more than 20% of an income of £25 millions in 1957. But part of the higher income which represents a catching up with inflation is self-cancelling so far as capital costs are concerned, and that part which represents payment for the operating costs of a greatly extended service is also self-cancelling in capital terms, since it is reflected in a very substantial increase in the capital installations required to provide the service.

What does constitute a proper level of capital investment for a television broadcasting operation? There are not many guides to this, and everything is affected by the jerkiness of the pattern of political decisions about television development. But it is interesting to look at the capital investment pattern of Commercial Television in this country. The Prices and Incomes Board studied the finances of the programme companies over the period 1969–1974. Their report suggested that the total income expected by the independent system over this period was just under £600 million. Deducting the levy as it then stood, together with the rental payments by the companies to the ITA, and the profit forecasts which were shown in that report – a total of some £250 million – and allowing for an initial injection of funds by the companies to start their capital programme of £20 million, the calculation yields a total available for operating and capital expenditure of some £370 million. On the basis of the forecasts made by the companies capital investment was expected to run at about £35 million – in other words, at about $9\frac{1}{2}$% of income. I have omitted from this calculation the investment by the IBA in the distribution system, but since the rental payments were estimated as a relatively small part of the whole – some £55 million – and

289

since the estimate of the proportion of this to be devoted to capital investment was about 25% – it would not affect too substantially my conclusion that the companies believe that a proper rate of capital investment in the system is something not less than, and somewhere near to 10%. By that criterion 7% by the BBC in 1975 was not enough.

I have mentioned the effect on the BBC's capital problem of a possible unexpected buoyancy in colour television receiver sales, which has been a continuing phenomenon. That raises another very important aspect of the total capital problem. I have dealt so far entirely with capital investment by the producers and distributors of programmes. But the major capital investment in any broadcasting system is made by the customers – by the viewers and listeners. Colour television offers the easiest illustration of that proposition because the figures are new, easy to trace and do not present a problem of the accumulated obsolescence of the equipment in the public's hands. By March 1972 there were probably one million colour sets in use. This represented an investment of some £250 million by the public. By 1975 the estimate was of three million sets in use – or one viewing home in six equipped with colour – representing a public accumulated investment of some £750 million. By 1977 investment by the public in colour receivers must have been at least £2,000 millions, not allowing for replacements. Comparing that with the historic cost at those dates of the BBC's capital investments it is clear how the proportions distribute themselves. The public pays by far the biggest bill in capital terms. Similarly, even in VHF for radio, where the public is equipped only as to 60% for receiving the signals, the three BBC national networks were built for £4 million in the late fifties and early sixties, whereas the public – rather less than 40% of them had probably paid by 1970 something like £175 million over the period of VHF transmission (that is since 1954) in equipping itself.

This represents an enormous element of inflexibility in the total system, from which considerable consequences follow.

The first is that having decided on a system of distribution, and having persuaded the audience to equip itself to receive the programme in a particular way, Government and broadcasters are committed to the maintenance of that system for a very substantial period. Thus the decision to begin television in 1936 on the 405-line electronic system needed a major policy change on a national scale 30 years later when the line standard had to be changed to 625. Because it was impossible to abandon overnight the 405-line system, the country was compelled to use precious frequency space in a network-duplicating operation in order to permit the changeover. The investment of capital by the audience in the system of reception first of all delayed the changeover to a more satisfactory standard and a more satisfactory system, and, secondly, required a substantial capital investment by the broadcasters and the public in the new system when the decision was finally made. That capital investment also included a very substantial and important part of the nation's inelastic capital – frequency space. The deployment of a given amount of capital, both by the broadcasters and the audience, is in itself a barrier to innovation unless one is prepared to invoke the total force of Government policy in order to bring about a change to something different.

This will apply over the years in the case of colour television. Now that the United Kingdom is committed to the PAL system of transmission it will not be possible to abandon it for a period which will be measured in decades rather than in years. Even if some more efficient method of propagating colour television is discovered it will be impracticable to use it. And once the nation has invested a given amount of capital in the broadcast mode of distributing television signals and receiving them there is an automatic discouragement to the development of any other system of distribution – such as cable vision – even though broadcast receiving equipment in the home could be adapted to meet the needs of the alternative system. It is not so much a question of the relative proportions of investment as between the broadcast mode and the cable mode. Broadcasting is a very cheap way of getting programmes to viewers in built-up areas. The capital cost of the Sutton Coldfield BBC-1 and BBC-2 station worked out at about 10 pence per viewer served. Broadcasting is also much less expensive than cable when it comes to the question of providing a service in thinly populated areas. It is without question much more economical though costly in these circumstances, even though it cannot be 100 per cent complete for practical reasons of frequency availability, and even though it may be, in certain circumstances and relatively speaking, inefficient because it is subject to a certain degree of interference and diminution of signal strength because of physical obstacles.

One recent example will show how the nature of the equipment possessed by the audience imposes restraint on the broadcaster in improving his technical efficiency. The BBC is now distributing the sound component of its television transmissions from the studio centre to the transmitter at the same time and on the same circuit as the picture signal. This holds out the advantages of a financial saving as well as a saving in circuit bandwidth. For an initial investment of something over £200,000 the BBC has been able to make very substantial revenue savings cumulatively over the years.

The logical thing would be to extend this mode of distribution to the domestic receiver, leaving the sorting out of the sound and vision signals to the receiver itself. This would save bandwidth at the transmitter as well as in the distribution circuits. But the fact that the audience is not equipped with receivers which will carry out this function means that the broadcasters cannot adopt this approach – and bandwidth will continue to be used because of the need to supply to existing receivers a signal with which they can cope. It would be impractical to demand that all viewers should re-equip themselves in order to make the technically possible saving.

What emerges from this concept of relative inflexibility is that the period of return on a capital investment by a broadcaster is now very long. The establishment of a transmission network on a particular system commits broadcasting to the use of that system, both in the studios and in the receivers, for a period of up to 20 years. In order to plan that kind of investment programme one needs a good deal of certainty, and in present circumstances, I do not think that broadcasters have it in sufficient measure.

First, and most obviously, we are uncertain about the cost of money, and even its value. Prices rise and replacement costs are correspondingly affected. Interest rates are relatively high. They may fall, but we cannot be sure. But further, the constitutional instruments under which the BBC and the IBA have been working had a span of 12 years. If we were to gauge the length of time of the next set of constitutional instruments by the length over which capital investments must be recovered we would be talking about periods of 15–20 years. That would make financial, economic and technical sense. The BBC-1 and IBA UHF networks will be, in their major elements, 20 years old in 1990. The BBC-2 network will then be about 25 years old. By 1990 it should have been possible not only to cease the 405-line black and white transmissions but also to re-engineer the bands released for additional services. Again 1990 may well be about the right sort of date by which it will be technically and economically feasible to broadcast a regular service direct from satellites to the viewer. The situation will be open enough for a number of real choices to be made. I do not expect that 20 years of certainty for the broadcasters will ever make political sense. But I do think that 12 years is a minimum period and that 15 years is a more realistic period.

I believe that this argument applies at least as much to Independent Television as it does to the BBC. They run a commercial operation which has to calculate in terms of the recovery of the capital investment both at the beginning of the contract, and during its currency. If the period of exploitation is short the return has to be quick and high. That is not the best formula for producing good quality programmes. I believe that my colleagues in Independent Television would agree with me wholly in this analysis of their position. A degree of certainty about the future is essential to the maintenance of decent standards in programmes.

There is only one respect in which a shorter contract period holds an advantage from the point of view of Independent Television. It is that when a contract comes to an end and is available for re-allocation there is a possibility of bringing into the industry a new flow of capital. New shareholders mean new money, and that is always useful if one is in a developing technology. But I do not believe that this adequately compensates for the disadvantages which follow from the need to produce a high return over a short period.

It might be supposed that the BBC was relatively safe from this kind of uncertainty. But as each enquiry approaches, or as each renewal of the constitutional documents draws near, the BBC is also subject to a degree of uncertainty, or at least of delay in implementing intentions. This is clear from the figures which I have given about the pattern of BBC capital investment at periods which were constitutionally and politically critical in the last 15 years. It might be thought that the BBC ought to cover these difficult periods by borrowing in order to sustain the momentum of its capital investment. But borrowing is no answer to financial uncertainty. It can only be safely carried out where there is a predictable financial future – and that is a condition which ought to be insisted upon as much by the lender as by the borrower.

Moreover, as I have indicated, the BBC's capital expenditure follows a pattern of peaks and troughs. What it needs is sufficient temporary accommodation, either by way of reserves or borrowing power, to see itself through the peaks. The BBC can recoup itself during the troughs, and ought desirably to be able to accumulate reserves to see it through the next peak of expenditure. The BBC have never been able to do that in the last 30 years. It used to follow this practice, because its income was sufficiently buoyant to cope with the problem. I cannot see that the BBC is likely to reach that kind of surplus position again in the future. The political pressures are too great for one to be entitled to expect it.

What are the consequences of a squeeze on capital expenditure imposed by the need to remain within a budget fixed over a period of years? First, there is no doubt that the BBC has to delay the carrying out of its public service obligations to provide a service to small pockets of population in the more remote areas – indeed, to precisely those areas of population which have the greatest need of its programmes. Second, it had to ask its staff to work with equipment which has lived beyond its full useful life. They have to work in out-dated buildings, or in others which are becoming obsolete, at a time when programme-making methods develop and the tools and methods of production are constantly changing. The BBC is prevented from introducing new technological developments at a rate sufficiently to maintain its competitive capacity in a highly competitive field. And finally, it loses the freedom to choose how to develop its technological installations because rising operating costs over the years progressively consume more and more of its available income. Capital programmes, in short, must be planned, because they are long term, against a secure background of continuity, both of policy and of finance. In any financial squeeze, capital plans are the first to be cut, because they yield a quick saving, and nobody notices the effects until some time later.

The conclusions which I draw from this analysis of the BBC's capital situation are that the period of validity of the constitutional instruments should have a closer relationship to the calculations which derive from an assessment of the investment life of the broadcasters' principal capital assets. Fifteen years represents two sets of television studio equipment, each having a life of about seven years. It represents three-quarters of the life of a transmission system. It represents half the life of the average building. I am not sure whether it exceeds the political tolerance of those whose duty it is to decide on the length of time for which the broadcasters should be left free of enquiry and therefore, from the point of view of the politicians, not strictly accountable to the public. That is the nature of the problem which has to be solved by those who assess the rights and wrongs of the renewal of the constitutional instruments – where to draw the line between what is politically tolerable and what is financially sensible.

CHAPTER XVIII

Appointments

WHAT EXACTLY do I mean by top management? The Board of Governors appoint the chief executive of the BBC – the Director-General. Under the Director-General, as I have explained in an earlier chapter, there are the three Managing Directors and four or five other Directors who constitute the executive Board of Management. The three Managing Directors are responsible for the three main parts of the BBC which actually produce the programmes – the Television, Radio and External Services. Alongside these are four Directors who manage the various technical, administrative and public relations services. They are, respectively, the Director of Engineering, who is responsible for the provision and operation of all the BBC's studio and transmission activities; the Director of Personnel who has charge of all the staff, contractual and property management functions; the Director of Finance who now has charge of Publications and Enterprises (that is, Radio and Television Sales) as well as the obvious Finance department; and, lately, the Director News and Current Affairs and, at certain periods, the Chief Assistant to the Director-General who has sometimes ranked as a Director and whose function can best be described as an extension of the mind of the Director-General. Either of these can expect to handle, either personally or through a senior deputy, all but the very highest discussions with the Government and political parties. The Director of Public Affairs is responsible for publicity and for audience research and correspondence with the public. These men are the BBC's top management. Each Director has, naturally, a supporting staff – and in accordance with good principles of management one might expect to find some six or seven such staff working directly to each Director. All in all, therefore, the top management of the BBC amounts numerically to about fifty people. What follows is an explanation of how these people come to be where they are, and how the BBC hopes to find their successors.

First, we should look at numbers. The BBC employs some 25,000 people. Like all public bodies it is frequently criticized for being a swollen bureaucracy, an overgrown giant, a colossus which no longer knows what its extremities are doing. It is almost as though the BBC was seen as suffering from Parkinson's disease in two senses – that of Professor Parkinson who argues that work expands to fill the time available, and that all organizations grow because growth is the law of being and has nothing to do with ideas of purposive activity; and in the sense of Parkinsonism as a medical syndrome in which there is a failure of nervous communication from the brain to the limbs. This picture of dual disease, as I have already argued, in this book, is nonsense. Those who criticize an organization simply on the grounds of its excessive size are forgetting that where size has in fact seemed to be a handicap the real fault has been a failure to organize properly. Bad structure can create a fallacious impression of excessive size. But size is a relative term and has to be considered in relation to the function concerned. So far as top management is concerned the pool on which the BBC draw for top management is comparatively small. Of the 25,000 employees some 5,000 work at above what the BBC regards as the basic professional grade – that is, the levels from which one would expect to recruit a member of one of the professions without previous experience – the equivalent of a university graduate or a qualified accountant. Effectively, this is the pool of men and women with the right kind of judgement to go through to management. I should not argue that no others can ever qualify. I do believe, however, that those others who come into management consideration will pass through this grade before they enter the management recruitment pool.

Of those 5,000 about 1,000 are professionally qualified engineers. I mean no disparagement to the professional engineer when I say that in an organization like the BBC, where editorial content is the final management preoccupation, the engineer is less likely to be considered as a candidate for the general range of top management, who are more likely to come from less technical spheres. Things have been different elsewhere – as for instance, in Canada, where the Canadian Broadcasting Corporation was headed for some 15 years between 1954 and 1969 by a distinguished engineer without whose leadership the Television services of the CBC could not have been taken, as they have been, from coast to coast by a live communications system. I exclude, then, the BBC's 1,000 engineers above the professional grade from my general consideration. Of the balance of some 4,000 a considerable proportion are in the service and administrative areas. They are concerned with those activities which are ancillary to programme making – contracts, property, accommodation, finance, catering and so on. Others are in publicity, audience research, publications and reference services. In my judgement these areas are somewhat more likely than engineering to provide recruits for top management, but, on the whole, they have been less frequent sources of management recruitment than the programme areas. We come down, therefore, in the last analysis to a pool, which I would put at a maximum of 2,500. This represents the potential top management employed at any time in all BBC's services.

This is a comparatively small field of selection. It is just big enough for the BBC to be able to offer a full prospect of career promotion to the very top to those whom it recruits, without laying itself open to the risk of debilitating inbreeding. But the fact that the BBC is just big enough to sustain its next generation of top management recruitment has some very important consequences for the BBC approach to a number of personnel problems. These consequences can be seen in the attitude towards the selection of staff for promotion, in which the BBC gives a very strong preference indeed to internal candidates for vacancies. The result has been that after 50 years of history, during which the BBC has grown to its present substantial size, it has established its virtual independence of outside sources of senior recruitment. The BBC does not, like the Police, frequently look to the Services, whether civil or military, for most of its senior appointments, though for specialist staff in, for example, law, accountancy, or organization and methods, it must obviously look outside.

In the specialist field in which it operates this internal recruitment is of profound significance. As might be deduced from the composition of the Board of Management, the editors are in charge. They are not only editors as to content. They are *managing* editors. They have the power of the purse – the power of hiring and firing. They are staff managers as well as the programme managers. 'Administration' is not in charge of the operation. It is the servant, and it operates on budgets delegated by the editors to provide the services they need. In other words top management is predominantly provided by professionals trained in the BBC's major field of activity. It is likely therefore – indeed I should argue inevitable – that the main line of management selection should run through the editorial grades. That is what now happens when the BBC is looking for its top men. This is not to say that a man must be at the top of the editorial tree in order to have a major chance of entering top management. It *does* mean that a man who has had editorial experience at some stage in his career is more likely to be a candidate for top management than one who has not had that experience.

It might be argued that it is easy enough to identify the field, but a good deal harder to spot winners. Anybody can find out the names of the horses entered for the Derby at the two-year-old stage. It is just as easy to identify the survivors at each stage of acceptance, right up to the moment when the runners appear at the start. The real secret is to identify numbers 1, 2 and 3 with enough certainty to place a bet. How does the BBC identify its winners? Naturally it is not a matter of sticking a pin in the list. The BBC does study the form. But it would be misleading to suggest that the BBC has nothing better than the form book to guide its choices. The BBC equivalent of the form book is the system of annual reporting. Every year each employee of the BBC is the subject of an annual report which is confidential in the sense that it is not made public to others, but completely open in the sense that it is communicated to him by the superior officer who wrote it. Moreover, it is communicated almost always in its entirety. The only circumstance in which parts of a report are not communicated is when there is a reference to some shortcoming which derives from an 'irremediable defect' of character, when that defect would not be remedied by the fact of communication. Such exceptions are rare. The risk of this system is, I admit, that the reporting may not be as efficient as it should be, and may, indeed, sometimes be less than wholly honest. The reporting officer may couch his phrases less trenchantly than would ideally be desirable. He may even conceal relevant criticisms for fear of damaging his future relations with the person in question.

But any sensible reporting officer will realize that such concealment will, in the long run, leave him in an impossible position, because if the shortcomings are such that the individual should be transferred to other work, or even dismissed, the previous reports will be on the record, and if they do not indicate the reasons for dismissal or transfer, the case will be impossible to sustain on appeal – for all this process rests upon the right of each individual to appeal upwards right to the Director-General, and then to the Industrial Court in cases of dismissal – against what he may consider to be unfair treatment by his superior. In a litigious society that would be a dangerous situation, but such is the reputation, established over many years by the BBC, for good staff management, that there are relatively few appeals on matters of annual reporting. More-over, the next man up in the line of management will know the capacities of the reporting officer, and he will be able to judge whether reports on staff are likely to be too lenient or too critical when they are written by a particular individual. On balance, the benefits of the reporting system as I have outlined it are great. Management has the means of saying what it thinks about a particular member of the staff, and on the other side the member of staff knows, without reservation, in what regard he is held by his employer. The BBC ought, perhaps to be con-sidering whether the analysis and distribution of the material contained in staff annual reports is as good as it might be in the interest of career planning and the best deployment of available talent. It may be that the information is not as much used as it should be. But the system is a good one in principle.

I have described this system of reporting because I think it is the key to the BBC's general solution of the selection and promotion problem. These reports form a basis for the selec-tion of staff for vacancies. The fact that they constitute a continuous and gradually developing record gives the BBC a better chance to make logical decisions about advancement than it could expect to achieve if it proceeded simply on the basis of *ad hoc* judgements when pressed by the need to fill vacancies or to repel outside competition for staff, or to allevi-ate internal disgruntlement. When there is a vacancy to fill the BBC usually looks, as I have explained, in the first instance, to the field of internal candidates. The fact that the vacancy exists is advertised on the internal notice boards, giving the duties of the post and the experience required, together with a clear indication of the grade and salary attached to the work. Some-times in order to check the standards of selection the BBC will advertise outside and take into account the applications which come in as a result. The applications are sifted and unless the selection is so obvious as to make further study pointless, the decision between those short-listed is made by a board com-posed normally of the head of the employing department, and one of the specialized staff management personnel who serves in that area of the BBC, and a representative of the BBC's central appointments staff whose job it is to see that candidates receive equal and fair treatment. The continuous record of service on internal candidates constituted by annual reports is available on these boards on request, and always to its Chairman. I do not claim – nor would anybody in the BBC – that the board is an infallible instrument of selection, but it is the best anyone had been able to devise as a routine method.

From this account it might be assumed that the BBC is satisfied that it is operating a system on the most liberal principles of free competition within the organization, and that it has a very adequate flow of information about its staff, on the basis of which entirely logical selections can be made. But the BBC is well aware of the deficiencies of the system. Its great advantage is that it convinces the staff themselves that they have had an equal chance to compete for the higher jobs. It also convinces them that if the BBC recruits from outside, the chances of people already on the staff will first have been fully considered. In other words it is a system in which the BBC can feel entitled to assume a very great measure of staff assent. That is a very important requirement in any institution which operates in an atmosphere of free discussion of policy, and which cannot call on the absolute power of command, as can the military forces.

That is the situation which prevails in the BBC. Programmes are free ranging. So is the behaviour of individual members of the staff of the BBC. Some people look upon the BBC as though its affairs were conducted in an atmosphere of almost complete anarchy. Every decision, they suggest, turns into a motion for debate. I preferred to put the situation in the way in which it was once presented by Sir Hugh Greene – that creative staff cannot do good work if their superiors are all the time breathing down their necks. The full yield of intelligence which can be drawn from a lively staff comes only in an atmosphere of freedom which contains within itself the recognition of responsibility and self control. That is as true of the BBC's administrative proceedures as it is of its programme output. It is hard to see how the BBC could maintain two different atmospheres in the same institution, and it does not try to do so.

But having gained the advantage of staff assent to the system of promotion the BBC must recognize that it needs something more. The basic weakness in a system which relies on applications for competitive appointment is that it may promote a situation in which only those who apply are available for consideration. In other words, it will rely, in the last resort, on a kind of self-selection. If good people are entirely happy in their jobs, as programme producers very often are, they may well not wish to apply for others – and yet they may be the best people for an appointment. Similarly, if a transfer from a particular post can take place only when the holder of that post submits himself for another, then every appointment can become a kind of freehold tenure until the age of retirement. It would not be wise for an institution which depends on continuity of standards, as the BBC does in the editorial field, to be constantly encouraging the turbulent movement of staff from one department to another. But it would be clearly disastrous to have a situation in which, because nobody *wanted* to move, nobody *did* move. There are, therefore, certain quite significant modifications to the absolutism of the BBC's competitive system. It can 'enrich' the field in particular competition by stimulating applications from other qualified candidates to whom it may not have occurred to apply. It can refuse to select from those who do apply, and then either readvertise or make an appointment after an exploration of the potential field. Moreover, the BBC has a system of training attachments, under which people of obvious capacity can apply, or can be invited, or transfer temporarily from their own post to some other department in which their experience will be extended and their capacities tested.

But the whole extent of flexibility is conditioned by the fact that the basic competitive system of appointment is a matter of agreement with the Trade Unions. It is right that it should be so, because their interest is greatly engaged in securing fair treatment of staff, even though they are well aware that the BBC has already placed a very high value on this same objective. Every modification of the competitive system of appointment must be carefully considered in order to establish that it will not undermine the basic accord with the unions and the general sense of fairness which is the first fruit of the system. But it is a matter of practical record that of all the BBC's internally advertised vacancies in the year 1965/66 over a quarter were filled without competition. Ten years later the figures were much the same. That is a sizeable degree of flexibility in what could otherwise be an intolerably rigid system.

Nevertheless, the inhibitions inherent in the competitive system do have important consequences in the process of identifying future top management. There is no system of posting, in order to ensure that a particular individual may gain wider experience. Such individuals do emerge, and manage to find for themselves the breadth of experience which is desirable in the general interest of BBC management as a whole. But the BBC recognizes that there is weakness, and it has considered various ways in which, without disturbing the basic structure, it could improve flexibility in this area.

The problem has been intensified in recent years because the business of broadcasting has become more specialized in different ways. For example, the technical equipment at the disposal of the television producer, and the specialized production skills which he has to develop are such as to make it very difficult for anybody who had not been trained in this field either to enter it as a producer from some similar capacity in sound broadcasting, or to assume a management post without having gone through the mill himself. I could quote other examples of the same kind of increased complexity of working. All these developments tend cumulatively to reduce the flexibility of management in arranging for promising

candidates to broaden their experience. It is one of the responsibilities of the Director-General of the BBC to make sure that
the ultimate field of choice for top management is not so
restricted by these built-in rigidities as to reduce it effectively
to no choice at all. I cannot suggest general answers to this
problem because I do not believe that they exist. One has to
take each individual and see how best to handle his case. But
that there *is* a problem cannot be denied.

The approach to the solution of the problem is eased to
some extent by an important modification of the general
principle of open competitive appointment. It is accepted by
the Unions – and has been for many years – that appointments
to the most senior posts in the BBC need not be subject to
the general principle of open competition through internal
advertisement. The area within which this freedom applied
includes some 200 posts, of which about 30 are engineering
appointments. It can be said, therefore, that about 170 posts in
the general area of senior management are open to appointment by management discretion, and it is from within this area
that the 50 or so top management posts will be filled. This
gives to management a limited power to move staff who have
already proved themselves in particular fields of management.
It offers a useful degree of flexibility. But I have some doubt
about the precise value which should be placed upon this
relaxation of the general system. It can be used only when
vacancies occur. It is not a 'posting' system, in the true sense.
By the time a man reaches this level of seniority he may well
have acquired in a special measure one of the particular skills
which I have just mentioned. But by the same token he will
have gone beyond the point at which he could transfer,
without embarrassment to himself or to others, to some other
skilled professional area. For example, it would be very difficult indeed for a man who had become the head of one of our
specialist language services, but who had no direct experience
of television production, to transfer on his own level of
seniority to a television production department. Ideally he

ought to be able to go to such a production department and do the normal job of a television producer for a worthwhile period, and then take up the proposed appointment. But the time required for such manoeuvres would be extravagant in terms of senior staff deployment. Further, there would be the terrible risk that a man proven in one field would turn out to be inept in another, and unable to gain the respect of his prospective subordinates. And finally there would be the realities of the embarrassments which could arise from the very difficult personal relationship during the training period. I do not think these difficulties can be brushed aside, and consequently I have, as I say, reservations about this limited freedom of appointment by management discretion in the higher levels of the BBC. It ought to be attempted from time to time, as when an Editor, External Services News, is transferred to edit a television news programme, which happened recently. But it is a risky business for all concerned.

Furthermore, given the effect of increasing complexity in the operation it becomes less and less likely that someone from outside the BBC will be able successfully to enter at the management level. Policy discussions, which are the substance of top management's life, cannot, in my experience, take place in a theoretical vacuum. They arise unequivocally from the day to day practice of the profession, and the solutions are bound up inextricably with the operation to be carried out today and tomorrow. There is no such thing in broadcasting as a body of knowledge which could be described as the theoretical principles of broadcasting administration. There are practical problems to be solved, and the solutions can be reached only through the intimate knowledge of the interlocking repercussions of a general decision as they are left throughout the operational machine. That is why I believe that, difficult though it may be, the BBC must, for the future, principally look to itself for its own top management. Purely on the technical level, as distinct from the general issue of staff confidence, it seems to me inevitable that selection must be from within.

I draw this conclusion from the recent history of broad-casting developments. But the whole pattern of our history is relevant to a consideration of the way in which the BBC has identified its top management. In its first ten years, from 1924 onwards, the BBC was a comparatively small body of enthusi-asts who were willing to stake their careers on the future of an unproven medium. They were pioneers, but because they were pioneers they were a miscellaneous group. I intend no dis-respect to them. They were men of vision. They provided the top management of the BBC until comparatively recently. Thus Sir Noel Ashbridge remained at the head of Engineering Operations until as late as 1952, B. E. Nicolls, who was in almost at the very beginning, was the Senior Programme Controller – and indeed, at the end acting Director-General – until 1952. Sir Lindsay Wellington, who joined in the very early days (1924), was Director of Sound Broadcasting until 1963. Harman Grisewood, who was also among this early BBC group (1929), was a member of the Board of Management until 1964. Sir Beresford Clark, my immediate predecessor but one as Director of External Broadcasting, whose service also dated from the early twenties (1924), was Director of External Broadcasting until 1964. There was, therefore, a historical layer of initial recruitment which provided the BBC's top management until well after the end of the Second World War.

There was a second wave of recruitment to the BBC in the 1930s, when broadcasting seems to have become a respectable target for young men leaving the older universities. By the end of the thirties the BBC had reached a strength of about 3,000 staff, and in that period of the thirties it acquired its second wave of top management candidates. One could see them on the Board of Management in the 1960s – the Director of Television (Mr Kenneth Adam) and the Chief Assistant to the Director-General, Mr Oliver Whitley. One could also see them in the next layer down – the Assistant Director of Sound Broadcasting, the Controller of Administration in the External

Services, the Controller of Programme Organization in Sound Broadcasting, and the Controller of Television Administration were examples.

The next wave of recruitment came at the beginning of the Second World War, by the end of which the BBC had attained a size of some 12,000. These were men of a vast variety of experience and age levels, brought in to meet a particular need – that of broadcasting overseas in order to maintain confidence in Britain at a critical point of history. Because of the rules governing National Service in wartime Britain, those who stayed for any length of time from this intake were mostly aged thirty or over. Younger people did not enter the BBC's services, or if they did, they left when their time came to be called into the armed forces. Many of these younger men volunteered for service. But the effect was the same in either case. Some of them came back after the war because they had enjoyed their experience of broadcasting and because they had, in many cases, a legal right to reinstatement. But the major effect was that the BBC acquired during the war a group of men and women of some maturity, many of whom stayed in its permanent employment when the war ended. But from all that wartime recruitment wave the names which later became prominent in top management were those of the younger people who returned to the BBC or stayed with it after tasting the excitement of broadcasting. Sir Hugh Greene himself was one of them. The point to note – a remarkable piece of luck – is that the war brought to the BBC an injection of people of talent whom it would not, in other circumstances, have expected to recruit. It was a happy accident on whose repetition the BBC cannot rely. There is, of course, the risk that when recruitment takes place in waves of this kind, the intake may include a fair proportion of recruits who are of less than top quality. But the BBC has been especially fortunate in its intake.

After the Second World War it became necessary to rebuild the structure of domestic broadcasting. Some of the recruits in the rebuilding process came from the wartime External Services, and the flow from that source continued until very recently. But the period between 1945 and 1950 was one in which the BBC was more preoccupied with re-deploying the existing material to fit the new needs of peace time, than with bringing to itself any new accretion of staff from outside.

It was not until the major expansion of television in the early 1950s that the next recruitment wave made itself felt. From that phenomenon there have come a succession of Programme Controllers in the Television Service and three Managing Directors. There were special circumstances at work, because, as I have explained, television is a business with its own professional requirements, and it was always likely that the management would come from within the ranks of the professionals themselves. I believe that this is likely to be a future pattern. But the new note has been the transfer of some of the Television professionals to the senior ranks of the Radio Service. There was a further recruitment wave in the early 1960s – that associated with the launching of the second television network, BBC-2. It is still early for this wave to have produced a major crop of top management recruits. But in due course the BBC will find itself equipped with another range of choices. And that range will be followed by another which will flow from the dedicated recruits who came into Local Radio from its beginnings in 1968.

This history of expansion suggests that the BBC's problem of establishing a field of potential managers has largely been solved by the fact of expansion. It has never yet had a situation in which, within a single entity, it has had to produce, by a deliberate process of selection and training, those who would evenutally run the whole organization. It is not that the BBC has been unaware of this need. I was myself selected in 1953 as the first of the BBC's internal trainees. I did not know at the time that I was being trained for future management. It was wise of those who re-elected me to say nothing of this, and it would have been arrogant for me to assume anything of the kind. But the problem has so far not been a general one for the BBC, which is therefore only now in the early stages of working out the possible process of deliberate management selection.

Among those steps the most important – because the most far reaching – was the recruitment each year until 1970 of a very small number of 'general trainees'. These were people from the universities who went into some aspect of the Corporation's work – usually in the programme field – for about two years in order to gain experience of broadcasting, and were then considered for appointment to an ordinary post on the staff. They also had to consider for themselves whether they wish to stay in broadcasting. This scheme, which attracted substantial numbers of applicants, made sure that in most years the BBC received a small but a significant trickle of recruits of clear potential. But it was a scheme which could easily run out of control. It was very easy, when seeing attractive candidates on these trainee boards, to take them on in such numbers as to create frustration among the staff already in the BBC – with whom they would be competing for jobs – and to create the impression that the BBC was interested only in arbitrarily selected 'high-fliers' who might in the end turn out to be not 'high-fliers' at all. Moreover, there was a danger in recruiting direct from the universities that the BBC could turn into an organization of people without direct experience of life in the outside world. Ivory towers are made of human bricks, and that kind of recruitment would have been the surest way to put the BBC in the ivory tower where, many people are only too ready to claim, it too easily finds itself already. In practice, the scheme had to be suspended in 1970, partly for reasons of general financial stringency, and partly because too many of the trainees finished up in a long queue of applicants for posts as documentary producers and proved difficult to absorb. It would be encouraging to see a resumption of the scheme, but the absorption problem would almost certainly recur unless strict control were exercised. As things have turned out, the BBC's journalists training scheme seems in large measure to have taken over the role of the general trainee scheme, as well as producing some very good new journalists.

I have outlined the elements of a three-sided problem, from some of whose difficulties the BBC has been spared by the accidents of history. First there is the problem of establishing an organization of sufficient size to provide a flow of recruits to its own top management. Second there is the problem of securing an age structure among the critical grades of recruitment which will bring on candidates for top management without causing bunching or gaps in the field. And third, there is the problem of ensuring a balance between the satisfaction of legitimate ambition among the existing staff of the organization and the need continuously to renew contacts with the outside world in order to prevent mental fossilization. This last problem can be resolved to some extent by internal action in arranging for suitable transfers of staff to other areas of responsibility than those for which they were recruited in the first instance; the organization of internal training courses whose primary purpose is to extend among the staff the knowledge of the activities of people in other parts of the organization; and finally by a limited recourse to outside courses in management skills – limited partly for financial reasons and partly by the absence of really relevant outside courses. The BBC is, after all, a unique business.

My argument so far has related to the size of the recruitment pool for top management, and to the way in which selections are made from it towards the ultimate end of providing the management nucleus, and – most important of all – the chief executive himself. I have said nothing so far about the actual choice of this management nucleus – in the BBC, the Board of Management.

I have suggested that the pool of staff immediately answerable to top management is of the order of 50 to 60 people. The

choice of these individuals is clearly crucial. Who chooses
them? To answer this I must refer again to the constitutional
background. It is not the only duty of a public corporation,
which is set up, by definition, to give service to the public, to
concern itself simply with the efficiency of its routine operations. There are basic issues of its general relationship with the
public, and particularly with the political representatives of the
public. It is at least as important that the operations of a public
corporation should be giving the public, in its various expressions, what it wants, as that they should be efficient in themselves, considered purely as technical activities. There can be a
great deal of argument about the wishes of the public – and
more so in broadcasting than in many other public service
organizations – but the essence of the matter is here. The BBC
was set up as a public corporation to provide broadcasting
services, and the general responsibility for seeing that those
broadcasting services were in line with the needs and wishes of
the public was given to the Board of Governors. It is with this
Board that the power of senior appointment in the BBC resides,
and must reside if they are to be in a position to fulfil their duty.
They alone appoint the Director-General. They alone can dis-
miss him. And they, on his advice, make the senior appointments which I have described as crucial. They may do so
either on the basis of oral or written report by the Director-
General, or, on occasion, by seeking the advice of a sub-
committee of their own members who can look into the
claims of the candidates proposed by the Director-General.
In recent years the full Board has more frequently considered
the Director-General's proposals – a method of approach
which I feel to be often inefficient because of a lack of detailed
knowledge of the candidates and the known weakness of large
selection boards. In addition, the process of interview by the
full Board of wider lists of candidates than can have realistic
hopes of appointment is demoralizing for those not selected,
and insidiously undermines the authority of the Director-
General. The Pilkington Committee identified this power of

appointment of senior staff as one of the two most important held in the hands of the Board. It is by this mechanism of appointment that the Board can ensure that those policies which it believes to be in the public interest – whether in matters of programme content or of the disbursement of public resources – will be carried out to their own satisfaction. The Board's deliberations in exercising this function constitute the final stage in the process of selecting top management in the BBC.

It is a key function of the office of the Director-General that he should ensure that the field of candidates for these senior posts will be adequate when the time comes to fill them, and it is also his responsibility to ensure that the claims of all are considered by the Board with equal fairness. If the Director-General is to carry out this duty effectively he must be directly involved, to a considerable degree, in the day to day editorial decisions about programme output. Clearly the pressures of his office will mean that he can concern himself only with the most important of these decisions, and probably more with those in the field of public affairs than with any others. But unless he has some such direct contact with the programme output he will have no chance of acquiring personal knowledge of the qualities of the senior staff responsible for operations. And that, to me, is an essential element in his armoury of staff assessment. He must also keep a close watch on those people who fall within the pool of the 200 or so whose appointment is open to management discretion. The easiest way for him to do so is to study their annual reports. This, I know, was done by Sir Hugh Greene. I also did it myself. Finally, the process is likely to be best carried out by a chief executive who has himself served, at some stage – preferably at as many stages as possible – within the programme editorial chain. This has been true of the BBC's last four Directors-Generals. I think it is likely to continue to be true in the future.

The BBC's experience suggests that the top management of a public broadcasting corporation is likely to be recruited from those areas which are most directly concerned with its principal activity – the making of programmes. The matter of size is probably critical. The BBC must be of a certain minimum size if it is to provide its own top management – and the arguments for internal recruitment are strong. The history of the BBC's development has direct relevance to the provision from within the organization of a field of candidates for top management. Now that the size of the BBC has been stabilized there may well be a need for positive steps to encourage a range of recruitment from outside, in order to maintain an adequate inward flow of ideas and attitudes from society at large.

There must be a systematic record of frank career information about the staff if sensible selections for senior management are to be made. The system of appointment must be such as to effect a balance between satisfying reasonable ambition by the demonstrable fairness of its procedures, and avoiding the creation of an excessive expectation among the staff that seniority or some other predictable formula will be used as an exclusive criterion of promotion. There must always be room in the appointment system for accidents to happen. From time to time they are necessary.

Finally the last stages in the selection of BBC top management must be subject to a discretion which is recognized to represent the interest of the public, as distinct from the interest of the public service. This is perhaps the most difficult proviso for public servants to accept, but it is not different in essence from the power which we recognize we must leave to politics and politicians who embody, however crudely, the sense of public will.

EPILOGUE

I HAVE TRIED to set down, after eight and a half years as Director-General of the BBC, and one year's rumination after retirement, some reflections on the practical matters which I was obliged to consider during my period of office. As soon as I tried to write about practical matters it became obvious to me that nothing could be sensibly written without explaining the formal constitutional framework within which I had to consider these practical questions, and the general philosophies which conditioned my thinking. But the prevailing consideration was always that of the personal relationship between myself as Director-General and the Chairman of the Board of Governors – and, to a lesser extent, with the Board of Governors as a whole. I start from the assumption that a Director-General has to be technically literate, financially competent, reasonably capable of resolving problems of relationships with unions, and, above all, having some capacity as an editor-in-chief. In this last respect he must be able to formulate a general intention for the programme services – of how they should fulfil the triple intention of entertainment, education and information. He must, from time to time, be prepared to elaborate on particular questions within that framework. It is his duty to give an informing spirit to the programme output. It is not usually his duty to say that a particular programme must be produced. It is his duty to create the conditions in which people will expect it to be produced, and will enjoy the conditions in which that can be done.

It is at this point that he will discover his relationship with the political establishment of the State. There is no area of programmes in which he will be free from political interest – and indeed, political pressure. Even light entertainment can produce dynamite. Drama in the permissive society offers an excellent opportunity for the moralizing politician to beat his breast publicly for the sins and omissions of the broadcaster. But most of all, of course, the public affairs programme will be the target of political comment. And in replying to criticisms the Director-General must remember that in maintaining freedom to broadcast programmes which have a critical approach to society he is, at the same time, making more difficult his own task of persuading the State to furnish him with the money to produce those programmes. In a longer term and more general sense it is also true that a Director-General who maintains the principle that his broadcasters are free to produce critical or independent programmes will be adding to the problems which he faces in persuading the State authorities of his capital investment needs, and particular developments involving the technical consent of Government may be made the more difficult to argue.

It might be argued that Directors-General ought to be cautious in such circumstances about the content of programmes. I believe that this would be a fundamental error. To shrink from the truth in a programme is always culpable error and I do not believe that it wins respect. The only restraint on truth should relate to the manner of its expression. Its presentation must be fair. But its substance must be complete. An organization which bought its revenues at the expense of its editorial independence would soon cease to have the respect which, in the long run, is the only qualification by which the public is made willing to pay for the broadcasting service. There is the nub of the problem for any Director-General – the temptation to submit to political blackmail, even of the gentlest kind, and the knowledge that there is an absolute necessity never to do so, because surrender destroys all worthwhile objectives. Of course, a Director-General must maintain a politically impartial stance when he is considering editorial questions of content in political programmes, but that does not mean that he can avoid an involvement in politics – the politics of broadcasting. I mean here the considerations which arise from the fact that broadcasting is an important medium for conveying opinions about politics, and that therefore any proposal for its development will be the subject of political arguments, and even suspicion. A Director-General – and a Chairman – have to assess what is politically practical and to devise the tactics which will secure the greatest benefit for broadcasting – not for broadcasters. They will therefore find themselves involved in political manoeuvres, trying to avoid commitments to a party interest, but taking advantage of the party situation as it develops. In my experience such matters are best conducted in private. No political party likes to be embarrassed in public by a broadcasting organisation which is assertive at the wrong moment about its own rights to development. It is more likely to agree if the credit for that development can be attributed to its own action in Government. The broadcaster's job is to keep an eye firmly on the interest of broadcasting and to make sure that it prevails. It is only when a defeat for the interests of broadcasting seems probable that it is worth considering – in my opinion – a possible appeal to public opinion over the heads of the party in power. And even then, it is a risky business, because the weapons of power in these situations nearly always turn out to be in the hands of Government. The broadcaster's life has to be one of continuous political ingenuity, offending neither the one nor the other, but seeking to secure the main objective.

In all things a Director-General must be prepared to listen almost infinitely, because advice is nearly always useful, even if it is to be rejected in the end. Advice which is rejected is, after all, simply the argument against a particular course of action put in its best form, so that if that course is rejected, the rejection will be decided upon in the full knowledge of what the decision means. But when all the advice has been heard, there is a point at which decisions must be made. At that point a Director-General must make up his mind and must then stick to his decision. Beyond that point delaying a decision becomes uncertainty, which throws the whole machine into disorder. Wrong decisions can wreck a Director-General. No decisions can wreck the organization which he directs. From time to time there will be a lot of noise. Sometimes it is necessary to be deaf. It is a very useful attribute in a Director-General.

In all his activities the Director-General is bound to operate by the devolution of authority, for reasons which I hope will have become evident through what I have written in earlier chapters. But the devolution of authority requires a recognition of the source of ultimate authority. In the BBC that must be the Board of Governors. The relationship between the possible, the practicable and the desirable is the result of the continuous dialogue between the Director-General, representing the executive, and the Board, representing the public interest. That contrast is, of course, too sharp, because the executive staff of the BBC are steeped in the necessity of identifying the public interest, and the Board is constantly illuminated in its thinking by the explanation from the professionals of what is possible.

The heart of the matter is that the Director-General works within the authority which constitutionally belongs to the Board, and that authority prevails. On the other side, the Chairman and the Board should remember that if they act in a way which diminishes the Director-General they are weakening their own power – and the BBC. A tolerance by the professional of the waywardness of laymen has to be combined with a tolerance by the laymen of the apparent arrogance of the professional.

There was a limit to what I, as Director-General, expected the Board of Governors to do. The line of definition will never be entirely clear. It is not that between policy and administration. Lord Normanbrook wisely observed that policy questions tend to grow out of individual day-to-day issues. Policy does not exist in a vacuum. Nevertheless, the Board of Governors is concerned with policy, and when it considers particular issues it is usually doing so with a view to drawing a general conclusion which will be of help to the executive, and particularly to the Director-General, in meeting similar problems in the future. It may be comforting to individual Governors to know that their views on individual programmes have been recorded in the minutes of the Board, but it is not often a useful exercise for those individual opinions to be communicated, as presumably they must be, to the producers responsible for the programmes themselves, unless they embody an opinion which has a recognizably broader relevance than to the content of the single programme in question. The Board of Governors has constantly to be reminded by its Chairman of the need for generality in its opinions about the programme service. Nothing is more entertaining than to spend an enjoyable hour as an amateur critic of broadcasting. For the professionals, the outcome can be very irritating and not very constructive.

The difficulty of hitting the right compromise between useful general opinions and idiosyncratic particularities was obscured, I believe, by the need which was felt by the Governors – and by others on their behalf – to reassert their authority after the forceful impact made by the open-hearted libertarianism of Hugh Greene. What he did to release creative initiative was very necessary for the BBC, and I regarded it as one of my functions to protect the freedom in which that creativity had emerged. Some people undoubtedly took undue advantage, and the advent of Lord Hill, with a mission to reassert the authority of the Governors, made a profound difference to the psychology of all who were concerned with public affairs programmes in the BBC. I believe that, within limits, this change was desirable.

I described in my Granada Lecture (1977) how, when I was being interviewed for the post of Director-General, I had said that I thought that there should be 'a minor resurrection' of the powers of the Board. It was my view that Lord Reith, having invented the idea of the Board, as the constitutional instrument by which the BBC's political independence might be uniquely protected, followed the practical course thereafter of limiting its activities in order to make it possible for him to run the Corporation at all. The general pattern of a powerful Director-General, relying on the advice rather than accepting the commands of a Board of Governors, persisted through the eras of Sir William Haley and Sir Ian Jacob. Sir Hugh Greene, with his powerful impetus for freedom, induced the Board of his day to work with him in developing freedom, and they did so with considerable courage. My problem was to withdraw, as Director-General, from some degree of the prominence which had been acquired by Sir Hugh Greene without abandoning either the authority or the initiatives which he had taken. It was not an easy task, but I believe that by the end of my time there was a reasonable reconciliation of the responsibilities of the Board and the executive. That reconciliation was not a little helped by the attitudes taken by Sir Michael Swann.

The character of the Board itself has a good deal to do with the way in which it has traditionally operated, and the implication of the Government White Paper of July 1978 is that the Board must continue to occupy itself with the general philosophy and policy of broadcasting, and avoid becoming too involved with the detailed management of affairs. One suggestion which has been made with increasing frequency in recent years is that the Governors should include identified representatives of the staff of the broadcasting service. Lord Annan, in a lecture on 'The Politics of Broadcasting', given in November 1977 (Encyclopaedia Britannica lecture) seems to me to have dealt with this question in a very final way. After disposing of the suggestion that broadcasting in the United Kingdom is in a state of crisis because it does not include any element of true accountability to the people at large, he noted that the proponents of a new control mechanism looked to some kind of 'broadcasting commission' which would exercise accountability for society as a whole by calling on the judgement of 'the workers' in the industry. The unions representing the workers would become 'the creative force', reflecting the theory expressed some years ago by Mr Tony Wedgwood Benn. The advocates of this theory suggested that editorial control was too important to be left to editors or producers. Real power must be transferred to the unions, who would exercise the controlling voice over the content of programmes. There would be no conflict of interests between the general interest and that of the workers, according to these theorists, because, since the unions represent the mass of workers in the industry, and since unions outside an industry do not complain about the actions and plans of those who operate within it, the ground of conflict would not exist. The management interest would have been reflected in the broadcasting commission, but as a minority whose views would be heard, taken into account, and therefore adequately reflected in the final proposals.

Lord Annan rightly denounces this line of argument as being an attempt to attack the ultimate power of the Minister over broadcasting, and therefore, through him, the power of Parliament. However ineffective Parliament may have become with its delays and compromises, it nevertheless represents, in a way which no other body can claim to do, the authentic voice of the people. Any other voice must represent a special interest, and therefore one which cannot respond to the requirement that broadcasting should meet the needs of the general mass of the people. Every argument put forward for the special reflection of worker interests in the control of broadcasting is a potential denial of the interests of the generality of the audience.

Yet the question of accountability is at the centre of concern for the Board and for the Director-General. Lord Normanbrook hit the nail on the head when he said that the Board must proceed almost entirely by retrospective review. The same holds good for the Director-General. For him the question that has to be answered when things go wrong is not so much whether an editorial mistake has been made but why the system of reference or consultation upwards has not worked. In a sense that is the more important question because it relates to future judgements rather than past errors. Looking back, I think it was probably a mistake for the inquiry into the production history of *Yesterday's Men* to have been launched by an initiative from Lord Hill. It would have been right for that initiative to have come from me. As it was, the report was one commissioned by the Board of Governors through its Chairman, and this, together with the knowledge that some of the Governors had seen the programme in question before it was transmitted, made it impossible for them to claim, with any public conviction, that they had been able to distance themselves in making their judgement about what had happened. My own proposed draft report on the findings, submitted by the two investigators, Mr Desmond Taylor and Mr Maurice Tinniswood, was a brief document on one side of foolscap setting out certain conclusions, which were substantially critical of certain elements in the programme and supportive of others. The document which was finally published went into a great deal of detail and bore the imprimatur of the whole Board of Governors. There were arguments for producing the whole information in order to convince the critics that the enquiry had been thorough. But I think that it would have been better for me to have produced a short verdict which could then have been the subject of criticism from the Board of Governors, who would have been truly in the position of detached judges, considering general matters rather than particular evidence. Lord Hill evidently considered at the time that he had to involve himself direcly in order to assert the authority of the Governors, the better to repel the attack which was being made by politicians who were not always careful about the accusations they were making. It was a difficult judgement to make. I think it would have been better made differently.

Every situation of this kind reflects the importance of the personal element in the relationship between the Chairman and the Director-General. Lord Hill came with a political history and a reputation for a robust approach to public relations. He also came from the Independent Television Authority, which rested on commercial finance. I had had a special opportunity of seeing Lord Hill at work in the early 1960s. He was then Chancellor of the Duchy of Lancaster, charged with responsibility for the Government's information policy, and especially for overseas information. He came to Bush House to visit the management group of the External Services when I was a junior member of that group under Sir Beresford Clark. Dr Hill, as he then was, felt the need to explain that in the early days of his Chancellorship he had had to favour the British Council because it had been so badly damaged by earlier Government policies in the 1950s. But he pointed out, quite fairly, that having been faced with strong Conservative representations that the External Services should be formally put under Government controls, he had, within six months, come to the opposite conclusion and had thereafter not wavered from it. Indeed, he explained, he was keen to initiate a period of re-investment in the External Services, and to carry forward, as a permanent programme, the emergency re-equipment of transmitters which he had instituted in 1957 in a preliminary phase. I thought at the time that he showed considerable courage and frankness in coming to face that very critical group to tell them exactly what he thought. I thought, moreover, that his case was a good one. I knew from the way he spoke that he had a genuine belief in the editorial independence of the BBC. Consequently, when he arrived in Broadcasting House as Chairman I did not have the same fears about his editorial intentions as some of my colleagues seem to have entertained.

Nevertheless, when I was asked at the Board which considered my candidature what I would see as my principal disadvantages if I were to be appointed, I replied that, after my lack of direct experience of television, I should find the most difficult problem to be that I should be working with a man with substantial public persona, whereas I myself had none. All my good decisions would be attributed to him and all my mistakes to me. I am not sure whether Lord Hill was entirely pleased with this reply, but it did embody the reality that the personal relationship between the Director-General and the Chairman, and their relative weights, is an important factor in the management of the BBC as it is carried on, and in the public understanding of that management.

Lord Hill was a man who was perfectly ready to throw his weight about, and there were several occasions on which we came into conflict, though there were many others on which I appreciated the strength with which he carried through a case. The first of these was shortly after I took over. He asked me to prepare the best case I could, with the best methods I could devise, for the BBC to accept advertising revenue. This was at a time when an increase in the licence fee was desperately needed, and when the Government's readiness to provide it was in doubt. My misgivings were very great and I knew that if the Board were to favour the idea – which I had been instructed to argue in the best way possible – I would have to go, because I did not accept in any way that advertising revenue could be used by the BBC without fundamentally affecting the character of its programme service. I did my best with the paper and with the construction of proposals to insulate the programmes from advertising revenue. I did so with no conviction and I approached the Board with great apprehension. At the very opening of the discussion Lord Hill at once said that he had no intention whatever that the BBC should accept advertising revenue. He had had experience of how the pressures operated in Independent Television and he believed that they would be multiplied if the BBC were to agree to go into the commercial revenue field. My relief was unbounded, but so was my astonishment. I should have expected that if this was to be the Chairman's line with the

Board he would have told me beforehand. He did not. I never cease to wonder at this – to me – strange notion of a relationship of confidence between a senior executive and a chairman. Sometimes the force of Lord Hill's support could, of itself, be an embarrassment. In the summer of 1971 I came to the conclusion that it would be better for the BBC's political relationships with the political parties to be transferred from one senior executive to another, whom I wished to assume what I saw as the increasing responsibility of fostering relationships between the various BBC regional establishments and the centre. I saw this as a developing field, though one full of organizational pitfalls because of the inherent difficulty in relating regional operations to the central activity of the BBC. The executive concerned wished to continue in the political field, and, in conformity with his rights and BBC practice, insisted on taking the matter to the Board, on the ground that duties allocated to him by the Board – as was indeed the case – should only be removed from him by their explicit approval. I was therefore faced, as Director-General, with an appeal to the Board against my decision, and which I had advised them to be in the best interests of the BBC. Lord Hill was enthusiastic about my proposals and pressed throughout the summer for speedy action. I knew that tense personal arguments of this kind between senior people take time, and that if they are pressed forward too rapidly, resentments are left behind which cannot be cured, because a sense of arbitrary haste confirms impressions, however ill-founded, of unfairness. The Board finally approved my decision, but only by a majority which reflected the divisions to which Lord Hill referred in his book, between those Governors who had served in Hugh Greene's day and those who had joined since Lord Hill's appointment as Chairman. The vote, in itself, was characteristic of Lord Hills' approach to the Board. He believed that things had to be settled with reasonable speed, and if there appeared to be continuing division, then a vote was the proper way to resolve it. It may have been true in this case. But I am much more doubtful about its general applicability in a body like the Board, which needs to develop a collective opinion as its normal means of proceeding.

My one really serious disagreement with Lord Hill, in which votes once more came into play, was when he sought to press on me the desirability of appointing a full-time Deputy Director-General. He believed, with some justice, that I was over-loaded as Director-General, and needed additional support. In his account of the outcome of the discussion the post of the Chief Secretary emerges as the resolution of the problem. In fact, there was a protracted argument between myself and Lord Hill, and within the Board, about the desirability of a full-time deputy and about the identity of such a person, should the post be created. I argued that while I certainly needed a deputy in absence – and a Director-General is quite frequently absent on international business – I could see no point in having such a post on a full-time basis. The effective deputies in each of the operating Services were the Managing Directors, and they expected direct access to me. To interpose a Deputy Director-General would mean either that he would be continually by-passed by the Managing Directors, who would refuse to take his word as final, or that he would be confined to performing relative chores – in which case it would be a waste of a good man's talent to appoint him to such a post. There was no structural requirement that I could identify. It would have been possible to appoint one of the administrative Directors (Personnel and Finance) as a Deputy Director-General to take charge of affairs in those sectors, but this would have been a retrograde step to the old post of Director of Administration, which had been found to be an unwieldy amalgam. Lord Hill's idea was that, having named a full-time Deputy Director-General, I should then allocate to him specific duties which I found that I could not handle myself. To me, this seemed to be an unsatisfactory way of proceeding. Moreover, I could see a major internal disadvantage in the appointment of a Deputy Director-General.

I may have an unduly suspicious turn of mind, but it seemed to me that if the Board were to appoint anything more than an administrative handyman, then they might virtually be naming my successor at a time when I had served for only four out of the 'about eight years' for which I had originally been appointed. That expectation would certainly have attached to him in the minds of others, if not in his own. And it is no answer to that argument to say that deputies do not normally succeed. The assumption is made that they may. In the end, Lord Hill persuaded the Board to agree that the post of deputy was a justifiable support for the Director-General, in view of his heavy load, and particularly in the light of the additional responsibilities that I was taking on at that time as President of the European Broadcasting Union. Some of those on the Board whom I regarded as my friends wanted to give me this help, even though I was reluctant to have it. Faced with the belief of the Board that the creation of a post of deputy was sensible, I said that I would reluctantly accept, but only on condition that the person chosen should be acceptable to me. The Board was then unable to agree, either on the appointment of the person I wished to have, if I had to have anyone, or of anybody else. The proposal therefore lapsed and the post of Chief Secretary was created in order to reinforce the Secretariat which worked for me. It did provide some relief, without the disadvantages of the Deputy Director-General post.

I felt throughout this discussion that the Chairman, perhaps with the best of intentions, was intervening in what was properly my sphere of operation – that of deciding how I did my own job. Potentially, this proposal from the Chairman represented a diminution of my authority as Director-General, and, as I have said, that is one step which the Board should always seek to avoid. The issue was central, because of all the functions exercised by the Board, that of appointment of senior staff is one of the most important. But no Director-General should be required to work with people whose aptness for their senior posts he does not accept. He may be willing to go along with an appointment while not being fully convinced that it is the best one. He should not be required to submit to the direction of the Board when he is convinced that the proposed appointment is wrong.

Lord Hill has said, quite rightly, that I was delighted by the appointment of Sir Michael Swann, to take office at the beginning of 1973. I felt certain that we could establish a good relationship almost from the very first moment when I met him. Lord Hill brought him in to see me as soon as he arrived at Broadcasting House, and tactfully left us alone for about an hour. I learned later that Mr Heath had come to the view that there were many similarities between running the BBC as Chairman, and running a university as Vice Chancellor. It is true that there is the same anarchist creativity in both institutions. I also learned, much later, that Sir Michael had formed the impression, during his conversations with the Prime Minister, that the time had come for a somewhat quieter exercise of the authority of the Chairman, though not for a retreat from the established authority of the Governors. Moreover, I knew quite early, through personal accounts of conversations between some of the senior staff at No. 10 and American News correspondents, that there was a deliberate intention to restore in some degree the authority of the Director-General. I was quite certain that this view would have been communicated to the new Chairman, and reassured by the fact that he saw fit to accept the office against the background of that intention.

There were one or two hesitations as the relationship developed between me and my new Chairman. He was, on occasion, a little over-anxious to apologize for the errors which occurred in programmes. From the public point of view that was an error on the right side. But so far as I was concerned, it was very necessary, in the new regime, to reassure the staff for whose errors the apologies were being made that a decent respect for public opinion did not represent an abandonment of the defence of their right to independence. One particular occasion arose over a programme called *A Question of Confidence*, in which half a dozen MPs were faced by a large audience, some of whom were violent in their attacks on politicians and in the expression of their disrespect for the political profession. Since Mrs Shirley Williams was one of those who were attacked, it was clear that things had got out of hand. Sir Michael wrote rather quickly to apologize to the politicians who had taken part, and I was able to save the situation only by being able to demonstrate to the staff and to their representatives in the unions that I had already expressed my displeasure to the responsible production department about the way in which the programme had got out of order. I had to give an undertaking to the unions that if public criticism was to be forthcoming from the Chairman about the work of their members, whose reputation might thereby be adversely affected, they should at least be given some prior warning. I felt this was a justifiable request and I had no difficulty in persuading Sir Michael to accept this view.

By the time he came to give his Lunchtime Lecture on 'The Functions of the Governors of the BBC' he had completely accepted that programme discipline was a matter of pride to the staff of the BBC, and that the individual freedom of programme-makers was the logical foundation for creativity within this discipline. He gave explicit endorsement to the long established system of reference upwards by the responsible producer as the most effective method of editorial control, and retrospective review by the Governors as the best means of exercising their trust for the nation in seeing that programme standards were maintained. Moreover, throughout our relationship he was always prepared to recognize that persuasion by the Director-General, carrying conviction with the staff, was the best way to proceed if effective implementation of the wishes of the Governors was to be achieved. He was willing to wait in patience for the process of persuasion to take effect.

331

Votes in the Board became a rarity. Indeed, if there were to be any criticism, it would be that Sir Michael was so devoted to the pursuit of agreement with his colleagues that he sometimes did not insist enough on the reaching of a decision at the moment when it was required. The cohesiveness of the Board to him was clearly an overriding consideration, and he took it that the influence of the Board would be the greater if it was known that they were agreed among themselves. This was a return to the earlier concept of the corporate character of the Board, not only in action, but in conviction.

So far as I was concerned, the essential difference between the period of Lord Hill's Chairmanship and that of Sir Michael Swann was that under Sir Michael I never had any occasion to consider the possibility of resignation on a point of principle. I believe that the normal approach of a Director-General to his relationships with the Chairman and the Board should be that of seeking agreed solutions to difficult problems, but occasions can arise when the differences are so acute that a parting of the ways is the only solution. In that case, it is my view that the Director-General should go.

Under Lord Hill each of the three incidents which I have mentioned forced me to consider the possibility. The first – that of the paper on advertising – raised the possibility, before I knew Lord Hill's mind, that advertising revenue might be introduced on the basis of a BBC representation in favour of such a course. I should have regarded that as totally contrary to my own convictions about the necessary financial base for the BBC's programme integrity. The question of resignation was, of course, completely disposed of from the minute Lord Hill made his own view clear. The second occasion – that of the appeal by my senior executive colleague against my wish to change his duties – raised an equally important issue. A Director-General ought to be free to define his own requirements of his senior supporting staff, and ought to be supported in them by the Board. If the appeal against the change of duties which I had proposed had been upheld by the Board my authority in this respect would have been fundamentally undermined and I could not have continued in office. Equally, the authority of my successor would have been undermined. Finally, the question of the Deputy Director-General raised, in principle, the same issue, except that in this case the argument was that the Director-General's view ought to extend to persons as well as to functions. In fact, when I realized how serious the intention was on Lord Hill's part to create the post and to name its occupant, I asked for figures to be prepared for the retirement pension which I would draw if I were, in fact, to submit my resignation. There is no point in submitting a resignation unless one intends to carry it through.

The difference between the two regimes was in the view which the two men took of the role of the Director-General. Both of them regarded me as Chief Executive in the fullest sense, and gave me strong support in many critical situations. But Lord Hill, perhaps naturally, saw me as playing the role of Permanent Secretary to his Minister. I think that Sir Michael saw me more in the role of Vice Chancellor to his Chancellor – though that is understating his conception of his own functions. He was a more active Chancellor, and legitimately so, than would have been regarded as normal, to judge by an external view of the practice of most universities. The'Permanent Secretary' role is an understatement of the degree of public accountability which is carried by the Director-General. He is required, in the nature of the programme operation, to make more, and more individually important decisions of public consequence than it would be constitutionally justifiable for a Permanent Secretary to take upon himself. Moreover, the Director-General is required frequently to state, on his own authority, the position of the BBC in matters of public controversy. The exact division of labour between himself and the Chairman in this respect is one which has varied from time to time in the history of the BBC, and is likely, in contemporary circumstances, to fall more heavily on the Chairman than it has done in the past. But there is the essential difference between the Permanent Secretary and the Director-General that the latter is, of requirement, a figure of public controversy at times.

Because of Lord Hill's prominence I was likely to be thought of as carrying the 'Permanent Secretary' role. In fact, Lord Hill encouraged me to take a public position, but it was not really a practical course until he had retired from the BBC, although I made several statements of importance, the substance of which I have recounted in some parts of this book. Sir Michael Swann, on the other hand, saw me as naturally speaking in public for the BBC, in parallel with himself. That, I believe, is what he would regard as being as natural for a Director-General as for a Vice Chancellor.

There was one problem in the Board which produced almost equal difficulties for myself and for my Chairmen. A hidden effect of the failure of Governments promptly to set in motion the processes for the appointment of a new Governor becomes especially evident to a Director-General when the appointment in question is of the 'trade union' member of the Board. Any group chosen from the list of 'the great and the good' is likely to under-represent the middle-of-the-road working class sector of opinion. There may be those on the list who, by liberal persuasion, will argue the case for this group, but they cannot do so with the conviction born of experience as well as inclination. Consequently, in the temporary absence of such a voice in the Board, the Director-General will find himself, in the pursuit of his editorial obligation to secure a balanced approach, having to argue the case of the absent Trade Union element, however inadequately qualified he may be to do so. This happened to me more than once, and on industrial relations matters as well as editorial. I felt a distinct risk that in having to raise a necessary sectional interest I might be written down by some members of the Board as personally committed, and whatever my personal views might have been, I could not afford professionally to have that opinion develop. The political risks were too great.

The relationship of the BBC with politicians and politics is always central, and always difficult. Under neither of my Chairmen was I ever embarrassed by weakness in the face of political pressure. Neither broadcasting organization ever had an easy relationship with Harold Wilson, whether he was Prime Minister or Leader of the Opposition. Sir Hugh Greene had experience of the difficulties as early as the election of 1966. My first difficulties arose, after an initial period of harmony, during the election of June 1970. The final *Panorama* of that campaign, to be broadcast on the Monday before polling day, was to deal with external affairs, with the emphasis either on defence or on the prospect of entry into the Common Market. Neither of these subjects had been prominent in the election campaign, but each was likely to be of major importance in whatever Government took office after the result of the poll was known. I had an arrangement, made personally with Mr Wilson, that there should be consultation between the two of us, if necessary operating through his staff at No. 10, about the selection of Labour speakers to take part in major programmes. I had agreed to this in order to avoid the risk that the BBC might seem to be choosing spokesmen for the Labour Party who would not be acknowledged by the Party as representing its official point of view. There was a danger, of course, that such an arrangement could degenerate into outright nomination by the Party of participants in programmes. The problem in such situations has always been that broadcasters depend on the willingness of spokesmen to appear, and at election time senior politicians are reluctant to incur the wrath of the Leaders of their Parties by accepting invitations from broadcasters in defiance of the known wishes of the Leaders. The device of the 'empty chair' in a programme in order to signify the existence of a dispute between the broadcaster and the Party on the selection of a suitable spokesman is possible, but does not add greatly to the illumination of the audience or the subject. It is also a hostage to fortune for relations between the broadcasters and the possible next Government. I asked Mr Wilson, indirectly, whether, in the event that external affairs were to be the subject of the *Panorama* in question, the then Foreign Secretary, Mr Stewart, or the Secretary for Defence, Mr Healey, would be the 'more likely to be available', making clear that the subject of the programme would be external affairs in general, including the possibility of the Common Market. The reply which I received, also indirectly, was that Mr Healey would be the more likely to be available. I had no illusions as to the possible political significance of that message. When the producer of the programme decided that the emphasis was to be on foreign affairs rather than on defence, and on the Common Market in particular, he knew of this message, though not of its provenance. He thought it right, in all the circumstances, in the exercise of his proper judgement as an editor, to invite the Foreign Secretary. Mr Stewart, clearly uninformed about Mr Wilson's views, accepted. The fat was in the fire. Mr Wilson made what I can fairly describe, with the greatest restraint, as the strongest representations to me that this was a breach of our understanding. I had to defend the action of my producer. In the end Mr Stewart was instructed by the Party to withdraw. In the circumstances, the BBC invited Mr Healey. But what was more serious than the reaction to the news of the producer's intention was the claim by Mr Wilson that the Parties had the right to nominate speakers in such programmes. Although the dividing line was, in practice, very narrow, the BBC had to maintain that in the end the choice of speaker belonged to the broadcaster and not to the Party. The alternative, after all, to having Mr Healey would have been to have the empty chair, and the broadcaster must always retain that option. At no time during this whole proceeding did Lord Hill give any sign that he wished me to change course. Naturally, I kept him fully informed throughout.

Lord Hill was similarly robust when, in 1969, Mr. James Callaghan, as Home Secretary, felt very strongly that some form of direct instruction should be imposed on producers in the matter of television violence. I accompanied Lord Hill, with David Attenborough (then Director of Programmes in the Television Service) to the Home Office in order to argue the contrary case and to suggest that what was required was a thorough self-examination by the broadcasters of what might constitute practical ways of evolving self-administered rules of guidance. If Mr Callaghan was firm, then Lord Hill can only be described on that occasion as having been durably resistant. We came out with no additional shackles, and a commitment, which would have been acceptable to us in any case, to look to our own affairs in the matter of television violence. That we did. The credit went largely to the determination of Lord Hill and Lord Aylestone (for the ITA was equally involved in this discussion) to avoid any imposition of a Broadcasting Council which would take away from the absolute editorial discretion of the Board of the BBC and the Authority. They were defending, before its time, the proposition of diversity and independent responsibility as the buttress of independence which was later propounded so effectively in the Annan Report. But much credit should also go to the lucid and practical arguments put forward by David Attenborough about the nature of programme control and the desirability of working on the basis of knowledge rather than instinct when considering questions of social behaviour. It was his proposal that we should call on experts in various disciplines in medical and social psychology in order to help us evolve rules of guidance which constituted the practical response for which Mr Callaghan was looking. I still believe that this is the right course for broadcasters to follow.

On a later occasion, when Mr Callaghan was Foreign Secretary in the Labour Government which took office in 1974, Sir Michael Swann was equally strong in reasonable resistance to representations from the Foreign Office, and in the end, from Mr Callaghan himself, that the BBC's External Services should not broadcast comment on a biography of Field Marshal Amin by David Martin. The Foreign Office view was that the author, a former BBC Foreign Correspondent, was so unacceptable to the Field Marshal that mention of the book in the BBC's Services to Africa would, in itself, be provocative and might perhaps result in the risk of pressure, and perhaps worse, against the remaining British inhabitants of Uganda. The BBC view was that while it was reasonable to consider the form in which mentions of the book might be presented, it would be unacceptable for a publication which was bound to be known to the audiences in Africa to find no reflection in the BBC's programmes. It is a requirement of credibility for the BBC, in addressing its overseas audiences, that the service of information should be reasonably complete, and should certainly include those matters which are likely to be the subject of common discussion among the audience themselves. The problem is one which must frequently arise. The Foreign Office is bound to consider the immediate practical circumstances, and the BBC is bound to hold to the long term issue of principle – that of editorial integrity – which underlies credibility. The representations which were made to me and to Mr Mansell (then Director of External Broadcasting) from an official level in the Foreign office were forceful. Those subsequently made by Mr Callaghan to Sir Michael were certainly not less forceful. Throughout Sir Michael maintained the position which any Director-General must always hope to find in his Chairman – that the BBC must take its own decisions on grounds of principle, and be prepared to accept the public responsibility for their possible consequences.

I have no doubt that there must have been many occasions when Mr Heath, as Prime Minister, would have wished that the BBC were not reporting matters of public interest in the way it did. But I cannot remember any occasion on which he himself, as Prime Minister, brought any undue pressure to bear, either on me or on the Chairman. We knew, through his Press staff at No. 10, that he was not always happy with our reporting of affairs. But it is always reasonable for that kind of communication to be made, leaving the BBC to take account of its own position. In a particular instance, when *Panorama* interviewed David O'Connell, the Provisional IRA leader, in June 1972, Mr Whitelaw, then Secretary of State for Northern Ireland, asked whether it was proper for O'Connell to have been allowed to say that negotiations had taken place between representatives of the Provisional IRA and a representative of the British Government. The inference to be drawn from O'Connell's answers was that the representative was of Ministerial standing. I said that since this was O'Connell's statement in reply to a question, it would be quite wrong to exclude it from the interview, but we were always ready to report any repudiatory statement from him or from any spokesman on his behalf. I am sure that Mr Whitelaw would agree that this conversation with me was somewhat tense. I add that it contained no element of undue pressure, and was followed by entirely reasonable conversations on the matter on the following day. I was supported, incidentally, in this matter by Lord Hill when I reported the circumstances to him.

The major conflict between the BBC and the Conservative Government under Mr Heath arose over the programme *The Question of Ulster*, which was broadcast on 5 January 1972. This was an example of careful and continuous consultation between the Current Affairs staff of the Television Service and myself in the earliest planning stages; continuous information from me to the Chairman, and subsequently to the Board, about the development of the project, and of violent protest from the then Home Secretary, Mr Maudling, within whose responsibilities Northern Ireland at that time lay. There was no question of irresponsible action by the editorial staff of the BBC, nor of the Board being uninformed of the progress of events. They were exercising their responsibilities to the full. However, Mr Brian Faulkner, whose participation was one of the essential ingredients in the make-up of the programme if it was to present a fair survey of the various strands of opinion affecting the development of events in Northern Ireland, declined to take part, and was supported in his protest by Mr Maudling who was against the whole concept of the programme. The BBC was faced with a decision as to whether an editorial venture which it had hitherto judged to be entirely responsible and within its proper range of public information activities should be abandoned because of the representation from Government quarters that it would be a hindrance to the progress of possible negotiations in Northern Ireland which had not then been initiated. The BBC's Board of Governors, after the most careful consideration, took the view that their responsibility for informing the public, both in Northern Ireland and in the rest of the United Kingdom, was of overriding importance, provided that a reasonable representation of all the relevant points of view could be ensured in the programme. They were satisfied that the preparatory moves in the making of the programme had been responsibly undertaken. The choice which faced the Home Secretary was whether to ask his colleagues in Government to approve the issuing of a formal veto on the programme – a veto which, of course, the BBC would then have been free to publish. In the event, he decided not to do so but to make a public protest against the obstinacy of the BBC. The public and Press response to the programme when it was broadcast was a complete justification of the independent line taken by the BBC, from executive to Board level, and the programme itself will remain as a historical example of how the independence of the Corporation has to be defended, even in circumstances of the hottest controversy.

On another occasion, however, after the defeat of the Conservative Government, I found myself in conflict with Mr Heath himself on a question which, although not central in itself to the conduct of programmes, did raise a vital issue. We met at the meeting of the Committee on Party Political Broadcasting, which had to consider the disposition of political broadcasting time in the circumstances of the new Government. Mr Heath decided to attend the meeting himself. The underlying philosophy about party political broadcasts is that the time is offered by the BBC and then shared, by agreement between the parties. The service is relayed by the IBA. The sharing agreement is reached within the Committee, which is chaired by the Leader of the House. The Liberals had gained substantially in the popular vote in 1974, and they claimed a greater allocation of broadcasting time. The view of the broadcasters has always been that the allocation of time should not be increased, and that, desirably, the number of broadcasts should not be increased. Consequently, if any party claims a greater share of the available time, it can only be at the expense of the others. If, therefore, the Liberals were to have an additional broadcast, it had to be at the expense either of the Conservatives or of Labour, or perhaps both. It was not to be expected that either major party would acquiesce in such an arrangement. I was able in the end, after the meeting had broken up with no agreement, to devise a formula which would protect the future for the broadcasters, while ensuring that the allocation of time within the quota would reflect changes in the popular vote. The formula involved a small increase in the amount of time available so as to accommodate what I felt was the reasonable case put forward by the Liberals. But that increase would be the last, as a result of the acceptance of the formula. The importance of the occasion lay not in the actual arrangements reached for the allocation of party time, but in a claim stated by Mr Heath that it was for the political parties to allocate what he described as 'our time'. In other words, he was maintaining that the broadcasting time belonged to the parties and not to the broadcasters, and it was for them to make or to withhold concessions about the amount of time and the number of occasions on which it might be used. I demurred at once. It was not for the political parties to dispose of our programme schedules. I believe that this editorial control over air time is an essential doint of resistance when the broadcasters have dealings with the politicians. It is not a question of plain obstinacy and awkwardness. It is an issue of principle. Who controls the programme schedule? In my view it must be the broadcaster. Clearly, Mr Heath's view was the contrary. To the best of my recollection it was our only conflict. Once again, I can say that I received complete support from Sir Michael Swann, backed by the Board of Governors.

The two examples of differences over programmes on Northern Ireland which I have quoted are an illustration of the different view which all Ministers take of the duty of information which rests upon the broadcasters from that which is followed by journalists. Broadly, Governments tend to expect that journalists will freely recognize an obligation to help in the sensible administration of affairs by telling the objective truth – which is, of course, in their eyes, the truth which they conceive to justify their policy decisions. Journalists will universally reserve to themselves the right to see the truth differently. They will maintain an obligation to tell that truth to the public, even if it is embarrassing to Government. And part of the business of telling the truth is to reveal that there are indeed differences about what constitutes fact. The public has a right to know about those differences, and the embarrassment which may arise from that awareness is a part of the democratic process.

Mr Heath, when out of office, made it very clear to me on one occasion that he regarded broadcast journalism as having been a definite hindrance to the process of Government, especially over Northern Ireland, and I have no doubt that he was sincere in his belief. Northern Ireland was the most difficult instance of this difference of approach between Government and journalism. I had to consider very carefully, on more than one occasion, whether an interview with a Provisional IRA spokesman might not amount to conceding to an illegal movement the chance to use a public medium to an extent which was not justified by the enlightenment of the public which might result from the interview. In eight years I agreed to only two such interviews, and was bitterly attacked on both occasions. I was also attacked by the exponents of free journalism for not allowing more. A Director-General has to live with such decisions. His criterion must always be the enlightenment of the public. Ministers, like Dr Conor Cruise O'Brien, will always believe that the 'legitimisation' of subversive movements by allowing their spokesmen to appear on the public media is always the major consideration, and a decisive argument against such appearances. No journalist could ever accept that view.

It might seem that I give a clean sheet to Mr Heath in the matter of Ministerial pressure on broadcasters. But I did receive representations from other Ministers during his period of office – notably from Mr Peter Walker and Mr Julian Amery about the documentary programme *Up the Rents*. What they appeared to be seeking was a change in the programme when, in my view, the editor was able to produce convincing evidence to support his report. They were reluctant to accept an invitation to appear in the second week's edition of the programme in order to confute what they took to be an opinionated presentation of the facts, but in the end Mr Amery appeared. It was not uncommon for members of Government from both major parties to object to what they saw as the 'slant' of documentary programmes and to regard an opportunity to be interviewed as an inadequate balance. I know of no other way of dealing with such representations short of yielding to the pressure to change the content of a programme to which the reporter has already brought his professional judgement as a journalist. The right remedy is argument before the public, not quasi-mandatory judgement on the journalist's work.

Politics, although an area of tension between the BBC and the outside world as represented by the politicians, is at least a field on which agreed judgements can emerge. Taste was a much more difficult issue, and it was here that the BBC most frequently found itself in trouble, and where agreement within the Board of Governors was most difficult to achieve.

We always have to come back to the question of divisions

within society over these matters of behaviour. And if we look within ourselves we can find the evidence of these divisions. For my part, for example, I accept my church's teaching on abortion – though I should be prepared to discuss definitions. Is it abortion, for example, to expel the fertilized ovum at any stage before implantation? That kind of argument must proceed in the light of the current state of knowledge. But although I accept that teaching, I am unconvinced about the teaching of Humanae Vitae on contraception. If my own mind, as a practising Catholic, is divided in this way about my Church's teaching, then I am bound to concede to others outside the Church what I claim for myself within it – the right to a fair and open discussion of the issues, without limits set by preconceptions. In my view, there ought not to be any limitation in principle on the subjects which can be discussed on the air. There are practical considerations imposed by the nature of the probable audience to be reached, and there must be adequate forewarning to the audience of those things which they might wish to avoid.

So I considered taste in terms of caution against excess. But a great deal of my thinking was taken up from time to time by resistance to the pressures of those who were concerned not merely with caution, but with exclusion from the screens of matters which they felt to offend against the canons of good taste. Although Mrs Whitehouse has repudiated any notion that she wishes to act as a censor, or to see anyone else do so, the effect of the criticisms which she levels against particular programmes is to suggest that a degree of exclusion should be practised which cannot sensibly be regarded as anything less than censorship. I was never able to share her approach to these matters. To take just one example – the play *Gotcha* – whose second showing was cancelled by the BBC following – but not because of – representations by Mrs Whitehouse which quoted my own comments to her on the nature of the programme after its first showing. I found it unacceptable that she should quote only that part of my letter which was critical of certain presentation aspects of the play, but which supported the intention of the author in writing on the subject of the inadequate adolescent at school. Freedom for authors to choose controversial themes seems to me to be essential to the creative and provocative role of the BBC in a society which is normally only too ready to acquiesce in silence about difficult problems. If playwrights and producers wish to present a view of the General Strike, such as that which was offered by Tony Garnett and his collaborators in the series *Days of Hope*, or if they wish to pose, from a particular point of view, serious questions about the enforcement of law, then it seems to me right that the BBC should give them an opportunity to do so, while insisting on the necessity for special points of view to be contrasted with others, perhaps in programmes of a different nature. But to exclude, because of difficulty, subjects which are essential matters of discussion in a democratic society, is the wrong approach to securing a reasonable level of information on which future policy can be based. Mrs Whitehouse has always under-rated the benefits of open presentation, and has emphasized unduly the arguments of taste which raise criticisms of what is essentially ephemeral.

Many people must have assumed, on hearing that a Roman Catholic had been appointed to be Director-General, that judgements about taste and about the discussion of difficult subjects, particularly in the matter of sexual morality, would be made on a more restrictive basis than before. Indeed, similar thoughts must have been in the minds of earlier opponents of possible Roman Catholic appointments to the post. It was accepted tradition in the BBC that at the time of Reith's departure the reports of his advocacy of the appointment of Graves, a Roman Catholic, as his successor, had provoked representations from the then Archbishop of Canterbury against such a step. H. A. L. Fisher, a former Governor, had earlier written in 1937 to Ronald Norman, then the Chairman, with the responsibility for the new appointment, to say that if Graves were made Deputy Director-General it would be difficult ever to make him Director-General because he was a Roman Catholic. 'I think', he wrote, 'it would be quite impossible that the supreme executive control of one of the most important organs of public education in this country should be placed in the hands of a Roman Catholic.' This was by no means an exceptional view for a liberal minded man to take, even as late as 1937. It is not surprising to find Queen Victoria asserting in a letter to her daughter, then Crown Princess of Prussia, that 'they (the Catholics) will not be conciliated and wish to persecute, by fair means or foul, to obtain the upper hand'. But it is perhaps not entirely according to expectation to find Archbishop William Temple writing in *Christians and the Social Order* in 1942: 'blindness (to freedom) is, as some of us think, the conspicuous defect of Rome to this day, leading to a never repudiated belief in persecution and a spontaneous sympathy with authoritarian regimes.'

When I was being seen as a candidate by the Board I knew that at the time of Hugh Greene's appointment the question had been raised in the then Board as to whether he was a Roman Catholic – presumably because his brother Graham was known to be a Catholic. His brother was, of course, a convert, and Hugh was not a Roman Catholic, but, as he said himself, 'a respectful agnostic'. When Hugh Greene had proposed me to the Board as The Secretary to the BBC I myself had pointed out to him that if I were to be appointed he would then be advised in the public relations field by two Roman Catholics – myself and Harman Grisewood. Was he sure, I asked, that this was a wise step? He replied that the matter was not to the point, provided I were capable of doing the job, and observing its professional requirements. Later, in an informal conversation with Robert Lusty, then a member of the Board, he put to me the possibility that I might become Director-General in due time. My reply to him was that since I was a Roman Catholic I regarded myself as 'not vulnerable' – that is, to appointment. So, as the interviews proceeded, my vulnerability to appointment having been demonstrated, I was prepared to accept that my religion might be an obstacle, and to accept also the consequences as a necessary price to pay for my faith. But I did not think it likely that the issue would be seriously raised.

I was wrong. I now know that the last objection to my appointment, after my relative youth and my inexperience of Television had been dismissed, was the fact that I was a Roman Catholic. The objection came from only one Governor, whose atavistic memories raised doubts in his mind. I think it does the Board, and him, credit that those doubts were overcome. But before leaving the subject it is worth considering the philosophical background to the thinking of any Roman Catholic who might in future be considered for appointment. Things have changed more than a little in recent years.

I had come to the post of Director-General, as I have explained, with a background of state education and a liberal university intellectual training, having never been submitted to the formalities of a Catholic education. My assumptions were therefore those of English liberal society and it was highly improbable that I would ever seek to bend the practice of broadcasting, even in the slightest degree, to conform to what were suspected as Roman Catholic predispositions. It was indeed something of a struggle in my earlier years for people like myself to keep ourselves within the Roman Catholic fold while still preserving our own good conscience, founded on our liberal indoctrination. Since the Second Vatican Council, that difficulty no longer exists. The evidence is in the text of the 'Pastoral Constitution on the Church in the World Today'.

Perhaps the central statement of that Constitution relates to the importance of conscience: 'Conscience unites Christians with other men in the search for truth, for solutions of individual and social problems of morality which shall be based on the truth . . . yet not seldom it happens that conscience can be wrong through invincible ignorance. In this case conscience does not lose its stature.' The theme is continued in phrases which could form part of any charter of

liberty. 'Man cannot embrace what is good other than freely.'
And further: 'Man's dignity demands that he should act in
accordance with a free and conscious choice, personally,
inwardly persuaded, and not by either blind impulse from
within or coercion from without.' Discussing even the extreme
opposite pole of atheism, the Constitution says that the
Church 'sincerely maintains that all men, believers and un-
believers, should work together to build properly this world
in which they live together. This certainly cannot be done
without sincere and prudent dialogue'. Later the Constitution
speaks of the 'respect and charity' which is owed 'to those who
think differently from us in social, political and also religious
matters'. Further, in a more directly political statement, the
document says: 'Admirable is the practice of those nations in
which the greater number of citizens take part, with true
liberty, in political life'. And if there should be any retrospective glances at the fate of Galileo, the Constitution
observes: 'Within the bounds of morality and the common
welfare, man should be free to pursue research, to express and
publish his opinions, to practise any art', and that finally, he
should be 'accurately informed about public affairs'. In a
further sentence: 'It must be insisted that culture must not be
turned from its proper purposes to serve political or economic
power.' On authoritarian government there is a sentence
which would have been unthinkable in the 1930s: 'It is
inhuman that political authority should take totalitarian forms
or dictatorial forms injurious to personal and social rights.'

With that background created in the 1960s it is not difficult
to see that most of the objections to a Roman Catholic
Director-General should have disappeared. In fact, during the
whole of my time in office I was attacked only once in public
on the ground that my Catholic beliefs were perverting my
editorial judgements. That occurred when Woodrow Wyatt
said that my Catholic affiliations were the cause of the BBC's
'pro-Biafran' attitude in the reporting of news. His accusations
were hotly repudiated in Parliament, and looked the more odd

in the light of the representations which I had received a few weeks before, when still Director of External Broadcasting, from missionaries who alleged that the news and public affairs programmes of the External Services, under my direction, were taking an excessively pro-Federal line. There was never any suggestion, during all the difficulties with which I had to deal in judging how best the affairs of Northern Ireland should be reported, that my personal origins, as a Roman Catholic of Southern Irish descent, were in any way influencing my decisions. I believe that it should now be possible for the question to be forgotten, should any Roman Catholic present himself in future as a potential candidate for the post of Director-General.

My Catholic background did have one positive effect in my performance of my duties. Although it was not a conscious reaction, there was no doubt that my European colleagues, and particularly those from the South European countries, regarded it as evidence of a common ground of interest. My relations with the Spanish broadcasters were, from the beginning, very warm, partly on this ground and partly because I spoke Spanish (learned, incidentally, from following BBC Further Education courses on radio). My German and Austrian colleagues seemed to feel the same response, as did the French and Italians. About the Irish, there was never any question! This fellow feeling turned out to be a very important beginning to a new aspect of my life and one which I had under-estimated when I first became Director-General.

The BBC is an immense force of international broadcasting. I knew this from my visits overseas when running the External Services, but I had not known how profound was its influence in Europe, both through the activities of the European Services, and through the direct professional contacts with the domestic Radio and Television Services. It was this foundation which brought to me election on three successive occasions as President of the European Broadcasting Union, and I believe that it was the force of the BBC's example in broadcasting which enabled me to create a solidarity of action between the broadcasters of Western Europe themselves, and between the European Broadcasting Union and other international broadcasting unions, when it came to the negotiation of major contracts for the coverage of international events such as the World Cup and the Olympic Games. It is an obligation for the BBC to remain active in this European and international context.

When I was elected for my third successive term as President in Helsinki in 1976 it was already evident to me that my time as Director-General of the BBC was coming to an end. I had been appointed, in the first instance, for 'about eight years', although there had been nothing precise about the definition of that period. It should surprise no one that any Board of Governors will always be eager to take part in the most important of its duties – the appointment of a new Director-General. The main problem in approaching this duty is to decide the moment at which the term of the existing Director-General should end. Mine had been fixed, to some degree, in advance. I never thought that the approximation of eight years was unreasonable, though I was always reluctant to see it too closely defined at too early a date, because uncertainty about the direction of an institution like the BBC is bound to result from immediate uncertainty about the length of tenure of the Director-General. Apart from Reith, whose situation was unusual, and the wartime Directors-General, whose circumstances were equally unusual, my predecessors had served for periods of between seven and nine years. Sir William Haley had told me that after just over eight years, and the experience of the Beveridge Committee, he had felt exhausted and ready for new things. Sir Ian Jacob had told me that seven years or so was long enough for anybody. Sir Hugh Greene had completed nine years and was anxious to continue when he left. My own view, having worked closely with him, was that the cumulative burdens of office were weighing heavily on him by the time he finally resigned. There did seem to be a periodicity about the job of Director-General. More-over, the Committees of Inquiry – Beveridge, Pilkington and Annan – did provide punctuation marks at which a change of Director-General seemed to be appropriate.

The important question for the Board was to find a successor. In this respect, too, 1976/77 represented a turning point. If I were to continue beyond that time, then I would have to go on until the immediate generation of potential successors – those around the age of 55 or so – had been replaced by the younger men who were coming forward. (All this assumes, as I believe to be right, a successor from within the BBC.) I doubted whether I could go on for as long as would be required for that process to complete itself. And so it came about that Gerard Mansell and Ian Trethowan were considered for the succession, and the date for the change was arranged for the latter part of 1977. For my own part, I would have liked to have gone on in order to see through the changes which might follow from the Annan Committee recommenda-tions. As it turned out, that would have been rather longer than I would have wished, and than would have been appropriate if my successor, as between these two, was to have a reasonable term of at least five years. My only disappointment was that the procedure of selection and preparation which I have described earlier in this book did not produce as my successor a candidate who had been through the full career succession of the Television Service. This is what I had hoped to see when I was originally appointed in 1968, and when I accepted the limitation of my term, proposed by Lord Hill and the then Board. It would have been unwise, had such a successor emerged, for me, by staying, to keep him too long waiting in the wings.

Looking back, the great virtue of finding one's career in the BBC is the enjoyment of the sense of public service without the corruptions which can follow from the search for profit. It is entirely possible for an institution with the standards of the BBC to produce excellence without the profit motive. This does not mean that those who operate in the public service feel no financial responsibility. There is no fear of undue extravagance in the future because there can be no fear of a disproportionate allocation of public finance to the BBC. Political reality suggests quite otherwise. What will remain a problem for my successors is the process of convincing the public, and their representatives, the politicians, that the price which is paid for a superb public service is, by any standard, absurdly low. The BBC has to sell itself, not simply as a bargain, but as excellence within the reach of everyman.

INDEX